Food

Encounters: Experience and Anthropological Knowledge

ISSN: 1746–8175

Series Editor: John Borneman

Encounters: Experience and Anthropological Knowledge is a series that examines fieldwork experiences of contemporary anthropologists. It aims to render into vivid and accessible prose the insights gained from fieldwork on topics such as money, violence, sex, and food. These short collections of essays are committed to:

- the subjective quality of sensual experience, tied to a particular time and place;
- curiosity in difference itself, in translating the strange, foreign, or unassimilable;
- storytelling that contributes both to the documentary function of the ethnographic encounter and to analytical potential.

Previously published in this series:

Money: Ethnographic Encounters
Edited by Stefan Senders and Allison Truit

Violence: Ethnographic Encounters
Edited by Parvis Ghassem-Fachandi

Food

Ethnographic Encounters

Edited by
Leo Coleman

Oxford • New York

English edition
First published in 2011
Berg
Editorial offices:
49–51 Bedford Square, London, WC1B 3DP, UK
175 Fifth Avenue, New York, NY 10010, USA

Berg is the imprint of Bloomsbury Publishing Plc.

Library of Congress Cataloging-in-Publication Data

Food : ethnographic encounters / edited by Leo Coleman.
p. cm. — (Encounters: experience and anthropological knowledge)
Includes bibliographical references and index.
ISBN 978-1-84788-907-2 (pbk.) — ISBN 978-1-84788-908-9
(cloth) — ISBN 978-1-84788-909-6 (individual e-book)
1. Food habits—Cross-cultural studies.   2. Food consumption—
Cross-cultural studies.   I. Coleman, Leo.
GT2850.F6   2011
394.1'2—dc23   2011017435

British Library Cataloguing-in-Publication Data

A catalogue record for this book is available from the British Library.

ISBN 978 1 84788 908 9 (Cloth)
978 1 84788 907 2 (Paper)
e-ISBN 978 1 84788 909 6 (Individual)

Typeset by Apex CoVantage LLC, Madison, WI, USA.
Printed in the United Kingdom by Biddles Ltd, King's Lynn

www.bergpublishers.com

Contents

Contributors

NINA BERMAN is Professor of Comparative Studies at The Ohio State University. She has written extensively on the representation of Africa and the Middle East in German culture. Her publications include *Impossible Missions? German Economic, Military, and Humanitarian Efforts in Africa* (University of Nebraska Press, 2004), and a book forthcoming from University of Michigan Press on Orientalism and practice theory (*German Literature on the Middle East: Discourses and Practices, 1000–1989*). She has conducted ethnographic research, pursuing her interests in humanitarian aid and travel writing, in Kenya since the 1990s, most recently starting a study of German settlers and tourists on the south coast of Mombasa.

JOHN BORNEMAN is Professor of anthropology at Princeton University. He received his PhD from Harvard, and has done ethnographic fieldwork in Germany, Central Europe, Lebanon, and Syria. He was appointed to the Executive Board (Beirat) of the Internationales Forschungszentrum Kulturwissenschaften in Vienna, and currently sits on the Beirat of the Max Planck Institut-Halle and the Forum Psychoanalytischer Wissenschaften of the Berliner Institut für Psychotherapie und Psychoanalyse. He has written on issues of intimacy, kinship, sexuality, nationality, justice, and political form. His most recent publications include *Syrian Episodes: Sons, Fathers, and an Anthropologist in Aleppo* (2007), (as co-editor) *Being There: The Fieldwork Encounter and The Making of Truth* (2009), and *Political Crime and the Memory of Loss* (2011).

LEO COLEMAN is Assistant Professor in the Department of Comparative Studies at The Ohio State University. He received his PhD in Anthropology from Princeton University in 2008, and his dissertation research included both historical and ethnographic work on the politics of electricity in India. His research interests include the changing uses of technology and technological goods (including food) in global contexts, urban anthropology, and the methods and theory of anthropology. He has published articles on ethnographic methods, especially in urban settings, including "Being Alone Together: From Solidarity to Solitude in Urban Anthropology" in *Anthropological Quarterly* (2009).

ELIZABETH CULLEN DUNN is Associate Professor of Geography and International Affairs at the University of Colorado, Boulder. Her work among displaced people in the Republic of Georgia has been funded by the Fulbright Commission, the International Research and Exchanges Board, and the National Council on Eurasian and East European Research. Her previous work on food, work, and private property in Poland was published in *Privatizing Poland* (Cornell, 2004), which won the Ed. A. Hewett Prize for the study of post-Soviet economies.

MARK HARRIS is Senior Lecturer in the Department of Anthropology at the University of St Andrews, Scotland. He was awarded a British Academy postdoctoral fellowship 1996–99, and the Philip Leverhulme Prize in 2004. He is the author of *Life on the Amazon: the anthropology of a Brazilian peasant village* (Oxford, 2000), *Rebellion on the Amazon: Race, Popular Culture and the Cabanagem in the North of Brazil, 1798–1840* (Cambridge, 2010), and various journal articles. He edited the collection *Ways of Knowing* (Berghahn Books, 2007), and co-edited with Stephen Nugent *Some Other Amazonians* (Institute for the Study of the Americas, 2006). He has also taught at the Federal University of Pará, Belém, Brazil, and the London School of Economics. His research interests encompass ecological anthropology, the anthropology of embodiment and experience, social science methodology, and the ethnography of the Brazilian Amazon and South America.

NINA HIEN's research interests include topics related to visual cultures, media and technology studies, nationalism, transnationalism and globalization, urban studies, and popular culture in Southeast Asia, Vietnam, and the United States. She is drawn toward finding creative links between these conceptual zones and geographical areas through ethnographic, historical, and theoretical inquiry. In her doctoral dissertation titled "Reanimating Vietnam: Icons, Photography and Image Making in Ho Chi Minh City" (2007), which received the Lauriston Sharp Prize, she examined the connections between visual technology and Vietnamese identity construction by the state and individuals. Forthcoming publications include: "Ho Chi Minh City's Beauty Regime: Visual Technologies of the Self, Subject and Body in the New Millennium" (*Positions: East Asia Cultures Critique,* Duke University), and "Reconfiguring the Dunes" (*Visual Anthropology,* Routledge). She is currently developing a new research project that explores the relationship between the body, vision, and tactility in new media practices.

JENNIFER A. JORDAN is a sociologist with expertise in cultural sociology, who has conducted ethnographic fieldwork in Berlin, as well as elsewhere in Europe. She is Associate Professor of Sociology and Urban Studies at the University of Wisconsin-Milwaukee, and is the author of *Structures of*

Memory: Understanding Urban Change in Berlin and Beyond (Stanford, 2006). She was a Fulbright fellow and a Senior Scientist at the Austrian Academy of Sciences in Vienna, Austria, and is the author of scholarly articles on topics ranging from collective memory to heirloom tomatoes (not to mention dumplings and historical kitchen gardens). Her research, writing, and teaching focus on questions of culture, collective memory, and materiality; she is currently at work on a book about the heirloom food movement and the sociology of kitchen gardens.

FRÉDÉRIC KECK is a researcher in social anthropology at the National Centre for Scientific Research. He has conducted four years of research on food safety crises in Paris and Hong Kong. He has published works on the history of French anthropology, from Lévy-Bruhl to Lévi-Strauss.

ANNE MENELEY is Associate Professor of Anthropology at Trent University in Canada, and the author or editor of a number of books and collections on cultural politics, dress, and food, in Yemen, Palestine, Italy, and contemporary North American culture. Dr. Meneley's current project, a comparison of the production, consumption, and circulation of extra-virgin olive oil from Tuscany and Palestine, is based on her fieldwork in both these places over the last decade. She remains engaged with her first project, based on nearly two years of fieldwork with Yemeni women in Zabid. Their competitive hospitality, fashion, and politics are the topic of her *Tournaments of Value: Sociability and Hierarchy in a Yemeni Town* (Toronto, 1996). Her work on olive oil attends to the material qualities that determine its semiotic potential. Her work on foie gras (with Deborah Heath) focuses on the tensions between nature and culture as humans and animals coproduce luxury foods.

CLAIRE NICHOLAS is a doctoral student in cultural anthropology at Princeton University. Her interests include the anthropology of labor/work, the anthropology of knowledge practices and expertise, colonial and post-colonial forms, and the anthropology of development. She completed her dissertation fieldwork in Morocco on contemporary incarnations of traditional textile craftsmanship and the various actors with stakes in its development. She has published two articles on the rationalization of Moroccan embroidery and contemporary iterations of colonial craft representations and policy.

KATHLEEN C. RILEY conducted ethnographic fieldwork in the Marquesas, French Polynesia, for her doctorate in linguistic anthropology, and has since published articles on topics ranging from language shift and code-switching to sex and gender in these islands. More recently she has become intrigued with the study of the intersection of foodways and discourse not only in the Marquesas but also in France and northern Vermont. She now teaches linguistic anthropology at City College and Queens College, The City University of New York.

CHRISTOPHE ROBERT received his PhD in cultural anthropology from Cornell University in 2005, with research fellowship support from Fulbright-Hays, the Social Science Research Council, the MacArthur Foundation, and the Wenner-Gren Foundation. He then taught at the Princeton Institute for International and Regional Studies and the department of anthropology at Princeton, the Council on Southeast Asia Studies at Yale, and the Chinese University of Hong Kong. Since 1999 he has conducted field research and consultancy work on urban planning and resettlement, migration, criminality, and poverty in Ho Chi Minh City and Hanoi. His academic research focuses on the political aftermath of war and state violence, and their long-term effects in urban areas throughout Vietnam and Southeast Asia.

PENNY VAN ESTERIK is Professor of Anthropology at York University, Toronto, where she teaches nutritional anthropology, advocacy anthropology, and feminist theory; she works primarily in Southeast Asia. Past books include *Beyond the Breast-Bottle Controversy*; *Materializing Thailand*; *Taking Refuge: Lao Buddhists in North America*; *Food Culture in Southeast Asia*; and *Food and Culture: A Reader*, edited with Carole Counihan. Research interests include food and colonialism in Southeast Asia, breastfeeding advocacy, and maternal and child nutrition.

Foreword

John Borneman

Food is a collection of essays about fieldwork experiences of contemporary anthropologists. Its focus, like that of other volumes in this series, is on personal encounters that reveal an intimacy with difference, but which tend to be omitted from standard academic accounts. The authors explore what anthropologists call "commensality," eating together, as a central activity in fieldwork encounters. Their stories of food exchange and interaction take us into diverse worlds of food production, preparation and procurement, cooking and tasting, illness and indigestion, in such places as Vietnam, Laos, Hong Kong, the Pacific Islands, the Brazilian Amazon, Georgia, Central Asia, Yemen, and Morocco.

Modern anthropology is different from the other human sciences because it takes the intimate experiences of fieldwork to be a primary source of knowledge. Anthropological and ethnographic knowledge is most often produced through "fieldwork," a form of long-term experiential study that brings the researcher into direct contact with an "Other." Anthropologists have, of course, incorporated methods and techniques from other disciplines—history (archival work), literature (reading texts), linguistics (discourse transcriptions), and psychology (controlled experimentation). And scholars in a wide range of disciplines have made use of ethnographic techniques. But while ethnography has become an important tool in many disciplines, its success has come with more than a few vexing questions. Is *any* place a field site? Should reading in the archives or in one's own office be regarded as an encounter with an Other who speaks back to the researcher through the text? Are all field sites and encounters equally valuable or productive?

The popularization of ethnography beyond its original contexts and use also challenges the assumptions of anthropologists about their own unique contributions to the understanding of culture, and about the relative value of the risks they take in ethnographic encounters. To the extent that anthropologists have succumbed to a professionalization and standardization in style of presentation, their accounts are often dismissed as obsessed with the everyday or, alternately, as overly ambitious theoretical renderings of simple things. The specific cultural texture of person and place is all too frequently sacrificed for a more streamlined theoretical account that focuses solely on a particular question or problem. Moreover, since the disappearance of "the primitive" as an object of study, the public tends to be confused about what it is, exactly, that ethnographers do.

In this third volume, edited by Leo Coleman, the contributors explore what Coleman calls the "meaningfulness of food cultures." Food in the field is never merely about hunger and nutrition, ingestion and digestion, edibility and sustainability, but about moral categories that embody and embed eating in potentially dangerous relationships of humans to land and water, to plants and other animals, and to each other. The authors arrive at understandings through their co-residence and co-presence with the people being written about. Learning through experience, they enter into commensalities that are an essential feature of culture itself, and make for the distinctiveness of a specific people in a specific place at a specific time. Under what conditions, they ask, can one enter into these already existing relationships revolving around food and eating together as a space of cross-cultural learning? This approach yields insights not obtainable through interviews, surveys, questionnaires, or laboratory and top-down approaches to the study of food.

Part of what is being documented here is shifts and problems encountered in various locales as the world food systems respond to changes brought about in the "food industry" by the powerful industrialized fossil fuel-dependent economies, based, as they are, on intensive energy use and long-distance transfers. The ethnographic approach demands that the anthropologist enter into other culinary worlds as an individual who must adapt, assimilate, and integrate, and frequently work against his or her own individual will and historical dispositions. As a collection, the essays demonstrate the importance for anthropology of comparison, which has proven more difficult since the anthropological critique of the concept of "culture" as too restrictively bound by time and place.

The focus here on the encounter itself—which cross-cuts domains, such as money, violence, food, and sex, as well as cultural and geographic spaces— suggests, as Coleman states, that ethnographic knowledge is not overdetermined by power differentials between researchers and their interlocutors. The question turns away from whether to confirm or criticize one's own cultural categories to how to be alert to mutual learning opportunities and surprises that exceed one's categories of pleasure or pain. In the space of commensality, one comes to understand what can and cannot be shared, with whom, and under what conditions.

We asked the authors to write with a particular concern in mind: to focus on stories of their own encounters with food in fieldwork, and to show how these encounters lead to particular kinds of engagements with cultural difference.

We also requested that they resist the temptation to let theoretical concerns dominate their writing. We encouraged them instead to allow their descriptions of fieldwork to show how and in what way cultural difference is learned in an encounter with food. We invited them, in other words, to write outside the current normative genres of anthropology, and of the academy generally, and to risk exposing themselves—warts, private pleasures, misunderstandings, and all—in the thick of it. Hence, contributors have elaborated their specific interactions and eschewed most of the conventions that today authorize ethnographic accounts, such as extensive historical contextualizing, footnoting, long bibliographies, or dense theoretical language.

Such omissions and rhetorical changes make new demands on our readers: We ask them to enter, openly, into the often threatening, sometimes embarrassing, but always educative situations of fieldwork. In return, we hope that the reading of these essays awakens appreciation for the intersubjective, and interdisciplinary, quality of sensual experience (personal, tied to a particular time and place); for curiosity in difference itself, in translating the strange, foreign or unassimilable; and for a kind of storytelling that contributes both to the documentary function of the ethnographic encounter and to its analytical potential.

Acknowledgements

For a volume focused on eating together—commensality—and encounters that take place over food, it is remarkable how much of this book was made through e-mail exchanges and in virtual conversations. This has been a greatly enjoyable and rewarding collaboration, in part because it was a highly networked and distributed one—contributors recruiting contributors—but it would not have come together without key meals and confabulations at the American Anthropological Association Meetings in Philadelphia (2009) and New Orleans (2010). My thanks as editor are due to each of the contributors for their willingness to write for this project and engage with its several purposes. John Borneman and Parvis Ghassem-Fachandi, and Anna Wright at Berg, together provided initial impetus and encouragement for the volume as a whole, while the comments of anonymous readers helped refine its purpose and aims. For myself, thanks to all those who helped me navigate the movable feast that is the anthropology of food and eating. Among many: Isabella Winkler and Ipek Yosmaoglu made key connections across fields, while Isabelle Clark-Decès and Sheila Bock provided further readings and tips about regional literatures at key moments. Finally, thanks to Jeremy, who long ago introduced me to the writing of M.F.K. Fisher, and to David, who gave me a cookbook when I started editing this book and has joined me in cooking and eating together ever since.

L. C.

Introduction

Leo Coleman

Nobody, not even anthropologists or other researchers, can go without food, and it should be obvious that food is somehow part of any attempt to understand social life and relationships. After all, we eat whenever we get together with friends or relatives—food is almost always an excuse for, if not the primary reason for, a social gathering—and varieties of foods are among the first things that come to mind when we think about other cultures. This book offers a collection of essays about eating in the course of cultural research, focusing on what you learn when you sit down and share food with someone else—and it is always much more than how to prepare or enjoy particular foods. We recount the pleasures, perils, and benefits of dining and drinking with others as a conscientious and conscious practice in the systematic exercise of ethnographic field research.

There are few areas of social life where the ethnographer's experience is more immediate and embodied, and where cultural learning requires more commitment, than eating. Food is the first medium through which each person, as an infant, learns to create and manage relationships with the outer world and the other people who populate it. These early experiences create tastes, customs, and habits, durable and hard to shake, which are the basis for our understanding or judgment of others' equally personal, and equally shaped, tastes. Because of this deeply engrained quality of tastes, food is also a cultural object, a thing we constantly alter and use to make new relationships. To be technical about it, both "cuisines"—products of long experimentation with the basic material of our sustenance—and "commensality"—structured ways of eating together or refusing to do so—offer some of the most important cultural arenas where we can learn about others, by experiencing how they communicate with each other by tasting, sharing, haggling over, or rejecting food.

Food: Ethnographic Encounters includes essays from widely varying parts of the world that focus on first-hand experiences of producing, procuring, cooking, eating, and sharing food in the course of learning about others and their lives.

Each essay recounts an individual researcher's fieldwork experience, usually in a part of the world that is not initially familiar to him or her, and often in pursuit of research questions that did not at first include food or eating as primary objects of interest. These essays explore the pleasures and perils of ethnography as an embodied, long-term engagement with other people where *they* live, with a special focus on how and what we learn when we cook and dine with others. But equally, these essays provide, individually and collectively, insights into the diversity and meaningfulness of food cultures in places ranging from South East Asia (Vietnam, Laos, Hong Kong) and the Pacific Islands to the Brazilian Amazon, by way of Georgia, in Central Asia, Yemen, Morocco, Kenya, and cities in Europe, including Vienna and Paris.

It should be noted at the outset that this volume is neither a comprehensive survey, thematic or geographical, of food cultures, nor of issues current in the broad field known as "food studies"—a vibrant field of research and writing in contemporary anthropology and related disciplines. There are many collections and monographs that address food and culture (Counihan and Van Esterik 2008), or the "cultural politics of food and eating" (Watson and Caldwell 2005), and much existing work on topics such as food and memory, industrialization of food production, and consumption and its contexts—from the kitchen to restaurants, with associated gendered and class-related meanings. Each topic could fill many volumes (and does—see the "Guide for Further Reading"). Meanwhile, researchers in nutritional anthropology creatively combine biological, sociological, and cultural approaches to food and eating, while folklore has always seen food as a special domain of talk, meaning-making, and storytelling (see Jones 2007). It is exemplary of the diversity and curiousness of anthropology as a discipline that no single "field" or "anthropology of food" can bound the range of interests that food attracts (fields, boundaries, and ranges, of course, all being food-related metaphors).

Across these essays we offer considerations of a number of topics important to the study of food in culture, politics, and contemporary global realities, but the essays dwell on the negotiation of different cuisines and systems of provisioning, delightful discoveries of new tastes and the exacting tasks of learning to cook with different techniques and tools, as well as painful experiences of food-borne illnesses and unpleasant reactions to unfamiliar tastes (both those of the ethnographers and their friends and family in fieldwork). They examine struggles over household tasks such as cooking, shared efforts to get food in insecure contexts, and the constant tasks of raising, processing, and eating food in the course of fieldwork and in the course of everyday life. In the range of ideas, contexts, and cultures encountered here, these essays reflect the breadth of ethnographic inquiry, while collectively they aim to demonstrate the particular methodological and substantive gains of doing ethnography—both as research and as a way of writing—from a basis in interpersonal experiences and encounters.

That is to say, this volume aims to provide a point of entry both for those curious about ethnography as it is practiced today, the kinds of knowledge and insights it can produce into social life in general, as well as to offer contributions to the study of food and its role in both personal and political relationships.

What Is an Ethnography of Food?

Ethnography relies on an assortment of research methods, which is part of the reason it can be so hard to define. Indeed, of the terms that make up the title of this book, *Food: Ethnographic Encounters*, "ethnography" surely needs the most explanation. Ethnography, like cooking, is both systematic and exploratory (often in different measures, depending on the kind of project being pursued). Ethnographers seek to find answers to research questions in everyday social life; questions such as: "How does industrial production change eating patterns?"; "Why does the price of different cheeses, or wines, vary so widely?"; or, more generally, "How does a national cuisine get invented?" Such questions can be framed and answered in a number of ways, and the research they support can be short-term, based on surveys and focused conversations (that might, for instance, collect remembered accounts of meals past). At the other end of the spectrum, ethnography can be a very long-term process, comprised of many return visits to a community, or a family, over years and even decades. Long- or medium-term research, which remains the gold standard for anthropologists, promises that research goals and orienting questions can be allowed to change over time, as more intimate and embodied knowledge is built up. Of whatever duration, ethnography in social and cultural anthropology always seeks to understand and explain both overt, discernible relations of cause and effect of the sort mentioned above, and also the underlying meanings, processes, and practices by which a whole pattern of human interaction is built up. This is not only a method that can be applied to discrete cultures (which only exist as abstractions), but indeed can be used to explore the cultural form and meaning of any social interaction, whether extended and mediated across great distances, or extremely local and of short duration.

Ethnography then is a process of research in which one actively seeks, learns, and shares cultural norms, habits, and meanings (whether at home or abroad). Ethnography in this sense is predicated on engagement in everyday habits and routines, and learning to discern important meanings and to communicate effectively in daily contexts (a process which is necessary even if everyone involved can already speak the same language), as well as observing both spectacular events (if the ethnographer is so fortunate as to be a witness to history) and the recurring festivals and rituals, which provide a rhythm for social life. Food is central to most occasions for learning and making social relationships, while it takes careful attention at first to master the particular ingredients, flavors, or patterning of meals.

Anthropologists seek out encounters with other people in order to learn something about them and about human social institutions, habits, and shared meanings, and are from the very first involved in feeding themselves and negotiating the food and the foodways—the complex of mechanisms for producing, procuring, cooking, and sharing food—of the place where they are doing research. This is equally true when the ethnographer is working in an office in a big city and has to finagle invitations to lunches and after-work occasions where people socialize, eat, and drink. It is also true when she is trying simply to get enough food to eat in a town or a village with unfamiliar foods, shops, and markets, and which demands a different set of "foraging" skills than she is initially equipped with. The work of getting food, the occasions at which it is shared, and the meanings it conveys both abstractly and in the course of strategic negotiations, are thus some of the aspects of food itself—as a complex object embedded in networks of exchange and interdependence—that these essays explore, in an array of locations both cultural and geographical, ranging from a family home in Kenya, to a vegetable market in Paris, to a settlement hastily constructed for displaced persons in the Republic of Georgia, the residents of which are provisioned by humanitarian food aid.

Encounters

At the outset of this project, the contributors were asked to write about encounters with food and eating, about episodes and incidents in their own experience of ethnographic fieldwork that revealed something to them—whether about the procedures and conditions of fieldwork itself, or about the people, place, or time of their encounter. Many of the contributors write about or research topics other than food and eating in their main professional work as anthropologists, sociologists, or literary scholars. They were asked to reflect, however, on how an encounter or set of encounters in which food figured prominently helped them develop insights into some more prominent research question they were seeking to answer, or forced them to grapple with some element of the local world that they had previously ignored in their research. This book was thus initially conceived as, and remains, primarily a forum for writing that emphasizes the experiential aspects of ethnography, and the often neglected or marginalized role of disgust, pleasure, and hunger, in the ethnographic task.

The authors were asked to focus on the encounters they had in the field and the way they related to other people and were related to in turn, which are conventionally treated as the "raw" data of fieldwork rather than the "cooked" product of reflection and writing. The relation between ethnography as experience, as writing, and as research process has been much debated by cultural anthropologists for over a generation. This is not the place to rehash those debates, but the essays collected here do speak to such debates—each is, obviously, "written," but written with an eye to interpersonal experience and the rich, personal content of social relations. The contributors have left intact the rough edges usually smoothed out by formal analysis: the interpersonal conflicts, thwarted desires, uncomfortable conversations, and often difficult instances of constraint—to eat, to receive gifts, to share potentially dangerous substances—as well as the affection, love, and labor of eating together with others.

In themselves, such experiences are of little intrinsic interest. The celebrated anthropologist Claude Lévi-Strauss famously warned anthropologists to steer clear of adventure for its own sake. In fieldwork, he wrote, "There are ... periods of hunger, exhaustion, sickness perhaps. ... [But] the fact that so much effort and expenditure has to be wasted on reaching the object of our studies bestows no value on that aspect of our profession, and should be seen rather as its negative side" (1973: 17). The authors demonstrate here, to the contrary, that the effort they expended to reach and communicate with others was much appreciated by their interlocutors, and the accidents and incidents of voyaging offered ways of understanding the kinds of effort their interlocutors already engaged in before the ethnographer's arrival, and the kinds of pleasures and dangers they, too, experience. It is not sheer exoticism that licenses the focus on encounters. Focusing on food as a material object, and on eating as a tangible, sensory, daily experience in fieldwork, highlights the embodied aspect of ethnography, with its incumbent pleasures and perils. More importantly, however, the travails and travels that ethnographers engage in produce a kind of knowledge that exceeds whatever one set out to learn and capture in the ethnography.

As Abdellah Hammoudi clarifies these concepts in a related context, "By 'experience' I mean an ethnographic encounter in which the anthropologist meets people as they engage in their own activities" (2009: 48). This is, thus, not simply a matter of writing down experiences or feelings: These essays all recount acts of engagement, encounter, and comparison, offered in the language of "perspicuous contrast," which has been identified in a previous volume in this series as a key aspect of ethnographic writing (drawing on the work of the philosopher Charles Taylor). "What is significant about the cultural encounter, as we use the term," Stephan Senders and Alison Truitt write, "is that it jars the anthropologist's subjective sense of social relations and social order, and even more specifically it brings the anthropologist and her 'subject' into a world of shared risk" (Senders and Truitt 2007: 3).

The essays here exemplify this effect of ethnographic co-presence, in highly material terms through exchanges of food. Such exchanges are not simply nourishing or material, but also always include intangible, even spiritual qualities, and sometimes are the occasion for agonistic battles over rights and statuses. That is, the experiences here are between subjects, not confined to the anthropologist alone. Not only are they shared encounters between researchers and interlocutors but also once these encounters are set down in essays they are available to be shared by the reader. There is a readerly aspect to the work of ethnography, which is necessary to training the ethnographic imagination and to building up a store of ethnographic accounts that can be used to make comparisons, between and within encounters. As Judith Farquhar says, ethnography "cultivates a reader," and readers "may compare what they see on the page with all manner of other practicalities and textualities" and with their own familiar settings (Farquhar 2002: 19). Ethnographic research can provide the basis for further imaginative engagements, sometimes from quite a distance, yet still be grounded in the process of encounter and engagement *in situ*. Both aspects of the ethnographic task are equally important—indeed, Mary Douglas once wrote that since anthropologists "have a privileged position for cross-cultural comparison, [we] also have a responsibility to exercise it" (1984: 7).

Exchange of Foods

Each of the essays focuses on a locale or a place, and an encounter between, on the one hand, an ethnographer usually identified (by those he comes to research with) as "foreign," and on the other hand, a "native." In that respect, the essays follow long conventions of anthropological representation, which have since been subject to some serious critique. This classical staging of the fieldwork encounter has been criticized for being over-determined by differences in power and location between the ethnographer, "authorized" to produce knowledge, and his or her research "subjects," who are left passive. Working within this very tradition, these essays often show this criticism to be overstated, and sometimes quite misplaced: Fieldworkers are often very dependent on their hosts both materially and emotionally, and material differences and inequalities of power always affect fieldwork relationships in sometimes surprising ways. On closer inspection, such power differences are among the aspects of the fieldwork encounter recognized by all participants, and can be among the strategic resources employed, by everyone involved, to negotiate new grounds of exchange.

The insights into fieldwork and its power dynamics extending across these essays are partly arrived at precisely through the process of reflecting on food as an object of exchange—how we get it, from whom, and what transformations it undergoes as it is made part of social relations. Exchange, and the comparison among substances that it requires, is central both to anthropological theory and to fieldwork practice, and anthropologists have developed elaborate schemas of knowledge about the various kinds of exchange and reciprocity—generalized, balanced, hierarchical, and egalitarian, to name a few types—involving various different media, from money to intangibles such as kinship.

Food presents something of a special case. Some forty years ago, Marshall Sahlins reviewed the legacy of economic anthropological studies existing at that time, in order to challenge some of the presumptions of classical economics about how people truck, contract, exchange, and barter and what the social meanings of these practices are. When it came to food he found, like many anthropologists before him, a realm of special need and special danger, in which moral and metaphysical qualities were produced and reproduced in the circulation, preparation, and ingestion of foodstuffs.

As several of the essays here attest, food is the primary object of sociable, hospitable offerings, and accepting and returning food requires a finesse that cannot be eliminated by recourse to cash payments. Indeed, within restricted circles of exchange of the sort that anthropologists are often either adopted into or already members of—families, households, and larger social units such as villages and even towns—there is an implicit taboo on accepting repayment for offerings of food. As Sahlins puts the point in anthropological language, "Food has too much social value—ultimately because it has too much use value—to have exchange value" (Sahlins 1972: 218); at least, that is, within specific social boundaries.

When it comes to such reciprocal, albeit often unequal, relationships, food is always more than food; more exactly, "whatever the utilitarian value" at stake in an exchange of food, *"and there need be none*, there is *always* a 'moral' purpose" (Sahlins 1972: 220, emphases added). Food is a "concrete," sensory vehicle of social relations, and by sharing and eating it, personal and collective ties are made and remade. Studying what people do with food as they exchange it with others and eat it together helps us understand local complexities and illuminates otherwise often mystifying cultural practices. For instance, food is used in many ritual contexts in order to make material connections with absent or divine persons; as Robert explores in his essay, in the context of a Vietnamese mourning ritual that involve "feeding" the lost family member. Such material extension of abstract or otherwise invisible social relations, captured by describing the specific ways in which food is tasted, ingested, and exchanged, also provides an avenue to understanding the complexities of national and personal identities, and of large-scale political and economic relations.

Locales and Processes

Each of the essays is located in a particular town or city or village, and is based on time- and place-bound encounters—though some of these encounters extend across decades. The one possible exception is Jennifer A. Jordan's peripatetic hunt for organic foods and heirloom tomatoes in the markets of Vienna and Paris. However, here too Jordan insists on the difference between her daily shopping routine in Vienna's markets, where she lived for several years, and her focused fieldwork in Paris, where she searched for what she had, by then, realized was the *elusive* heirloom tomato. She seeks local, stable food cultures, inspired by the recent efflorescence of popular books on the contrast such local and "slow" systems of production offer to industrialized and corporatized food production, and she fails to find them. Instead, she discovers how each of the neighborhood markets she visits is differently situated in more- or less-extensive systems of production, transportation, and preservation, and, equally, systems of symbolic value-production—which together give "old" varieties much of their marketability. Jordan's research is exemplary of a certain way of examining large-scale systems that otherwise would escape the grasp of encounter-based research. Indeed, all of the contributors to this volume document ongoing historical and cultural changes in their field sites, and each addresses how processes of change are experienced in specific locales. Jordan's methodological question of how and when ethnography can illuminate large-scale patterns of consumption and change is to some degree shared by all these essays. Each author makes a particular contribution, for instance emphasizing conversations she has had in the field about global political economic inequalities (Meneley), or exploring the visible and edible traces of colonial histories (Harris, Riley).

Indeed, industrialized food systems and processes such as globalization are only addressed in the following essays as they are experienced and encountered in particular places: Several essays document changing food systems through the lens of markets now full of new and exotic foodstuffs, as places such as Kenya and Vietnam become ever-more integrated into the global economy (Berman, Hien). Frédéric Keck explores sites of production and sale of live poultry in Hong Kong, as they are changing to meet the threat of epidemic contagion with avian influenza. This threat demands ever-greater surveillance of the (cultural) systems in which this living being is produced and novel negotiations of the boundary between animal and food (as well as of the boundary between mainland China and Hong Kong). If none of the essays here records multi-sited fieldwork to track the "flows" of food commodities in global networks, all record the comings and goings of their research interlocutors, the movement of others' desire for foods from elsewhere, and the borrowings and adaptations through which cuisines are made: We have here an Indian community in Africa whose foodways reflect centuries-old patterns of Indian Ocean commerce and exchange (Berman); an ethnic Chinese cook in Vietnam experimenting with cosmopolitan tastes and flavors from elsewhere (Hien); and even baguettes in the Marquesas substituting for the traditional breadfruit (Riley). The anthropologist may not move much once she arrives in her field site, but the "culture" and cuisine written about travel widely, are adapted and transformed, and there are no clear boundaries or static conventions.

On a related point, most of the contributors write about the "non-West," or about places in "the global South," but even within that global rubric, they take relatively marginal positions. Even in "major" regions discussed here (East Asia, North Africa, Latin America), encounters with "minor" people in provincial towns or agricultural backwaters become the vehicle for thinking about national histories and even imperial networks. The apparent omission of data from more central or prominent sites of global cultural production provides the basis for illuminating recastings of over-familiar stories. Thus, Mark Harris's contribution from South America is about riverine peasants in the Brazilian Amazon, people who are seldom included in official histories and "regionalist" narratives, but whose cuisine, routines of hospitality, and elaborate theories of food-borne pollutions can be analyzed for their traces of both Portuguese imperial economies and indigenous cosmologies (or rather, and more meaningfully, imperialist cosmologies and indigenous economies).

North America is largely untouched as an ethnographic field here, except in Anne Meneley's article, where her Yemeni hosts constantly attribute her maladroitness to the fact that she is Canadian, producing their own ethnography of North America based on their encounter with her. Yet the crucial contemporary concerns that dominate North American conversations, including nutritional poverty amidst caloric affluence, genomic modifications, and food safety in industrialized food production, are by no means neglected in the essays that follow. However, whether it is Keck's concern with how biosecurity regulations intersect with cultural understandings of the act of eating animals, Penny Van Esterik's report from a deeply food-insecure country, or Elizabeth Cullen Dunn's account of how displaced people in Georgia dealt with the glut of boring, empty calories delivered to them in the form of humanitarian food aid, the analytic issues of food policy take on a distinctive, local valence.

Ethnography as it is practiced here seldom produces clear recommendations for change, or advocates one alternative over another. The ethnographers are all astride large and long-term processes, but their primary effort is to register the conditions and impacts in which people seize these processes and make them their own, for better or for worse—not to critique the processes themselves but to better understand how they are lived. Clearly iniquitous and humanly damaging conditions are described here—most intensely by Van Esterik and Dunn. The local impacts of food insecurity, of displacement and violence, and of industrialized and commodified production are registered (the latter, most often, striking the note of sorrow for something lost, the elegiac mode in anthropology). But equally, the pleasure of night fishing (Riley), delectation of carefully saved honey or jam (Dunn), and cycles of work and leisure associated with places we might otherwise describe as deficient in nutrients, money, and global connection must be registered. Ethnographic encounters always happen between whole persons, who aim to know and relate to each other in the round. This aspect of ethnography is the basis for a gain in knowledge which might empower critique, but it is not itself that critique. That said, one important contribution that such ethnography can provide is to underwrite what has been called the "anthropological veto": the challenge to abstractions which says, "No, not here [or there]; it is not like that where I work." Or, as Sahlins insisted in the passages quoted above, food is not just about nutrition, for distinctive moral meaning and community are made in each exchange of food, too.

Small Morals

Meneley's essay on learning to comport herself in appropriate ways, in the face of the almost over-generous hospitality of her Yemeni hosts, introduces many themes that resonate throughout this volume. Adapting to local food customs is revealed as a key aspect of learning what those customs in fact are, not as an abstract table of "dos and don'ts," but as a way of expressing ongoing, changing, mutable relationships. Meneley takes us through a fieldwork experience which is shared, with differences, in many of the essays here: fieldwork as a constructive, pedagogical process which starts with one's own body, where learning occurs in the constant, everyday practice of elaborate and yet flexible systems of etiquette and expectation. Moreover, this is a mutual practice—her Yemeni interlocutors commented on what they took to be Canadian norms, and on the difference from their own ways of eating, sharing, hosting, and indeed being. At its best, this mutual exchange reveals the flexibility and communicative breadth of both cultural systems. Moreover, as Meneley is at pains to point out, and as Nina Hien explores in more detail in her essay here, people everywhere navigate within their own food systems, and have their own personal preferences and dislikes. Often, the first thing a fieldworker has to learn is how to say "enough," to end a meal without losing face or shaming her hosts. Meneley does arrive at that point, learning that "as long as you [had] established that you did not disdain all Yemeni food, saying that you did not like a particular dish was fine."

Much of what Meneley writes about is specific to Yemen, even to the milieu of a particular town, and that is what gives her ethnographic writing its texture and motivates her, and her hosts', comparisons. Specific dishes, particular ways of preparing and taking *qat*—a chewable leaf with stimulant properties—and the conversations and encounters that occur during and over these meals all are recounted with zest and flavor intact. We encounter many of the same habits and even ingredients in the next essay, Berman's account of cooking and eating, over thirty years of visits she has made to Kenya, with a Muslim Gujarati family in Mombasa. This cultural similarity, with important differences, between provincial Yemen and cosmopolitan Mombasa reflects Indian Ocean cultures and how they have been shaped by generations of travel and exchange between East Africa, the Middle East, and India. These travels maintain continuities, too: The family and community Berman lives with in Kenya cook and eat a distinctive cuisine, and an identifiably Indian one, characterized by fried flatbreads and coconut rice served with aromatic curries.

Yet, the context Berman describes is fast changing. She conveys much of the specificity of the food through careful accounts of the actual cooking, with attention paid to the work of the household and the techniques with which the food is prepared, and then recounts the ways in which the changing socioeconomic circumstances of this family, and for Mombasa at large, have introduced new habits, tastes, and desires—as well as allowing some of the women of the family to direct their work of cooking toward the marketplace, and earn income. All of this change and flux is understood within the framework of care, affection, and mutual curiosity constituted over a long friendship, and even as food habits change (and as each individual's dietary needs also change) cooking and eating for and with each other remains a site of intercultural exchange and understanding. Here, as for Meneley, Harris, and other contributors, food is the vehicle and the substance for forging connections, and Berman's essay folds out from the compact descriptions of techniques and routines of food preparation to indicate some of the contemporary urban changes her friends are living through.

That is to say, food habits, or simply table manners, are indeed "small morals" (a phrase, and a comparison, coined by the seventeenth-century English political philosopher Thomas Hobbes in *Leviathan*). Meneley recounts an exacting training in another morality and set of moral and social relations through the constant talk about, monitoring of, and generosity with food and cooking. Likewise, Harris's essay about *panema*, or contagious threats to masculine skills of hunting and fishing among Amazon-basin riverine peasants, demonstrates how the social world that links humans to their natural environment (through "edible" relations with, and ideas about, animals, spirits, and the like) is managed through prohibitions and taboos both minor and great. Harris's focus on the historical production of the norms and habits now embedded in ideas like *panema* presents some very interesting comparisons with Keck's very different topic of biosecurity measures and the control of trans-species contagion in Hong Kong. Both authors are drawing, critically, from the tradition of structuralist studies that mapped conceptual schemas and symbolic interrelations hidden in meaningful uses of foods. Harris and Keck produce novel insights into how such schemas are not only expressions of logical or conceptual problems, but are actively drawn upon and reshaped to meet challenges and threats in the widest social environment, including dangers presented by the proximity of animals and humans, when both are equally seen as living beings and moral subjects in a world of interdependence.

One theme that reoccurs across all of these essays, mostly in illuminating asides that emerge from the conscious focus on various fieldwork experiences, is the negotiation and navigation of fieldwork ethics. This emerges here as a matter of subtle negotiations of hospitality, reciprocity, and both social and biological boundaries, rather than as a question of adherence to bureaucratically defined human subjects' protections. The co-presence and co-residence entailed by ethnographic fieldwork of this kind brings both ethical and biological burdens, and moreover often exposes the fieldworker to disease and infection, or at least the threat thereof. For Harris, it is a *cafezinho* made with suspect river water; for Meneley and, likewise, for Claire Nicholas and Van Esterik, the water presents quotidian dangers, the results of which are both unpleasant and ultimately, for Van Esterik, very serious. For Hien, it is a matter rather of pungent, and to some people repellent, ingredients such as fish sauce and durian, which pose no danger other than to the taste buds of the ethnographer. It is the standard advice, only half-jokingly offered, to fieldworkers: Make sure your water is boiled. The essays here openly discuss how these hygienic requirements, imposed by the unskilled body of the Western ethnographer who is "not used to the food," lead to the negotiation of different demands, the distant one of medical advice, the proximate one of reciprocal engagement. In all these cases, one's fear of disease, one's disgust, is no match for the obligation to accept gifts when they are offered.

Safety and Security

The conventional narrative in food-related social science has it that countries on the up-swing of development will move from concerns with food security—adequate nutrition for the whole population—to new concerns with food safety that are particularly associated with large-scale industrial processing and anonymous chains of food production and packaging. Ethnographic research puts these assumptions in a new perspective, highlighting the interdependence of food safety and food security, and further drawing attention to broader moral and political concerns that are also involved in seemingly technical questions of nutrition and safety.

In his account of biosecurity measures implemented to control the spread of avian influenza, Keck works with chicken farmers, hangs out in the part of a marketplace reserved for selling live chickens—and now for killing them as well, so that chickens will not be slaughtered in home kitchens, which risks wider contamination and spread of the disease—and follows the practice of Buddhist groups that buy live animals at the markets and release them back into the "wild" (though, as he discovers, this could be seen as another form of consumption, especially since the wild into which the animals are released is a densely urbanized area and not all that hospitable). The biosecurity and food safety measures that Keck follows from farm to market to consumer, not only raise public health and epidemiological questions about the different practices of farms and food-producers on the two sides of the border between the Hong Kong SAR and mainland China, they also raise questions about how we view and understand animal life, and how we manage the relationships we have with those we eat.

Like Keck, Van Esterik's consideration of food security in Lao PDR also uses ethnography to ask questions about the assumptions built into public health studies. Van Esterik uses a very serious food-borne illness that she herself experienced—a physical collapse brought on by cumulative infections—as a way to understand the embodied reality of the inequalities she has always been conscious of in her fieldwork in Southeast Asia. However, her experience of illness did not diminish the importance of sharing food and care with the very food-insecure Lao with whom she works. She ultimately returns to Lao PDR, but with a new, tangible sense that the standard distinction between food security and food safety is a very limited one, and both are embedded in very complex cultural assumptions about food sharing. Van Esterik reveals that food safety, most especially clean water, is an integral part of any analysis of food security, while the embodied travails and illnesses, which helped her arrive at this insight, convey a strong moral message about the responsibility that comes with ethnography, and with an awareness of our shared humanity amidst research.

Food, Reciprocity, and Fieldwork

Jordan's account of her sociological search for the heirloom tomato (discussed above) provides a bridge into a set of papers that return to the theme of cultural learning, moral entrainment, and table manners, with a sharper focus on moments of exchange and reciprocity in fieldwork, and how these can structure our opportunities to learn and form relationships in fieldwork.

There are both opportunities and limits that come with the highly interpersonal and relational process of field research. Nicholas, for example, writes about a women's weaving cooperative in Morocco and her struggles to maintain a certain autonomy from her (female) host, in order to have a freedom of movement and encounter denied to her host's daughter (though Nicholas's own freedom of movement remains largely within a female sphere). Meneley's and Berman's similarly nuanced accounts of how food-labor is socially organized also focus on women's work and highly gendered patterns of segregation. All three essays are by women who researched in areas with strong norms of gender segregation (though not ones that are by any means immutable, as all three essays show). In many ways, forms of segregation are presented as an opportunity and a benefit by all three: They engaged in the life of the household in ways their male companions and co-workers could not. By contrast, Harris's essay dwells on a particularly masculine contagion, which only affected him in his occasional journeys with the men in his field site on hunting and fishing trips.

Gender is something lived and experienced in these accounts not as a pre-existing identity or fixed set of cultural norms, but as a result of exchanges, relations, and (sometimes highly unequal and exclusionary) impositions on the body of the ethnographer. The contrast here between what different fieldworkers are able to experience and understand opens up the other half of the observation that encounter-based fieldwork is about encounters with other people where *they* live; it is also a method that involves the social body of the ethnographer, a body that is differently marked, bounded, vulnerable, and put in relation in varying contexts.

Hien dwells on a learning process that affects and involves both ethnographer and ethnographed (as it were), here in a time and place—globalizing Ho Chi Minh City, Vietnam—where both seemingly settled national identities and habits of consumption are being transformed, as signaled by a new availability of and interest in the exotic. Hien asks here the key anthropological (and sociological) questions for any study of food and culture as tastes travel, and cosmopolitan opportunities become an urban, and urbane, norm for a large, affluent strata of global citizens: "So how exactly does something strange become adopted in or adapted to the local 'menu'? How does it get included in the repertoire of acceptable and agreeable flavors and tastes, and possibly even cherished? . . . And furthermore, what does not make the cut onto the plate and the palate, and why?" Broad in scope, such questions can only have local answers, attentive to national and personal histories, as well as to the remarkable pertinence of embodied boundaries, as Hien herself experiences and as her relatives in Vietnam also do, when she tries to cook an Italian meal for them. It must be said that Hien is herself an accomplished cook; while Meneley and Nicholas did not entirely have to feign their lack of cooking skills in the field, and Kathleen C. Riley and Harris had to learn new ways to gather, fish, and hunt for food, Hien underscores that these are not just deficits in technical knowledge—ethnographers also have to learn, or at least negotiate their lack of, skills with tastes and relationships internal to the cuisine.

It is not accidental that these issues of both boundaries and reciprocities come to the fore in food-related contexts. All the essays, in different ways, provide examples of the place that food can have in social life, both and at once an object of exchange and an object of sociality—nutritional thing, object of experience and thought, and a tool to wield in social relations with others. It is a general point supported by these essays that exchanges of food are especially fraught occasions for the ongoing negotiation of social relations and relative position. As Sahlins noticed, "Direct and equivalent returns for food are unseemly in most social settings: they impugn the motives of both the giver and the receiver" (1972: 215). Thus, for Nicholas, payment for her room and board was never enough to put her in a straightforward relationship with her hosts. Yet her struggles to define her own autonomy, as a separate member of a household with a strong female head and patterns of communal cooking and eating, help Nicholas clearly identify issues and sources of tension in the weavers' cooperative, which was the main focus of her research. By the end of her essay, a residential arrangement that was at first simply a necessity and sometimes an inconvenience becomes the basis for highly personal, and affecting, portrait of the head of the household. As Riley says in her essay here about the crucial connections by which people ensure access to foods in the French Marquesas, "Repayment is not the issue, relationship is." Nicholas registers just how difficult, or at least awkward, this can be in practice, but also just how essential this ethnological fact, cross-culturally applicable, is to the possibility of ethnography in the first place.

Food and money are not, of course, the only thing exchanged in fieldwork—so is language, as Riley emphasizes here, and learning to exchange words for food is one of the first tasks of any ethnographer. The processes by which the ethnographer learns to exchange words for food, or food for words, can reveal wider patterns of socialization, as well as whole economies of food production and consumption embedded in long histories of culture, contact, and change. As a linguistic anthropologist, Riley brings a special sensitivity to language to her work, while situating her study of language socialization in a richly described context of social labor related to provisioning and consumption. Work, food, language, and learning are woven together with the historical specificity of a fascinating context in which routines and rituals are heterogeneously composed of indigenous precursors and old and recent imports (mostly French). In Harris's essay, economies are shown to be intensely personal, infused with moral and social substance, not the least elements of which are the tastes and flavors of the foods this economy delivers. Riley focuses in conclusion on the specificities of how children learn to navigate this context by managing specific exchanges of words for food, offering a demonstration of how table manners both reveal and form the basic units of social being. As she describes the reciprocal relationships here (both analytic and practical), "Children learn through socializing interactions not only how to deal with food and how to talk about it, but also how to use it to negotiate social relationships within a society in which one's access to food depends primarily on one's social relations."

For Robert, the connections forged through eating together are not just a matter of sustaining the living; in the Buddhist practice of his friends in Hanoi and Ho Chi Minh City (Saigon), they are also a matter of connecting with dead ancestors and recently lost family members. This creative vitality, at the heart of the work of mourning, is compared with the ways in which he, himself, as a foreigner and someone strange to many people he met in Vietnam, both was incorporated and learned to incorporate himself in more durable social relationships (though not without some misunderstandings along the way). Ritual gifts of food sustain a distinctively Vietnamese Buddhist way of mourning and composing a human community (which includes both the living and the dead), and these remain powerful customs within the urban landscape of Vietnam, across many, sometimes violent, social changes. Robert registers these changes visually and in asides, while discussing how certain foods and habits are adopted to navigate both personal and social relations.

The tastes and complex relationships—of memory, desire, custom, and comfort—that make an edible object food are at the center of Dunn's concluding essay on the humanitarian food aid distributed to displaced persons in the Republic of Georgia, and how it becomes the quintessential "non-food," a symbol of abandonment, loss, and lack of relationality. It is a terrible paradox that efforts by aid organizations to reach out to the displaced, precisely to link up the charity of affluent others elsewhere with the need of those displaced by war, must be so material and embodied and therefore so open to mistranslation; such translation is always a risky endeavor, even when the object of translations seems as innocuous as macaroni.

Dunn's essay also offers a stern lesson about how difficult it is to apply utilitarian calculations in any endeavor involving human beings and their needs and desires. Ultimately, the displaced persons with whom she works find innovative new uses and values for their humanitarian macaroni (though, sadly, at a steeply discounted rate given its sheer plenty), and manage to salvage some old tastes and memories from their erstwhile homes. If the macaroni is perceived as a non-food, Dunn learns this through rich, sensory, embodied sharing of *other* foods, learning to appreciate honey and jam in the way that her interlocutors do. In this contrast, and what it helps Dunn see, this essay offers quite a strong, local image of a wider reality: the suffering and struggle that accompanies an artificially produced and inedible plenty flown in from overseas. Adequacy of food supply is never enough. Humanitarian aid here offers a mirror for our own cultural preoccupations with calories rather than satisfaction.

Food there should always be and yet it is never just food, or merely food, with which we deal. This is a sentiment and an insight long underwriting food studies, and which the contributors to this volume share with many, from diverse fields, who choose to write about food. The journalist, epicurean traveler, and food writer M.F.K. Fisher once said (in the midst of World War II) that she wrote about food not *instead* of writing about putatively more important topics, such as war or love, but because such themes were all gathered together in the acts of eating, cooking, and sharing food: "There is food in the bowl, and more often than not because of what honesty I have, there is nourishment in the heart, to feed the wilder, more insistent hungers. We must eat" (Fisher 1943: ix).

–1–

Food and Morality in Yemen

Anne Meneley

I was sick and moaning after our first meal upon arriving in Yemen's capital, Sana'a. I may have unwittingly taken a sip from the water glass set out on the table. It was not the food, but the water in which the food was washed or cooked that made me sick, as Yemen's water supply was certainly not safe at the time. At the American Institute for Yemeni Studies, a hostel where many academics stay on their way to and from their field sites, a seasoned American scholar of religious studies hurled a bottle of Pepto-Bismol at me, and berated me for being so naïve as to travel without it. Soon, I was carrying the pink bottle with me everywhere, furtively taking swigs as one might from a hip flask. Our three months in the capital were spent studying Arabic with a tutor every day, and making countless trips to the Yemen Center for Research and Studies and the visa office, in an attempt to get permission to go to Zabid, where I had planned to carry out my field research. My husband and I and the director of the institute often had lunch at a somewhat depressing little spot down the street from the institute, run by the son of a Vietnamese mother and a Yemeni father who was said to have fought in the Vietnam War. They served a lukewarm, watery sort of Vietnamese soup without spices and slabs of fried *dayrak* (kingfish), an oily fish which to this day I cannot abide.

My main culinary pastime in the capital was an endless quest for meals that would not make me sick: With our Arabic tutor, Ibrahim, we often went out for *ful* (fava beans) which was made in stone pots in a furnace so hot no parasites could have possibly survived. *Salta*, a meat stew seasoned with fenugreek, was cooked in a similar fashion. We also made occasional trips to a beloved Lebanese restaurant for hummus and French fries; I am sure they served more exciting dishes, but my tender stomach craved something safe and bland. I later heard that this restaurant, sadly, had been destroyed in the 1994 Yemeni Civil War. My husband sampled the deep-fried locusts in the *suq*, which he said were like a salty, crunchy snack, but I stuck to getting my salt and crunch from pistachio nuts. Another culinary specialty, from the coastal plain of the Red Sea, the Tihamah, where we would eventually end up, was fresh fish, slapped on the side of a wood-burning furnace and served with delicious round flat wheat loaves adorned with *hubb as-sawda* (black cumin seeds).

We were eventually allowed to make our way to Zabid in June 1989, after a three-month delay in the capital. While most of Yemen is mountainous and cool, Zabid is located on the humid Tihamah, where T. E. Lawrence, among others, suffered mightily from the blistering heat. We arrived while Zabid's torrid summer was in full swing, which was a shock to our Canadian physiology. Had we not had such difficulty getting permission to go to Zabid in the first place, I would have been tempted to flee the first day. The hottest season was also the most beloved social season: the wedding season. Almost immediately after moving into our house, I was invited to dozens of parties, including wedding lunches, which I initially viewed with absolute dread. One of the reviewers of my book *Tournaments of Value* noted that, while I had plenty to say about competitive hospitality in Zabid, I did not actually mention much about food itself.

When I contemplate why it was that I published so few of my own stories about Zabidi food, I am sure it was because they were often, at least at first, narratives of humiliation. I hated eating in public in Zabid for at least the first four months of my stay. This was not because Yemeni food is inherently hateful or even that unfamiliar, aside from the above-mentioned deep-fried locusts (and sheep's eyeballs and camel-hump fat). In fact, in Zabid, a formal lunch included boiled lamb, rice, potatoes in a tomato sauce, a salad of green onions and tomatoes, okra, and a *maraq* (lamb broth) in which freshly made bread (made from wheat or sorghum, both delicious) is dipped. Dessert consisted of a pastry dish called *bint as-sahn*, or "daughter of the plate," a thinly layered pastry adorned with honey and *hubb as-sawda* (black cumin seeds).

My discomfort about eating in public, therefore, was not really about the food, for which I eventually became quite nostalgic. Nor was it merely because of the food's uncomfortable physiological aftershocks: I was plagued by a parasitical infection I'd gotten from the water, so the ingestion of food was not always followed by a gratifying fullness, but by pain, embarrassing rumblings, and wild-eyed searches for a bathroom, in case my regular doses of Pepto-Bismol or Imodium failed.

Rather, in retrospect, it seems as if my dislike of mealtimes stemmed from my anxiety about being unable to accomplish feats that were ordinary for everyone else I was with, and hence feeling like I was sticking out like a sore thumb. I spent the first few months trying to acquire the everyday "techniques of the body," to use Marcel Mauss's evocative phrase, which are so engrained that the Zabidis take them for granted. I would join the women squatting on the ground around large communal dishes, each person helping herself from the many plates of food. My problem was that squatting was not a technique of the body I could easily accomplish, so I lived in constant fear of flipping over backwards. Like many Muslims, Yemenis eat only with the right hand. My Yemeni hosts often plunked down a large portion of steaming lamb right in front of me. I found myself struggling to tear off a bit of boiling meat with only my right hand. And I was befuddled by the Yemeni technique of tucking a small handful of rice between one's forefingers and thumb, which was then popped elegantly into one's mouth with nary a grain wasted. In contrast, I ended up with a few grains in my mouth and the rest on my dress. Of course, techniques of the body such as eating are so deeply inculcated as to be taken as natural, so the Zabidi reactions to their awkward guest (my status as an anthropologist was never very interesting for them) from Canada would inevitably include a murmur of surprise: "My God, they don't even know how to *eat* in Canada." Someone else was likely to holler to my embarrassment: "Bring her a *spoon*" (a utensil which I never found of much use when addressing the boiling meat). A child might be sent to bring me a cushion when my wobbling got too obvious. Also be aware that at mealtimes, as at all times in Zabid, I was too hot, and the relentless humidity rendered me a good deal sweatier than is optimal for social engagements.

Any pause in my pace of eating would prompt the hostesses to urge me, the guest, to eat. The cries of "Eat, eat!" would ring out. Or else indignant questions such as, "Why are you being shy?" or, "Aren't you comfortable here?" often made me struggle to continue, despite my difficulty in keeping food in hand as it travelled to mouth. When I had had enough, or at least enough trying, I would rise, saying the only acceptable thing to get oneself out of eating, "*Al-hamdulillah* (Thanks be to God), I'm full" and escape my hostesses' protests that I had hardly eaten a thing. While I was self-conscious about being the center of attention, this urging of the guest to be comfortable and eat her fill was integral to proper moral comportment in Zabid.

Even the young children were trained in this generous behavior: Children as young as three years of age would offer me bits of food or join the others in urging me to eat. This, I might add, is in stark contrast to our own children, who are taught to consider their own needs first. Children were often sent over in the mornings by their mothers or fathers to bring my husband and me fresh limes, dates, or other fruits from their agricultural estates, which surrounded Zabid. I kept a stock of gum, candies, and *batates Nom'an*, small bags of potato chips adorned with the characters from *Ifta ya-Simsim*, the Arabic Sesame Street (the show from which I first learned to count in Arabic), to gift to the young food deliverers. In this way, I entered into food exchange relationships with my tiny, curious neighbors, who loved coming over to our house.

Gender and Food

In Zabid, we faced a different set of circumstances than we had in the capital, because we began to conform to local gender segregation practices, which were essential for proper moral comportment. In Sana'a, it was possible for foreign women to go to restaurants (although I would not have tried it without male accompaniment) that Yemeni women would not have gone to, or to go to male *qat* chews, which no self-respecting Yemeni woman would ever have done. But in Zabid, by conforming to gender segregation, I learned much more about how food is prepared and ingested along gendered lines. While it is still commonplace for people to assume gender segregation is the worst form of oppression, it has its advantages. While women do all the cooking in the home, men do all the shopping. So that meant that in the late morning, while I was hanging out with my friends in cool, dark rooms of the old mud-brick houses with their distinctive elegant facades, cracking *zayaka* (toasted watermelon seeds) with my teeth to get the tiny seed-meat, my husband was out in the sweltering sun at the open-air fruit and vegetable markets, haggling over a few cents for a bunch of bananas or a papaya. For the most part, he enjoyed bargaining, but there were occasions when he would have been happy to pay a little extra to get out of the hot sun. If he had, however, he would have been berated by his friends for being a fool *and* driving the prices up. Since food, aside from dry goods, is never kept in the house (very few people had refrigerators and those who did turned them off at night to save electricity), shopping for fruit and vegetables, and fish or meat (caught or slaughtered every morning) was a daily event. After that, men went to the *qat* market to haggle for *qat* for their families, including their wives; women in Zabid, unlike in some parts of Yemen, were daily chewers, at least the married women.

Some older women, over sixty, who had been through much in their lives, no longer cared about gender segregation, or veiling for that matter. Our neighbor across the street, Alia, was one such woman. Her husband had died several years before, when her now twenty-year-old daughter was still very young. Her daughter wore the all-enveloping black *shaydar*, like the majority of young Zabidi women. But Alia and my elderly landlady wore short-sleeved, midriff-baring shirts and ankle-length skirts while at home or in our neighborhood, dressing more formally only when they left our narrow street. We parked our small jeep outside of Alia's front door; whenever my husband drove up, she would come out and yell, "Whoaa Faidhallah," and they would have a small chat.[1] Alia made and sold *lahuh*, delicious sorghum bread—rich and chewy with bubbles on top. As soon as we moved in, we became regular customers.

The food was bought and delivered by men, but everyday food, such as rice and potatoes, was prepared over tiny propane burners by women. The key spice was a *zahawig* (chili relish) made of hot peppers and garlic, which were ground on enormous mortars and pestles. If invited for lunch by close friends, I would go over early to "help" prepare the meal. I would usually be given some simple task, such as peeling garlic or chopping onions, but it was always clear that they thought that I was monumentally incompetent in the kitchen, an opinion which was not unfounded. One of my favorite dishes was made of ground camel meat prepared with onions and hot peppers and covered with a pastry topping. It was then sent out to a bakery that had huge wood-burning furnaces. The other pastry dish, *bint as-sahn*, was also sent out to these local bakers. I realize now that I never actually saw one of these bakeries, because while women always prepared the food, the bakers were men, so one of the young boys in the family would be assigned the task of taking the prepared food to the oven and bringing it back after it was baked. Like shopping for food in the market, interacting with the male bakers was a job for men or teenage boys. While in small families, men, women, and children would eat together, in Zabid's *kabir* (so called, great families), they never did, because men would always have to be prepared for unexpected guests to drop by. Some poorer clients ate with the men of the great families every day. So the women and children would eat separately, often entertaining female guests or neighbors for lunch.

I really did not know much about cooking at that stage in my life so, just as Steve Caton recounts in his lovely ethno-memoir of fieldwork in Yemen (2005), we ate a lot of odd tuna conglomerations when we cooked in our own home. While I still like tuna-fish sandwiches, which got me through writing my dissertation, combining heaps of tuna and rice and whatever vegetables we could find into a kind of hash did not constitute a dish that we have ever remembered fondly. When I was given a portion of meat on *'id al-adha* (the feast after Ramadan where sheep are slaughtered), I protested that I didn't know what to do with it. My landlady was appalled by my lack of culinary skills, and because she insisted that it was *baraka* (a blessing), I felt compelled to take it. The other food that was offered on religious occasions was *shafut*, (sorghum bread soaked in watery yogurt and covered in green onions). I literally could not eat this dish without becoming immediately sick, so for months I would accept it and then throw it out, until I realized that it was perfectly acceptable to say that certain foods did not please you. After all, Yemenis, like people everywhere, have particular food aversions and preferences. As long as you established that you did not disdain all Yemeni food, saying that you did not like a particular dish was fine.

Yemenis, like other Arabs, are famed for their generosity and hospitality, which was always dispensed in gender-segregated contexts. What counted for hospitality in Zabid was not necessarily the food itself, as the meal was fairly standard. For the most notable hospitality events, the wedding feasts, the meat and rice were cooked in enormous caldrons by the *muzayyinah*, a status group comprised of butchers, barbers, and circumcisers. The female neighbors would join the women of the host family to prepare the rest of the dishes, the salads and pastries, in evening work parties, which were usually a great deal of fun. The men would have their wedding meal and *qat* chew on one day, and the women would feast the following day. What was really important, for both men's and women's feasts, was the quantity of the food: It was a great shame for a host family to leave a guest hungry. At one wedding, a low-status man, who was one of the last to eat, exclaimed loudly after lunch that he was still starving. The higher-status guests are served first, but it is a great shame not to have enough food even for the lowliest guest. In this context, a guest is a guest and should be well fed, regardless of status. The neighboring families who heard this comment (it went quickly from the men's gossip circuit into the women's) displayed a certain *schadenfreude*, even glee, at the host family's failure and the besmirching of their honorable status. Despite wealth, considerable landholdings, and influence in the schools and local politics, there was much back-talk about how the family was miserly, how the house was never prepared for guests and that it took forever for guests to even be brought a glass of tea. Talk about the stinginess of the offering of food and drink was skillfully managed: A gossip was careful to know her audience. Had this kind of gossip become known to the host family, there would have been hell to pay, as stinginess, the opposite of the much-praised generosity, is considered a sin in Islam. Proper moral comportment in hospitable behavior was essential for a family's honorable status.

The food product that was used to make qualitative distinctions between guests at weddings was honey. Each region of Yemen has its own honey, the taste of which varies according to the kind of plant on which the bees feed. The honey from the Hadramawt region of Yemen was most prized, and the most expensive. The higher the status of the guest, the higher the quality and more expensive the honey he or she was served, usually poured over the pastry dish *bint as-sahn*. At one wedding, a host eager to show his hospitality to the foreign guest, or perhaps to make sport of him, poured honey directly into my husband's mouth, practically drowning him; this was not at all a regular practice. Yemeni honey has an international reputation: At a honey store in the Old City in Jerusalem, Yemeni honey was accorded a place of honor and was of the most expensive for sale in the shop, which featured honey from all over the Middle East.[2] When I returned to Yemen in 1999, I was surprised to see a very fancy honey store on one of Sana'a's main shopping streets. It resembled the designer olive oil and gourmet food shops found in North American and European cities of late: clean, uncluttered presentations of expensive food items, elegantly packaged. It stood out quite markedly from the usual Yemeni food shops, which tend to be cluttered or presented in the old style of the *suq* [market]. I later heard that this business was a front for Osama bin-Laden's shady interventions in Yemeni politics, although like many rumors in Yemen, this was never confirmed or denied.

Social interactions involving food were occasions when people would position themselves in solidarity with or opposition to others. Over time, one neighboring family started to send one of its young children over in the morning to invite us to join the family for lunch. These casual invitations were an index of closeness, as was the meal itself: We would often be served fish in a tomato sauce, whereas a more formal lunch, as described above, would always include boiled lamb. The family would say, "See how much we love you? We're comfortable to invite you no matter what we're eating!" A family with whom there was a more competitive relationship would never be invited under such circumstances. A guest would never offer to bring a substantial dish, as this would imply that the host family was unable to afford to feed guests properly, or worse, that the guest feared the host family would be stingy with food. Nonetheless, I felt the need to bring something; we could not reciprocate with a lunch because no one, not even me, had faith in my cooking skills. I was also "alone" (i.e., the only woman in my house), and hosting meals required considerable female labor. When we were in the capital, I would stock up on the kinds of candy, chocolate, and nuts that could not be purchased in Zabid. Upon arriving to someone's house for lunch, I would, without ceremony, hand over the superfluous treats to my hostess, who would chide me saying, "Shame. Why did you trouble yourself?" I would reply, "Oh, these aren't for you, but for the children," which was acceptable.[3]

Food and Global Political Economies

Practices surrounding the acquisition, preparation, and consumption of food in Zabid are inflected by gender and religion, although people never actually discussed it in such a fashion, as it was simply a part of "practical consciousness." But food production and consumption were also idioms by which moral judgments about global political economies are made. A Zabidi social norm I found it difficult to conform to was the practice of not talking during meals—proof that techniques of the body, once acquired, are as difficult to let go of as new ones are to acquire. The Zabidis tend to eat swiftly and silently. My inclination to chat while eating was indulged but perceived as somewhat bizarre. Yet these mealtime chats, though atypical, were moments when my Zabidi friends made moral evaluations about life in the West. The Yemenis would note that we eat from separate plates, whereas they eat communally, implicitly criticizing the individualization of our society versus the communalism of theirs. A Yemeni friend who married a Dutch woman said that the most jarring thing for him was to go to someone's house for dinner and to have the plates already made up. So instead of allowing the guests to eat as much as they want, the host rations the amount of food that the guests can consume without asking for seconds. To have to ask for more food in Yemen is embarrassing both for the host and the guest.

As I was told by my Yemeni Arabic tutor in the capital, Yemenis find it discomfiting when they are asked by North American or European hosts if they would like something to drink. If a Yemeni guest did agree to a cup of tea, he would further be discomfited by the question, "Do you want sugar in your tea?" Sugar is an index of generosity; to ask if someone wants sugar implies that the host or hostess is a *bakhil* or *bakhila* (miser). In Yemeni households, the tea would simply be brought to the guests. Any time a visitor enters the home of another family in Zabid, he or she (hosted by family members of the appropriate gender) is brought something hot and sweet to drink, or something cool and sweet. The hot drinks are either tea or *gishr*, a drink made from coffee husks and flavored with ginger, cardamom, and sugar. The cool drinks include a vile fruit syrup called Vimto mixed with water and added sugar, fruit juice, or Canada Dry Cola. This last drink constitutes Canada's sole fame in Yemen, and it is not even sold in Canada. In fact, when we first said we were from Canada, the children would giggle madly and intone, "Canada Dry Cooola"![4]

While it is the height of rudeness to ask a guest if they want something, as it implies that the guest is not really welcome or the host is reluctant to give, it is also insulting for a guest to refuse to consume what is offered. When I was in Zabid in 1999, for only a short visit, I was accompanied to the home of my former neighbors by a friend, Aysha, who lived in another neighborhood. Aysha seemed very uncomfortable. I later found out that the two families had been involved in a dispute over land, and when the hostess did not ask after Aysha's parents and family, she was so indignant that she left without accepting a glass of tea or *gishr*, deliberately insulting the family.

Sugar is what makes a drink an appropriate item for hospitality. As in our own lexicon, "sweetness" is thought to be a positive quality of a person. In Yemen, as mentioned above, it is also thought to be an indication of the generosity, and not to put sugar in tea or *gishr*, or to ask the guests to help themselves, indicates that the host or hostess is a miser, which is one of the harshest terms of moral opprobrium. An exception is that when visiting following a death, *gishr* is served without sugar; guests appear without makeup or gold jewelry, and sit on couches shorn of their comfortable cushions. All of this signifies that it is not a time for generosity, comfort, or display of any kind. A host family that serves sweet drinks at a funeral reception will be the subject of much negative talk.

If I ever slacked in eating when invited out for lunch, women would ask me, "Do you think the food is better in Canada?" which usually led to a discussion of what in fact we ate in Canada. They asked me if we served lamb to guests, and when I admitted that in my Albertan family, beef was a more common prestige meat, they looked disgusted. I never once was offered beef in Zabid. (I understood why when I later saw the very sad looking Yemeni cows, staggering about in the sweltering heat, if one can forgive the small ethnocentric judgment about the cows of the Other.) I noted that camel meat was completely unknown in Canada, whereas it was common enough in Zabid. Because camels are so big, they are not slaughtered every day as are sheep, since all the meat must be sold and cooked very soon after it is slaughtered or it will go bad. The day before a camel is to be slaughtered, it is marched around Zabid with a long necklace of jasmine flowers around its neck. The butchers ring bells and announce the forthcoming slaughter loudly. The cynical amongst my friends swore that the butchers would march a nice, young, plump camel around the town, and then slaughter a stringy old beast the next day!

Elsewhere in the Middle East (see Limbert 2010 on Oman), or even elsewhere in Yemen (see Maclagan 2000 for highland Yemen), women's parties tend to be occasions where food is served, but Zabidi women's parties, held in the evening, center around *qat*. *Qat* is a leaf that contains a mild amphetamine-like substance that tastes roughly like what one would imagine chewing a hedge might taste like. Guests bring their own *qat*. The hostess' hospitality focuses on an initial glass of tea or *gishr*—thought to be appropriate for countering the dehydrating effects of *qat*—and the *mada'a*, which is a tall water pipe in which uncured tobacco is smoked. While I recognize that the consumption of strange, preferably mind-altering substances may be part of an anthropological desire for exotica, I loved *qat* chewing, which I found much less difficult than mealtimes. And a little mild amphetamine after a long, hot day in Zabid was welcome. In Yemen, *qat* chewing is a practice that people are attached to affectively and which represents positive sociality among human beings; it is said to define "Yemeniness" in a distinct way. Talk, food, and *qat* all occupy the mouth, but there is a complex relationship among them. The verb *khazzan* (to chew) is used to refer to the activity whereby one consumes *qat,* but instead of chewing and swallowing as one does with food, one stores the chewed leaves in one's right cheek. One obviously cannot chew and eat at the same time, but chewing *qat* without eating a proper, hearty meal beforehand was thought to be dangerous for one's health. *Qat* is also an appetite suppressant, so people eat very lightly afterward, if at all. Its other effect on the digestive tract is to cause constipation, which I actually found to be a useful antidote for the consequences of my parasite-ridden intestinal tract.

In the capital, we mainly chewed with Ibrahim's friends, male university professors, and the more mature Peace Corp volunteers who were ready to accept the local stimulant and the sociality associated with it, as opposed to those who were trying, probably futilely, to get high by smoking nutmeg or banana peels. As I began chewing *qat* on a regular basis in Zabidi women's circles, people would say to me, "You chew *qat*, you smoke the *mada'a*, you dress modestly, *khalas* (it's over), you're a Yemeni now." For an anthropologist, *qat* chewing is a godsend: Amongst women, *qat* is exchanged fast and furiously and observing and participating in these exchanges revealed much about local alliances and hierarchies.[5] When people chew *qat*, they are also just sitting around chewing the fat of their daily existence, which is what we as anthropologists want to hear. Along with eating Yemeni food, chewing *qat* indicates that you are not a sanctimonious Westerner, as every Yemeni is aware that foreign aid donors routinely describe *qat* chewing as the source of the myriad Yemeni problems.

Women did not chew as much *qat* as men, approximately one-third to one-quarter of what their male counterparts chewed. Despite the fact that *qat* is an appetite suppressant, they felt it was important to have something in one's stomach after chewing, sometimes only a glass of milk and cookies, or sometimes a teenage boy would be sent out to fetch *mudarbash* (deep fried spiced sorghum balls). The women and girls would squat around this beloved local fast food and break off bits of the steaming dough and dunk them in the accompanying thin, but spicy, tomato sauce.

Despite ambivalence about *qat* chewing—several times I heard people, happily chewing away, say that *qat* was responsible for Yemen being *ta'ban* (tired)—they still claimed that *qat* was superior to our leisure drug, alcohol. Although several of my field note entries began with "Vaidila is talking about cold beer again," neither my husband nor I drank publicly in Zabid. We did admit to doing so in our home country. The use of ingestion practices—the use of food, alcohol, tobacco, or drugs of various ilks—to define and differentiate one group or people from another is well documented in anthropology. So, too, is the use of consumption practices to make moral evaluations of people. To say someone was a bad person in Zabid, one would say, "He drinks." Although some Zabidi men did drink alcohol, especially after chewing a great deal of *qat* (which can cause sleeplessness), it was generally considered to be a grave moral flaw.

After the Christmas we spent in Yemen in 1989, my father sent me a photo of the familial Christmas dinner table in Alberta, replete with roasted turkey and full wine glasses. When they saw the picture of the twenty-five-pound turkey, the Zabidis exclaimed, "What on earth do you feed your chickens?" I tried to deflect questions about the content of the wine glasses, knowing that the consumption of alcohol was not approved of by pious Zabidi Muslims. But I noticed that the mere mention of Christmas was enough to evoke shocked glances from Zabidi women, followed by averted eyes and a quick change of subject. I was quite mystified by this reaction, thinking that surely they must know that we celebrated different religious occasions, and after all, Jesus plays an important role in Islamic theology, although he is described as a prophet, not the son of God. Eventually, a Zabidi man told my husband that he knew all about Christmas: the excess food and drink that would drive people to turn off the lights and have sex with anyone, their mother or their brother, anyone. This apocryphal story had gained a foothold amongst Zabidi women, although I eventually managed to convince them that Christmas was actually a much tamer affair where I grew up!

Videos of Bollywood movies were a common backdrop to women's socializing; the movies, even though no one understood Hindi, were popular for their music, dancing, and fashion. Also popular, for reasons still not entirely clear to me, were videos of the World Wrestling Federation (WWF), which one would not have thought would appeal to pious and proper Zabidi Muslim women. These shows were considered the epitome of vulgarity by my Irish Catholic mother, so I was mystified as to why similarly pious folk would enjoy them. When I pointed out that these wrestling competitions were all staged, I elicited an indignant response. An elderly woman sharply contradicted me: These wrestlers were made wild and violent, she said, by the vast quantities of *lahm al khinzeer* (pig meat) that they consumed. The consumption of pork, which is forbidden to Muslims and a meat that is virtually impossible to purchase in Yemen, had a reputation for causing uncontrolled and irrational violence. While they recognized that not all of us were WWF stars, this was an implicit critique, or explanation of, Western intervention in the Middle East, which did seem to them irrational and violent. The first *intifada* in Palestine was going on at the time and daily we would see news reports of armed Israeli soldiers shooting small children for throwing stones. I was routinely asked how the U.S. and Canadian governments could support such irrational, brutal violence toward children. I had no good answer then, and I still do not.

Ramadan presented particular problems for us as everyone knew we were not Muslims, yet for more than a month before Ramadan, they all kept asking us if we would be fasting alongside them. We did not know what to say: We wanted to fit in as much as we could, and we honestly thought that the questioning meant that they thought we should fast. On the first day of Ramadan we tried to fast. We made it until about noon—not so much because of hunger but because of thirst, which we could not tolerate in Zabid's sweltering heat. As a compromise, we decided that we would not cook anything in the middle of the day. Our kitchen, as in many houses in Zabid, had high walls surrounding it but no ceilings, and we did not want the cooking smells to torment our fasting neighbors. We subsisted quietly on tuna fish sandwiches and boiled water furtively drunk. We were invited to a neighbor's house to break the fast on the first day of Ramadan: When I was asked if I had fasted, I confessed that I had not and the woman replied, "That's good, because if you had fasted without converting to Islam, we would have thought you were a *himaar* (donkey)!" I would have appreciated knowing that before I spent a month worrying about it! I was also told that Westerners were too morally *da'if* (weak) to fast as the Muslims did. Nonetheless, Ramadan turned out to be one of my favorite times of the year. I took to going over to my friends' house in the late afternoon to help them prepare food for *iftar* (the special meal to break the fast). As we prepared the food and waited for sundown to break the fast, we also lit coals in preparation for those older women who wanted to *yishrub* ("drink") the water pipe, after having a quick glass of water and a date. For many of them, the prohibition on smoking demanded more of a sacrifice than giving up food for the day.

Even though I was not fasting, I still got a sense of the community generated by this collective ritual. After the *iftar* meal, groups of women from the same neighborhood or family would go to make short visits to all the families in Zabid with whom they had connections. Generally, one would stay only for a quick glass of the dreaded Vimto with added sugar. I could not abide it, and my best friend, Magda, whom I often went out visiting with, told the hostesses that I was prone to a condition known as *barud* ("cold"), where one's extremities would suddenly become cold and clammy despite the heat. According to Magda, this condition is brought on by having too many sugary drinks, so with her intervention, I was allowed to drink incensed water instead of Vimto.[6] (Another time when I had been diagnosed with *barud* by Magda, she and her mother burned the soles of my feet with hot coals to warm up my limbs. Once was enough for that treatment!)[7]

Shortly before I left Yemen in 1990, Magda's sister showed me an Egyptian magazine with a picture of George Bush Sr., who was then U.S. president, holding a bunch of broccoli, a vegetable which was unknown in Yemen at the time. She asked me, "Why doesn't he like this *shijara* (tree)?" The irony of this question struck me forcefully: The vast majority of Americans (and Canadians, for that matter) would not even know the name of the Yemeni president, let alone his food preferences or dislikes. This small, seemingly insignificant anecdote seemed to me to capture the inequities of global political economies, where the everyday food habits of a U.S. president become global news, while the news from Yemen would suggest that Yemenis "eat" only *qat* and bullets, giving no sense of how everyday social reproduction through food is accomplished. Yet, for the Zabidis I worked with, how one interacted with food was a central way in which one constituted oneself as a Muslim and as a properly respectful gendered social being, as well as being a powerful medium for commenting on, and making moral evaluations about, power inequities between the West and the Middle East.

Acknowledgements

My first thanks go to the friends in Zabid, who fed me and taught me about food and much else. Thanks to our American friends who fed us in the capital, to the American doctor, who cured me of parasites and much more, and to my parents-in-law and my parents, who thought it was their duty to feed us as much as possible when we unexpectedly had to return home for a month, sick and emaciated. Thanks to Vaidila Banelis, Bruce Grant, Paul Manning, and Donna Young for their comments on this paper. Thanks to Leo Coleman for inviting me to join this volume. Writing this paper sparked a memory: The two beautiful frying pans in which we cooked our meals in Zabid were given to us by Cynthia Myntti, who had been charged with closing down Selma al-Radi's house in Sana'a and disbursing her belongings. I did not meet the indomitable, unforgettable al-Radi until I went back to Yemen in 1999. It was with great sadness that I heard of her recent death. This paper is dedicated to my mother-in-law, Nijole Banelis, who finally taught me how to cook. My Zabidi friends would appreciate her gracious hosting.

Notes

1. My husband's Lithuanian name, Vaidila, seemed less confusing in Arabic than in English. People simply substituted an "f" for the "v," which doesn't exist in Arabic.

2. Honey is also valued for its curative properties, especially in curing stomach ailments.
3. I would also bring perfume from the capital, where there was a much wider selection than in Zabid. This would be tucked away and eventually used as an element of hospitality, as it was sprayed on guests' hands after they had washed from the meal, and any female guest arriving for a visit would be offered perfume.
4. Political posters of the president of Yemen, Ali Abdullah Salih, also featured Canada Dry Cola, "blending domestic kitsch with global capitalism" (Wedeen 2008: 73).
5. For greater detail about *qat* exchanges, see Meneley 1996.
6. After one particularly bad bout with giardia, we went to Sana'a, where I was given the awful Flagyl to treat it. This drug is very harsh, making one feel as if one had had one's stomach cleaned out with a toilet brush. When we returned to Zabid, I was determined not to get infected again, but after a twelve-hour wedding party where I refused anything to drink, I was so dehydrated that I could hardly think straight. We boiled water in our own home, but drank water in the homes of our Zabidi hosts, as we did not want to reject what we were offered, and in any event, dehydration was more of an immediate threat than parasites. We finally got cured after we returned to Canada.
7. A further analysis of this treatment, as well as the use of food avoidances in the case of illness, can be found in Meneley 1998.

–2–

It All Started with the *Bhajias*

Nina Berman

It all started with *bhajias* back in 1980. After finishing high school, I was living for a few months in Mombasa, Kenya, working as a gofer assisting John, a medical doctor and close friend of my family. John had bought what was then the Tower Hill Hotel, and was pursuing his plan to turn the facility into a rehabilitation clinic. I lived at the hotel, and over time struck up a friendship with the plumber who took care of the ever-nonfunctioning pipes and drainage systems in the colonial-era building. The plumber, Kassam, loved to talk while drinking beer. So while he downed his *Tuskers* one after another, I listened to his stories on the veranda overlooking the port in the Port Reitz section of Mombasa—an area nobody would think of today as having recreational value. One day, Kassam asked me if he could introduce me to his wife, Kulsum. Of course I agreed, and the next day he brought her to the hotel. I can still see Kulsum just as she was that day: sitting outside on a bench under cashew-nut trees, and after a few first words, offering me *bhajias* from a cloth-covered bowl. These crisp, little patties—a deep-fried mix of *dal* lentils, onions, and spices—were delicious. I can no longer remember if Kulsum had brought the coconut-based dipping sauce that usually accompanies the various types of *bhajias* in Mombasa, but from that day on, these delicacies became a food I would dearly crave. We ate together and exchanged our first few words, Kulsum at times asking Kassam to translate for her, as her English was rudimentary. Before I said good-bye and thank you to Kulsum and Kassam, we all agreed that I would visit them at their house the next day.

So it all started with *bhajias*, with a gift of food, and by now, my thirty-year-long friendship with the Sameja family (which is part of the larger Sameja clan) is one filled with stories of scrumptious food and affectionate encounters. Food is central to understanding the life of the family; its preparation and consumption structures the day; it is a vehicle facilitating social encounters; and it also provides opportunities to earn a little money on the side. As is the case with cultures around the world, conventions concerning food in the Sameja family also, over time, tell a story of change and continuity, of modernization, social mobility, and the preservation of tradition.

Before I talk in more detail about the role of food for the Sameja family and for my relationship to them, let me offer some detail about the family's cultural background, economic situation, and social relations among family members. The Sameja clan is part of the Muslim Bhadala community of Mombasa. The Bhadala people, who speak Kachchhi, can be traced back to the area of "Kati *bandar* [Katiport near Karachi] of Sindh from where they migrated to Koteshwar" and various locations in the present-day state of Gujarat in India.[1] When exactly the first Bhadala came to Kenya is unknown. Hussein, the oldest brother of the Samejas, claims that their ancestors were already in Kenya by the time Vasco da Gama came to the area in 1497. One version of how Vasco da Gama found his way to India gives credit to a local Gujarati man who was familiar with the monsoon winds, and passed on the knowledge to the Portuguese explorer. Since the term Bhadala "means seaman or fisherman or one who earns a livelihood by catching fish and navigating the sea," it is not unlikely that this Indian man was in fact a Bhadala.[2] Economic relations among the peoples of the Indian Ocean have existed for centuries, so my friend's claim to this longer history is not at all surprising.[3]

In the 1980s, the Samejas lived in a very modest home in Sparki. Usually, one would not find Indians in this area, as this small neighborhood close to the center of Mombasa was, and is, mostly populated by black Kenyans and a few poor Arab families. (When I returned in the 1990s after twelve years away, I couldn't find the Samejas's house right away, and was laughed at when I asked for the house of a "Muhindi" family: "No, Indians don't live here!" But that was not true.) The father, Kassam, was a bit of a black sheep in the family: Most of his and his wife's brothers had managed to become quite wealthy through their work as car mechanics. Some owned their own workshops, while others worked for well-to-do family members and received a comfortable salary. Kassam's situation was less fortunate: His main employment was a job as a plumber with the city of Mombasa, which brought some benefits but only a meager income. He did some freelancing on the side, but the main reason for his dismal financial situation was the fact that he had drowned whatever ambition he had in his substantial beer and occasional marijuana consumption.

But Kassam was lucky to have married a resilient and resourceful wife, Kulsum. In fact, theirs was a love marriage, as opposed to the customary arranged marriage. Because Kulsum often questioned her own wisdom in having married Kassam, she was not particularly open to the idea of a love marriage for any of her nine children. All of their marriages were arranged.

When I met the Samejas, the three oldest daughters, Hawa, Selma, and Najma, had already married and left the house. Yet money was scarce, and a large family still had to be fed. Six children remained, four daughters and two sons. The oldest child of the family was Hussein who had just married Mariam. Mariam turned out to be as hard-working, warm, and practical as Kulsum, and was thus a good match for Hussein, who had begun working at a very early age. In fact, these days, after having worked himself, not from rags to riches, but certainly to a comfortable middle-class life, Hussein likes to tell the story of how small he was when he started his first job. He was about ten years old, and he was so small that when he locked up the workshop at night he had to move a little stool to the door in order to reach the key and turn the lock.

To supplement the scanty salary of Kassam and the eldest son, some of the women of the household sewed clothes for various stores in town. Kulsum would also occasionally be hired as a singer for engagement and wedding parties. I loved every opportunity to accompany her on those occasions; it was a pleasure to hear her beautiful voice and to be able to observe the ceremonies.

Together, these various activities enabled the family to pay for the basics. The house had electricity and water, but no flush toilet. Two of the four small bedrooms were occupied by the couples—the parents and the oldest son and his wife. One room served as a living room, and had a sofa and two chairs. The last of the four rooms was shared by the four girls and the youngest child, a boy, and the occasional visitor. Along with two beds, there was a simple mat that could be rolled out on the floor. One night, when we came back from some event or another, I found a note on one of the two beds that was written by Rehman, the youngest son: "This bed for Nina only!"

At this time, the family did not have a refrigerator. The only piece of electronic equipment was a boom box, which was turned on as soon as the men of the family had left the house. Music from popular Indian movies provided the soundtrack for most of the activities in the house. No refrigerator meant that food had to be prepared fresh at almost all times. Shopping for food, preparing it, and sharing it structured the day of the family, particularly the women. Being a woman, my interaction with the family was primarily with the women, and thus food was central to my experience with the family. If I was spending time with the women, it was in one way or another always connected to food. At breakfast, Mariam or one of the sisters would prepare *maani*, an unleavened flatbread that is also known as *roti*. *Maani* is made from whole-wheat flour, salt, and water. The dough is kneaded for quite a while, and then divided into small balls that are rolled out with a rolling pin. The family prepared three different types of *maani*: *ossi maani* (cooked in a pan without *ghee*, or clarified butter), *pacheli maani* (with *ghee* spread over the bread after the dough is baked), and *tareli maani* (where the dough is fried—the most delicious version in my opinion). *Tareli maani* was rich enough that when dipped in tea it was sufficient for a satisfying breakfast. Another version of breakfast consisted of fried eggs prepared with chili peppers and onions that were scooped up with *ossi maani* or *pacheli maani*. Sometimes, leftovers from the night before were heated up and eaten with *maani*. At other times, the family bought beans cooked in coconut sauce from a vendor across the street.

For me, the best part of breakfast was the tea. Spices—ginger, cardamom, and a little cinnamon—were ground by using a small stone rolling pin on a large black stone. The water was heated together with the spices, sugar (lots of it!), and milk (unless somebody requested black tea, the standard was *chai*, tea with milk). Kulsum and Mariam made the best tea in the world!

The family usually ate in shifts: The men were fed first, and then left for work. Afterward, the children and women ate. There was no table in the house in Sparki. Instead, a large woven mat was rolled out on the floor, and everyone sat in a circle around the dishes. Each person had a plate, and the *maani* and beans and fried eggs were presented on larger plates placed in the middle of the mat. We didn't talk much during meals; usually we ate in silence, and conversation picked up again toward the end of the meals. Lunch and dinner were arranged in similar fashion. Vegetable, meat, shrimp, or fish curries were served with rice and pickled mangoes, yoghurt, and, always, *maani*.

Shopping for and preparing the meals took up a significant part of the day. Dishwashing, cleaning, sewing, ironing, and washing clothes by hand were done in between meals. But there was always time to lounge on the beds, talk—and snack. I remember very well how the atmosphere changed once the men left the house. Suddenly the noise level rose, the boom box was turned on, work was dropped for the moment, and everybody started chatting, arguing, and playing. "Guards" were posted outside to watch for the men. When they were spotted, the boom box was turned off, brooms picked up, dishes washed, and clothes ironed and folded, all of it in earnest silence. That diligence continued until the father, older brother, or uncle left, and the house began to buzz once again.

Sometimes visitors came, and twenty people would suddenly fill a small room with their bodies and voices. Visitors had to be served food and drink. Among the everyday snacks between meals were *mabuyo*, which are made from the dried pulp around the seeds of the baobab tree and prepared in a mix of sugar and red dye. The taste is sweet and sour. Among the more special snacks were baked foods, roasted nuts, and cassava chips. Water was offered, sometimes tea, and at other times *Vimto*, a dark red soda that contains berry juices and spices, and is extremely sweet.

After lunch, it was usually time to nap, and then it was time to shower and change into new clothes. In the late afternoon, the family would either visit another part of the family to share afternoon tea, or visitors would stop by and be served tea—and *bhajias*. My favorite *bhajias* are those made from chickpea flour. Potato pieces, chili peppers, herbs, and onions are cut into the liquid dough and deep-fried. A dip made from grated coconut, chili peppers, salt, garlic, cilantro, and lemon juice perfected the delicious fritters. All visiting was accompanied by at least sharing a drink, mostly tea, and some food.

Food was, of course, central to all festivities, be they engagement or wedding parties, or religious festivals. The Bhadala community in Mombasa built a community center at which many weddings were and are celebrated. Women cook all night to feed up to four hundred people, working huge pots, chopping tremendous amounts of potatoes and onions, and talking into the wee hours.

One food item that deserves special mention is coconut rice. In the 1980s and still today, the Samejas made coconut rice the way it has been made for centuries. In fact, the Moroccan traveler Ibn Battuta, who visited East Africa in the late fourteenth century, provides a description of the preparation of coconut milk that captures all the essential steps.[4] First, a coconut is split in half, and then the halves are grated, using a special stool. One sits on this stool, which has a protruding grater attached to the middle of the front part of it. The coconut flakes are put into a small pouch made from raffia fibers, which is then submerged in water and squeezed until the water turns into a white, fatty liquid. Rice is cooked with equal parts water in a large pot, and once the water is absorbed, another part of coconut milk is added. A lid is placed on the pot, and hot charcoal is added on top of the lid. This way the rice can slow-cook with heat from the bottom and top, similar to how it would cook in an oven. When the rice is ready, the crunchy top layer is always a favorite with the children.

I visited Mombasa and my friends six times in the early to mid-1980s. After a twelve-year hiatus, I returned in 1998. Much had changed in the intervening years. Kassam and Kulsum still lived in Sparki, together with the family of one of their younger daughters, Shenaz, whose husband was out of work at the time. All the other sons and daughters had married and lived in various places throughout Mombasa, but usually not too far from the parents' house. Hussein, the oldest son of the family, was doing well, and had moved his family to a nearby middle-class neighborhood. He rented two two-bedroom apartments on the second floor of a house to accommodate his own family and that of his youngest sister, Maimuna, who had lost her husband, and had moved in along with her three children. In addition to the pick-up truck he had already owned in the 1980s, he now drove a Toyota Corolla. In Hussein and Mariam's house, the lonely boom box from earlier years had been replaced by a large arsenal of appliances: a TV and DVD player, a stereo system, fans, a blender, a refrigerator, and even a freezer. During my next visit a few years later, Hussein was proud to show me his latest purchase: a computer. Hussein stopped attending school after third grade and doesn't write or read well, and his main use of the computer is to play card games. We both marveled at the change, from the modest house in Sparki to the flats that were equipped with all kinds of electronic gadgets.

With a freezer and refrigerator came white bread, butter, jam, and soda. *Maani* is no longer made every day. The coconut dip is now prepared in a blender, as are the mixtures of spices for the curries. Spices for the tea are sometimes ground fresh, but often a ready-made mix is used that is bought in the local supermarket.

That tea is still delicious, but no longer tastes the same. Mariam maintains a traditional home, but the next generation is eager to try out new foods. The youngest son of Mariam and Hussein, Abduli, often refuses the traditional food, and opts for white bread with butter and jam. At lunch and dinner, soda has replaced water. Shamaila, Hussein and Mariam's middle daughter, tells me that she likes to cook pasta. Raziya, the oldest daughter, and Sabira, the youngest daughter, are quite interested in pizza and hamburgers, and Mariam herself craves hamburgers once in a while. But when we went out one day to an Italian restaurant in Malindi and ordered chicken, everybody agreed that Mariam's roast chicken was much better. And it is. The family eats out once in a while or picks up take-out food. During my last visit, in winter 2009–10, we ate at one Indian restaurant (something we had never done before) and, in addition to the Italian joint, at a couple of barbeque places that have sprung up all over Mombasa's sidewalks. The food was always good (with the exception of the tourist-oriented place in Malindi), but quite expensive and never as good as Mariam's cooking.

The curry, *pilaw*, and *biriani* prepared by Mariam, and also by her daughters, are still the best that I know, as are the rice dishes and the soups. These days, Mariam also cooks *ugali*, the staple food of all of Kenya. For *ugali*, white maize flour is cooked with water and salt until it turns into a thick dough. Mariam adds some fried onion and spices and then fries slices of *ugali* in *ghee*. When we share our meals, we no longer sit on a mat on the floor, but on chairs around a round table that can accommodate up to seven or eight people. We still eat in shifts, but I have moved up, since now I belong to the senior generation.

However, one sociable and culinary activity has remained unchanged since the early 1980s: the visits to Mombasa's Lighthouse area on weekend evenings. All along the waterfront adjacent to the lighthouse, on Mama Ngina drive, vendors sell roasted corn, sweet potato, cassava, hearts of palm, coconut water from young coconuts, cassava chips, soda, and ice cream. A mix of chili powder and salt is sprinkled on the roasted cassava and sweet potatoes, and the snack is perfected by a drop of lime juice—mouth-watering as I write about it (and mouth-burning if there is too much chili!). The Samejas, especially the younger family members, enjoy the trip to the Lighthouse each time, as it is one of the few social activities outside of the house. Buying snacks is the official reason to make the journey, but meeting friends and family is always one of the main objectives. The extended family is large, and every visit to the Lighthouse area will result in exchanges of gossip and gazes; for the unmarried teenagers it is one of the few public places where they can eye potential mates.

Memories of my thirteen visits (so far) to the Samejas always connect food to social activities. When, in the early 1980s, we visited Hawa, the oldest daughter of Kassam and Kulsum, who lived at the time with her family in Gongoni, we stopped in Malindi and bought some refreshments. That's when I was introduced to *paan*, a unique digestive snack. There are many different types of *paan*, but the basic principle is always the same: on a fresh leaf of betel, various seeds, shredded areca nut, sometimes dried fruit, spices, and syrups are spread. Then the leaf is rolled up, and the mixture is enjoyed in small bites. My first *paan* was bitter and made me throw up; most likely it contained tobacco. But I came to love sweet *paan*; buying two or three of that variety, with the sweet sticky syrup oozing out of the leaf, was always one of the first things I would do after arriving in Mombasa. In the 1980s, *paan* sellers, *paanwallas*, enjoyed telling stories about the effects of the various seeds and tiny pills they added to the individual *paan*: This one will make your skin look radiant; this one is good for your breath; this one will make you attract your lover, and so forth. I have not heard anybody tell stories while preparing a *paan* in a long time. The next generation of *paanwallas* no longer seems to be interested in continuing a tradition that requires both customer and vendor to enjoy banter and extended interaction.

During our last visit to Malindi, we bought fresh *halva*. We had to wait quite a while for the store to open after the lunch break, but it was certainly worth it. I am not exactly sure what kind of grain was used to create the gelatinous dough (but I made sure that it wasn't wheat, as I am gluten-intolerant); I do remember that it was made with almonds and was absolutely scrumptious. We immediately devoured a large piece; the rest was saved for the evening, when we lounged on sofas, pillows, and the carpet, and nibbled on the *halva*, fruit, and other sweets as we watched one of the four-hour Bollywood movies that have often filled our Saturday evenings since the 1990s when the first VCR arrived at the home of my friends.

As life for my friends has changed, so, of course, has mine, but we have succeeded in adapting to new circumstances in very satisfying ways. An example of this aspect of our relationship involves, once more, food. I was surprised to see that my friends adjusted quite easily when I came back in the late 1990s and told them about my recently diagnosed gluten intolerance. Their reaction was much more accommodating than that of my relatives in Germany, who would either simply ignore my condition or pity me for having to eat the dry cookies they bought for me while everybody else was feasting on triple-layer cakes. In general, Indian cooking is much more conducive to a gluten-free diet, so there wasn't really a problem anyway. I just could no longer eat the *maani*. But, and this is a good example of how food preparation was a way to create and strengthen our connection and friendship, Mariam went out of her way to find additional foods that I could enjoy. That's how I got to know *kibibis* and *mkate siniya*. They are both made from the same basic dough: white rice is soaked for several hours and put in a blender with coconut milk. Then eggs, sugar, ground cardamom, and yeast are added to the thick liquid. After the dough has risen, little pancakes are fried in *ghee* to make the *kibibis*. For the *mkate siniya* (which is Kiswahili and means "Chinese bread"), the dough is poured into a baking dish, and baked until golden brown. It turned out that *mkate siniya* is one of the favored Ramadan foods, and through another friend, I found a woman who prepared it extremely well. I put in an order almost once a week and loved having it for breakfast.

Food structures the day and creates social relations. Food preparation is also a source of income for the Samejas. In the 1990s, two of Hussein's sisters, Najma and Selma, made and sold *bhajias* on the side of the street in front of Najma's house. During my last visit, the Sameja women, including Hussein's sisters Faiza and Shamshad, prepared an order for two hundred *samosas*, the triangle-shaped, deep-fried pastry that is filled with a meat or vegetable mix. But the most impressive food-selling operation of the Sameja household is Mariam's ice cream business. Mariam started making ice cream a few years ago. She boils a mix of condensed milk, milk, and sugar in a big pot, and then adds various flavors. She packages her ice cream in little cups, and adds a small wooden stick to eat it with. She does not advertise, but has won a large clientele by word of mouth. Her husband is not so fond of Mariam's entrepreneurial ambitions, so to avoid conflict, Mariam managed to hide the business for three months by placing the freezer she was using out of the way. Once the husband discovered the secret operation, it was already so successful that he gave permission to Mariam to continue her work. She enjoys running her business very much; as her children have grown up, married, and left the house—only the handicapped son remains at home, although the girls love to visit their parents for extended visits—she itches to be involved even more in some sort of business. If she were given a chance, she would run a restaurant, and it would surely be popular.

On my last evening in Mombasa in February 2010, we Skyped with my daughter, Milena. When Mariam asked what Milena would like from Mombasa, my daughter, who has visited Mombasa four times, immediately said: "Your cooking!" My friendship with the Samejas began with *bhajias*, and it has continued over many years, during which we shared countless dishes, teas, and sodas. Food was the catalyst that started a deep friendship. In some ways, the food is an end in itself: I just love eating it. But without the people I am connected to through it, without the warmth of our interactions, the hilarious, serious, and enlightening conversations, the movies and the music that accompanies it, I would surely not crave Mariam's food so much, nor with so much affection.

Notes

1. See, Mohidden, Md. Azeez (2003), "Bhodala," in K. S. Singh (ed.), *People of India: Gujarat*, vol. 22.1 (Mumbai: Popular Prakashan), 234.
2. Ibid.
3. For a history of the Indian Ocean trade, see D'Souza 2008.
4. Gibb, H.A.R. (trans.) (1958–2000), *The Travels of Ibn Battuta* (London: Cambridge University Press). The description of making coconut milk is in volume 2 (1962): 389–90.

The Enchantments of Food in the Lower Amazon, Brazil

Mark Harris

Fieldworkers often struggle to find the most opportune time to visit their informants at home. When I was doing fieldwork on the floodplain of the Amazon River, I soon discovered that mid- to late afternoon was the best time for me to call on people. The end of the day was approaching, and if the heat had not exhausted my potential hosts, their work had. So they could be found at home doing odd jobs, or snoozing in a hammock. As I approached a house I would clap my hands loudly and shout, "*Oba!*" in order to announce my arrival. It could be a rude awakening! If anyone was around, I would tell them the purpose of my visit and hope to get invited in.

Each visit followed the same pattern. I was offered a *cafezinho*, a little coffee, and I knew that refusing was unthinkably rude. But when I started living on the floodplain, I was extremely wary of accepting. Many houses had one glass for all to share, and the coffee itself was made from river water that may not have been boiled. It contained large amounts of sugar, not added according to individual taste in each cup, but poured in liberally when first brewed. The coffee would come, poured from a thermos flask, and I would be asked if I wanted even more sugar. Bitter tastes, such as unsweetened coffee, are not generally appreciated here. While I sipped uncertainly, I knew at least I would have a calorific jolt that would help sustain my side of the conversation. I would like to think that the muddy waters of the Amazon improved the taste of the coffee.

This ubiquitous sweet cup of coffee, and its entangled history of taste, invention, and colonization, is a gateway to understanding the world of ribeirinhos—the people who live along the banks of the Amazon River. The sweet coffee is created from local and distant ingredients, and it is part of a form of etiquette associated with hosting visitors. Above all, it represents a small, but hard won, cultural peculiarity, familiar enough to outsiders but strange enough for them to comment on the experience.

The three elements in my glass—coffee, sugar, and river water (forgetting the microbes for a moment)—make an interesting trinity. Coffee is a very popular local drink. It has been served in much the same way for a couple of centuries, according to the scientists, naval officers, and chroniclers who have told of their adventures along the river. Even though the economic significance of coffee was only realized in the mid-nineteenth century, it has been exported from the Amazon since the 1730s; indeed, the Amazon was the first place it was planted in Brazil. Now it is unusual for floodplain dwellers to grow coffee, but if they do, they roast it themselves—in sugar, of course. Mostly it is produced in the southeast of Brazil, near São Paulo, and bought from shops in a nearby town, already roasted and ground (the nearest shops were about five hours boat journey away).

Sugar has an older provenance, and was central to the colonizing effort, the conquest of territory, and the work of slaves. Another well-liked drink is a liquor made from fermented sugarcane juice. The liquor, known as *cachaça*, was an important form of currency in trade relations between Indians and the Portuguese. It is still used as a form of payment, sometimes by anthropologists.

River water is naturally and abundantly available. It is seen by riverine people as a source of their strength. By drinking it, they become protected against certain diseases, quite the opposite of my own view of these things. One man told me that he would not get cholera because he always drank from the river. Only upper-class people suffer from such diseases, because they drink bottled water and do not build up their bodies with local produce. Indeed, the people who live along the banks of the river draw their water directly from the river many times a day. They are peasants in the sense they are in control of their labor and have to sell goods to local markets in order to raise money. Many are dependent on bosses for the extension of credit. They fish most days, invariably traveling by canoe, even short distances, and observe the river's ebb and flow on a daily basis as they wash clothes, pots, and themselves at the riverside. Their lives are organized around and on the river so it is not surprising that its water is seen as a kind of fortifying tonic, whether consumed plain or in coffee.

The coincidence of the local and distant, the dependent and autonomous, in culinary matters brings to light otherwise hidden features of social life. The complicated historical pathways that have contributed to making contemporary Amazonia are manifested plainly here: Ribeirinhos draw their cultural traditions from Amerindian, African, and European influences. And yet, in the standard view of Brazilian history and social sciences, they are seen as cultures "in between" and therefore without their own pasts, at least ones officially recognized. Yet, their perception of food, and the rules surrounding its consumption, demonstrates the vitality—and the historicity—of their way of life.

Food, for ribeirinhos, represents a relatively free expression of taste and preference. It has not been subject to direct ideological and material control by powerful outsiders as has most of the other areas of their lives, such as family and gender relations, labor power, land ownership, religious beliefs, and so on. Of course, it has been subject to indirect shaping, as outlined with reference to the glass of coffee. During the centuries of direct colonial rule in Brazil, the Portuguese brought in a series of laws to order social life, including an end to multifamily housing (the indigenous big house, *maloca*), and compulsory labor service. These laws were difficult to enforce, but they left traces in the political consciousness of these people; memories of exploitation, injustice, and violent punishments figure prominently in their oral histories. Ribeirinhos continued to be subject to forced labor obligations until 1850, and thereafter were tied to patron-client networks (particularly through creditor-debtor relationships). Since this time, a large part of their production has been oriented toward their own consumption, allowing them a degree of autonomy, especially in choice of diet. For example, "real food" is composed of either freely available or locally produced ingredients: fish, hunted meat, and manioc. These foods are a source of pride, as is the work that goes into providing the raw materials. Food behavior then offers a privileged access to features of social and cultural histories that may not be so easy to see elsewhere.

How we get, and share, food—even something like the *cafezinho*—also indicates the ethnographer's reliance on his or her hosts. I did not catch fish or hunt, or grow crops, and yet shared the food of my friends on the floodplain. Some of it I bought, but most was provided by their work and offered freely. In fact, my hosts' generosity extended to my then partner (and now wife), Anna. During my first period of fieldwork in the early 1990s, Anna accompanied me, carrying out her own investigations into women's lives and sometimes making visits with me. After a few months of living in the house of a middle-aged couple with grown children, we were allowed to build a small wooden house, perched, as all floodplain residences must be, on stilts. We gained a small measure of independence but still remained dependent on our neighbors for gifts of fish. "No one should buy food here," we were often told.

Over time, Anna and I became the subjects of the ribeirinho worldview. Our behavior was judged as less and less exotic, as it came to obey a local set of rules. About half way through our eighteenth month of fieldwork, Anna became pregnant. In the first months of her pregnancy, her tiredness seemed to rub off on me. We both felt a listlessness that could not be put down to a state of tropical repose. As far as I was concerned, it was a quite distinct feeling. I complained to my male companions. They all said it was quite normal, and that they had the same experience: I was undergoing an empathetic pregnancy, and this laziness could cause *panema*.

According to dictionaries, *panema* is defined as ill fortune in hunting or fishing and is part of ribeirinho culture in Brazilian Amazonia. This idea of contagious bad luck is thought to derive from Tupi-speaking Amerindians, though whether there is a direct correspondence between Amerindian concepts and *panema* is far from clear. Above all, *panema* is dangerous and feared because a man suffering from it may be unable to catch fish or game and therefore have no food to bring home to his kin. The term will be partly familiar because of the song, "The girl from Ipanema." There it refers to the beautiful beach neighborhood of Rio de Janeiro, the name of which originally meant "bad water" because it had few fish.

As a consequence of Anna's pregnancy and my capacity for being *empanemado*, or with *panema*, many of the questions we were asking about gender, pollution taboos, and livelihood-making took a less abstract turn. Suddenly, we both— but especially her—were the recipients of unsolicited advice about all sorts of activities that should be restricted and foods that were prohibited. I was not exempt: The father of the fetus was subject to controls similar to those put on the mother (a common practice known as the couvade). My incapacity became obvious to my fellows after my third unsuccessful hunting trip. I had accompanied four men to gather turtle eggs and catch *capivara* (capybara, a large rodent) at nighttime on the beaches surrounding the lake near the village, as I often did. These trips are some of my most enduring fieldwork experiences: the warm night sky with lightning always somewhere on the horizon, the relaxed banter between men working together, and the search for food. After the third trip in as many weeks with little to show for our efforts, the men blamed me for our bad luck and said I was *empanemado*. Anna was pregnant, thus affecting my capacity to hunt, which in turn "poisoned" the whole group. The situation was not intentional, but it was clear that my presence was no longer welcome.

In order to understand *panema*, it is necessary to outline the ribeirinhos' perception of the natural world. The nonhuman environment is understood to be guarded by the spirits of the animals, which are invisible to human beings. Humans are alerted to the presence of such spirits by the senses—hearing, smelling, and feeling. The spirits, too, can sense human presences. When a person enters this world guarded by the "mothers" of the animals, distinct rules apply to personal conduct. Men have to be careful when they are out hunting and fishing. They should not shout, but talk quietly amongst themselves, and not laugh too loudly, for fear of alerting any spirits to their presence. Neither must fishermen nor hunters take too many fish or game, which would anger the animals' guardian spirits. These spirits are offended particularly by human sexuality. This means that a woman who is menstruating or has just given birth should not go to the river's edge or into the forest; the same applies to a man whose wife has just given birth: he should do no active work for forty days. A woman who is merely pregnant, by contrast, is in a different position, as we will see.

Ethnographers of Amazonian peasant life say that, in general, *panema* is caused by contact between raw or freshly caught meat or fish (or the hunter) and a person or an object in an ambiguous relationship to "nature" and "culture." They understand *panema* to be an impersonal magical power, which can infect anybody, animal, or thing, but is incorporated and manifested by a man at a particular time and under specific conditions. Men only discover their bad luck after a series of unsuccessful hunting or fishing trips, where their failure cannot be attributed to lack of knowledge or generic misfortunes. The question is then, why does *panema* reside in certain kinds of foods (fish and game)?

Panema is embodied in a man, until it has been cured or his partner has given birth, and it is in his role as a hunter and fisherman that a man is subject to *panema*. A hunter of fish or game, by definition, traverses between the domains of the animal spirits—the forest, lake, and rivers—and the village. By using his equipment, he catches his prey and then brings it back into the house. He then gives it to a woman, who distributes it and turns it into food. Thus, it is in his actions connecting the world of animals and spirits with the community that he may have *panema*. A skillful hunter can outwit any animal or fish, but no hunter can defend himself against the forces of an angered spirit. In other words, fishing and hunting occur within the territory of spirits, who can cause harm, one manifestation of which is *panema*.

From the list below, we can see that the basis of *panema* is like an equation: If we have this and that, we might have *panema*. As Da Matta (1973: 70) notes, there are two active elements in the equation, the ones which cause *panema*, and a passive one, the person who or object that gets *panema*. All the cases are directly or indirectly related to food coming from the wild. Animals raised by humans or salted fish are not affected. Furthermore, the person who gets *panema* is the one who uses the hunting or fishing equipment and catches the game or fish.

Its causes, according to my informants, are various:

1. If a pregnant woman eats hunted meat or fish caught by a man, then he could get *panema*.
2. If a menstruating woman comes into contact with fishing or hunting equipment of a man, then he could get *panema*.
3. If the bones and entrails of a fish or animal are thrown from the house and eaten by domestic animals, then the man who caught the animals or fish could get *panema*, as well as the dogs that ate them.
4. If the blood of the game or entrails of fish are stepped on by someone, then the person who caught the animal or fish could get *panema*.
5. If someone urinates or defecates on bones or entrails that have been thrown away, then the hunter or fisherman could get *panema*.
6. If a friend or kinsperson is envious of the success of another person in fishing and hunting, then this could cause *panema* to that person who is the object of envy and the evil eye.
7. If a highly desired fish or hunted animal is not supplied to a woman or child, then the husband/father could get *panema*.

In this list, examples one and two involve a pregnant or menstruating woman. The invisible entities, sometimes in the form of an animal, are angered by the smell of blood and will magically harm a woman who comes near them. The spirit needs only look at the woman, and her shadow is taken away, leaving her ill or mad. A pregnant woman is in a position similar to that of a menstruating woman, though the pregnant woman has more power: She can fend off spirits, kill snakes by looking at them or by spitting on the ground, and can even make flowers wilt. She can also wash in the river. The pregnant woman actually poses little danger to herself. However, spirits angered by the presence of a pregnant woman can do harm to the developing fetus and occasionally to other people. Moreover, an expectant woman can affect an animal or fish after it has been killed, but before it is turned into consumable food. Hunting or fishing equipment, too, can get *panema* in much the same way that men can get it: by contact with a pregnant or menstruating woman.

Substances other than human blood continue to be important in examples three, four, and five. Fish bones, animal bones, and blood should be disposed of properly by either throwing them back into the river, or lake, or putting them in a hole, so that dogs will not eat them, and people will not urinate or defecate on them. Examples one through five thus share one aspect: fertility, either human or animal. It is the proper ordering of fertility that allows for food to be produced and consumed without posing dangers for the future.

Examples six and seven focus on jealousy and evil eye and are linked, since they both involve seeing something for real or in the mind. If one person has a strong urge for a particular type of fish, then it should be eaten in order to satiate the desire. If this desire is not fulfilled, the person responsible for bringing food into the house would, in effect, be refusing to recognize the other's desire for the food. As such, animals are dangerous, even in people's heads. With a pregnant woman, her desires are those of her baby, and those desires should be satisfied; otherwise, the baby will suffer and forever want things when it is born. People who are envious of the success of another man are said to be dangerous, because they can cause *mau olhado* (the evil eye), which results in illness or madness. Albeit unintentionally, the envious person causes harm to another, by stopping him from catching more animals or fish.

Cures for *panema* are applied once someone is convinced of his condition; these do not include banning women from contact with men, specific places, or activities. Indeed, women's participation is necessary to the cures, which involve herbal baths and fumigations, women running garlic over the affected hunting equipment, or biting the four corners of the fishing net. Another cure involves a man putting a very hot pepper up his anus. Fortunately, I was not forced to seek a cure; I merely exempted myself from hunting and fishing.

These are daily concerns for ribeirinhos, because *panema* puts the means for living at stake—work is no longer productive—and endangers the availability of food. If *panema* is about the process of making food from animals, the related concept of *reimoso* is about the qualities of different foods. *Reimoso* can be loosely translated as oily, fatty, and strong tasting. Foods with these characteristics cause sickness, and should only be consumed by people in very good health, and not by those in a transitory state such as puberty or pregnancy or poor health. The opposite of *reimoso* is *manso* (tame). There is a connotation of "poisonous" with *reimoso*, but only a few foods are considered intrinsically so, such as some game and catfish. *Reimoso* is neither subject to precise rules nor can it be predicted a priori. So a food, such as chicken, which is not normally considered *reimoso*, can be made harmful if it is prepared with too little salt or it tastes of smoke from the cooking hearth. Similarly, a pubescent child, someone in the process of bodily change, can become sick from the eating of a potentially *reimoso* food. In that situation, a person who is not in a stable corporal state can somehow expose the hidden qualities.

Both *panema* and *reimoso* work as a kind of sanction to ensure that food is dealt with respectfully. The conceptual core that *panema* and *reimoso* share is the sense of a dormant power or poison-like trace. The traces can be passed around and activated in particular contexts. This is revealing, given the fact that they have been shaped in and through the historical pathways mentioned at the beginning. The kind of analysis that concepts such as *panema* and *reimoso* normally lend themselves to, is, not putting it too strongly, antihistorical. Typically, avoidance of *reimoso* foods would be interpreted not as an isolated behavior but interpreted as a part of a larger system of ideas, symbols, and meanings. In turn, this analysis reveals the structures underlying the thinking characteristic of a culture or the coherence among functions of an interrelated totality. Each society then can be understood on its own terms. This perspective assumes the homogeneity and cyclical repetition of sociocultural beliefs and practices. But the analysis of riverine peasantries in the Amazon cannot be undertaken without reference to political, economic, and ideological influences since the colonial conquest, and how events have shaped the formation of particular groups over time (anymore than any other society). This is particularly so in the ribeirinho context because their social and cultural histories are intertwined with so many others: There is no integrity, or singular logic, generating cultural practices.

Panema and *reimoso* do not fit into a system of connected ideas or fundamental functions in ribeirinho life. They are two of many other behavioral complexes which have haphazardly come together in an inventive world of colonial and postcolonial Amazonia. I don't think it would be valuable to search for coherent structural patterns and its timeless reproduction. For human subjects do not pick their symbolic resources on the basis of how those resources fit into a preexisting totality, like arranging flowerbeds in a garden. Rather, such meanings are fought for, imposed, invented, lost, or perhaps they seep down to the present. Some might say they are the degraded complexes of Amerindian nations; others would argue they are European in origin and have acquired Amerindian terms and associations. This would be speculation and would be difficult to prove either way. It is helpful here not to assume an automatic connection between term and practice or belief. Nevertheless what *panema* and *reimoso* demonstrate is the historical resilience of particular cultural complexes. We do not need to know about their origins, just that they each exist in their own time, as their own strand of loosely associated cultural dispositions. In no simple sense should they be seen as locally generated concepts about food pollution. Rather *panema* and *reimoso* have a substance-like presence in the way they move along personal trails, which ultimately are part of historical and continental movements. They remain with the people whom they infect. Thus, where these people go, and those influenced by them in the intimate moments of life, will pass on these substances with new offerings of food.

What I find attractive and powerful about this approach is that it allows for features to be repressed or submerged, only to be reactivated if the context changes. A concept like *panema* is complicated, relational, and dynamic, and open to new influences. So, in any one historical situation, it is underdetermined, and its meanings go beyond a singular expression. *Panema* implies many other ideas and practices, involving nature, spirits, and gender. And food, being an area of social life not subjected historically to strong outside manipulation in peasant Amazonia, means that as a cultural activity, it has acquired various layers of meanings and associations more than others. It is a rich area to explore the legacy of conquest and colonization.

Aside from this historical perspective, the anthropological point is that the ordinary business of provisioning the household is bound up with extraordinary social—magical—forces. Fishing, hunting, and cooking are not simply technical activities but have cultural meanings that demonstrate how embedded they are in everyday life. It is difficult for us moderns to appreciate how much time, effort, and energy goes towards producing food. Anna and I calculated that, on average, about 60 percent of the day, for both men and women, was devoted to food-related activities. In addition, we found that about 70 percent of food consumed was locally caught or grown. This figure depends on the time of the day of the meal and whether it is a special one or not. Moreover, the availability of food is seasonal; hunger is an ever-present threat during the flood, when fish are more dispersed, no crops are available, and travel is more difficult, and the work that goes into securing food is accordingly greater. Such sustained activity associated with providing food gives force to culturally elaborated beliefs such as *panema* and *reimoso*. Buying food in supermarkets disconnects consumers from these preoccupations. It is not just a matter of losing touch with where our food comes from but a whole matrix of ideas about the different properties of food, and what kinds of food can be mixed. In turn, these relate, as seen in *panema*, to relations between men and women and the environment. And they have effects in the social world, since women's behavior, for example, is controlled in this way, or people become sick and cannot work.

In the end, Anna decided not to give birth in the Lower Amazon and returned to Europe. We were told that because our child-to-be was conceived and produced on the floodplain, he would remain connected to the river, and its people, all his life. According to ribeirinhos, there is an affinity of matter between food, body, and the place in which it was grown. And these residues will remain, as a kind of calling. The same sentiment is expressed by ribeirinhos when they talk of the enchanted city at the bottom of the river where invisible *encantados* (spirits) dwell. On warm equatorial evenings, they tell of the city's unlimited wealth and the cleanliness of its spirit inhabitants, who are dressed in white clothes. Shamans travel in their spiritual form and can even take visitors down to see the beauty. But it is imperative that these travelers not be tempted to eat any of the delicious food lying around. If they did, their spirits would remain in the watery underworld and their bodies, lying in their hammocks, would die. They would become enchanted and transformed into an invisible entity. We see again the perils of contact between strange elements. It may not be too much of an exaggeration to compare this to our hosts' presentation of a sugary cup of coffee: With our first sip, part of us became inextricably attached to the small village on the Amazon floodplain. Food is never quite what it seems.

Acknowledgements

My research has been supported by the Economic and Social Research Council of Great Britain, The Leverhulme Trust, Arts and Humanities Research Council, and the British Academy. I am grateful to all of these institutions and to Leo Coleman for his editorial guidance in the preparation of this chapter.

4

Live Poultry Markets and Avian Flu in Hong Kong

Frédéric Keck

In 1997, eighteen people in Hong Kong were infected with a new flu virus, called H5N1, and six of them died. All of them had been in contact with live poultry. The H5N1 virus was soon found in farms and markets all around the territory. This was the first time that a new variety of the flu virus had jumped directly from birds to humans, without first passing through the "mixing vessel" of pigs, and this virus caused huge respiratory distress in the organisms—human and otherwise—that were not immune to this new mutation. In a massive demonstration of public health power, one-and-a-half million chickens in the territory were culled, live ducks were banned from chicken farms (because they were "sane carriers," not sick themselves but carriers that could spread the virus from waterfowl to poultry), and all other live poultry (chickens, geese, and quail) were kept under intense surveillance (Greger 2006).

China, of which the territory of Hong Kong is a "special administrative region," raises 70 percent of the world's poultry, and has long been considered the epicenter of the most virulent of twentieth century flu pandemics (Shortridge and Stuart-Harris 1982). Between 1968 and 2008, the number of poultry raised in China increased from thirteen million to thirteen billion (Greger 2006), while the country passed from scarcity to abundance, and from food security to food safety concerns (Farquhar 2002). It is no wonder then that China's live poultry are under scrutiny, as the animal reservoir of the next pandemic.

What does it mean to raise, cook with, and consume live poultry in the context of intense animal surveillance? My work aims at describing how "biosecurity measures" introduced by global experts for the last fifteen years have transformed the daily life of local people (Collier, Lakoff, and Rabinow 2004). I don't take these biosecurity measures as a form of "biopower" imposed from above, but as a way of revealing the work of humans interacting with animals. I am interested in how the "bios" become problematized on the frontier between humans and animals, as traced and reconfigured in the act of eating. I first encountered these issues when I studied how mad cow disease has transformed food safety in France (Keck 2008); the study of avian flu then became a way to compare the perception of biosecurity measures in different localities. Live poultry in China after avian flu doesn't have the same meaning as beefsteak in France after mad cow disease, but I believe they highlight the same problematic tension in the human act of eating animals.

In China, dishes made with live poultry (*huoji*) are considered delicacies, and having them served to you is an honor, because the flesh is perceived as more tasty when it is fresh (*xinxian*). Live chickens are most often used in the preparation of soups, as is fish, which are also bought live (the character for "fresh" includes the character for fish), whereas pork and beef are bought post-slaughter, roasted and in pieces. For big festivals such as Chinese New Year or Mid-Autumn, a whole chicken in a soup is seen as a symbol of family completeness. And at the time of big festivals, authorities are as much concerned by the circulation of humans as by the circulation of poultry (*renliu wuliu*), since the risk of avian flu is as high as that of social unrest.

Fowl domestication probably started in China four thousand years ago, not for reasons of consumption (pigs provide more protein with less investment), but because fowl were valued for use in divination (Simmons 1991). Nowadays, when Chinese consumers inspect live poultry to see if it is healthy and will be tasty, they reproduce at the level of daily life both the gestures of ancient oracles who dug into the guts of birds to guess the future, and of modern scientists, who take oral swabs to look for flu viruses. Indeed, this act of inspection was traditionally done in the domestic kitchen, but in the present context of biosecurity measures, live poultry must be inspected and killed in the retail market because of the risk of avian flu. How can live poultry be perceived at the same time as good food for banquets, and as signs of future threats? What does this intersection of disease and augury reveal about the web of relations that constitute Chinese daily life?

Relying on two years of research in Hong Kong, I will describe live poultry markets as a place of encounter for different actors dealing with this ambiguous being: a sick bird. Killing and eating—but also refraining from killing and eating—do not carry the same meaning for each of the actors in the food chain, from producers to purchasers of live poultry. My work, relying on the methods of ethnography and social anthropology, is therefore different from that of public health studies of risk perception. Those studies concentrate on the opinions of consumers, to see how they introduce a bias in knowledge and recommendations produced by experts (Fielding 2005). Starting from the act of eating as problematic, I am interested in how, through different interactions between humans and animals, these tensions are solved variously. An ethnography of food practices is therefore compatible with an epidemiology of representations of contagion, but it follows a different logic; it is more attentive to the varieties of forms of interaction with, and to the contradictions of, that strange being circulating along the food chain: a sick, live bird.

The Wholesale Market

My first encounter with live poultry markets was at the wholesale market of Cheung Sha Wan. Built after 1997 in the middle of Kowloon, the most populous part of Hong Kong, it was designed to centralize inspection and distribution of all the live poultry sold in the retail markets. Chickens coming from the territory of Hong Kong and those imported from mainland China entered the market at different points. A street separated the poultry trucks coming from China and those coming from Hong Kong. Every day, ten thousand chickens passed the frontier at Sheung Shui, where twelve veterinarians inspected them; an equal number of chickens came to the wholesale market from farms in Hong Kong. Cheung Sha Wan market is not a vibrant and visually arresting place like Tsukiji in Tokyo, with its displays of fresh fish, nor as easily accessible to visitors (Bestor 2004). Chickens arrive around midnight, and the auctions take place between one and four in the morning, under the gloomy lights of the high buildings that surround the market. The only moment when the market comes to public light is when massive cullings are organized.

During the period of my research, two outbreaks of H5N1 occurred: one in a duck farm in Guangdong province in September 2007, and the other in a chicken farm in Hong Kong in December 2008. On the first occasion, the Chinese side of the market was closed for a month; on the second, there was a public culling of all the live poultry of the day on the Hong Kong side of the market. Ten thousand chickens, geese, and quail were put into plastic bins with gas, and crushed when they tried to flee. Indeed, culling was a regular practice in light of the threat of avian flu. After the fatal outbreak of 1997, a team of civil servants from the Agriculture Department was detailed to the regular practice of culling. "Most of them had never seen live poultry before. They had to learn. Now some of them have become experts in poultry culling," said the head of the Agriculture Department (Kolata 2006: 240). Note that culling is distinct from killing: You kill animals to eat them, but you cull trees to get rid of their malign parts.

The fear of avian flu is a way to express mistrust about China, even as Hong Kong increasingly depends on its products. The Chinese border has a strong affective value for Hong Kong people, and it is understood that the H5N1 virus emerged in 1996 on a geese farm in Guangdong province, across the border. Meanwhile, raising poultry was a major source of income for Chinese immigrants to Hong Kong in the 1950s, as the then British colony exported the Chinese breed of chicken to the United States, which had imposed an embargo on imports from the People's Republic of China (Yeung 1956). After the massive culling of 1997, only thirty poultry farms remained in Hong Kong; poultry farmers were encouraged to drop this dangerous activity by a Voluntary Surrender Scheme, and backyard poultry-raising was forbidden. Hong Kong chickens could no longer be bought directly at the farm but had to pass through the centralized wholesale market, where they were inspected as thoroughly for disease as their Chinese counterparts. In addition to the wholesale market, the government tried to build a central slaughterhouse for poultry coming from Hong Kong and China (there are three such slaughterhouses for pigs and cows), but the inhabitants of Hong Kong protested against this as posing further threats of pollution—leaving the wholesale market to its central role in the live poultry economy.

The Chicken Farm

After watching the culling of December 2008, I got in touch with the farmer who had been hit by the H5N1 outbreak, Mr. Wong. His farm was located in Yuen Long, in the northern part of the New Territories, an area where immigrants arrived from China and established early poultry farms in the territory (Liu 2008) after crossing the Deep Bay where container ships now cruise by with their cargos destined for the rest of the world. After the 2008 outbreak on Mr. Wong's farm, experts debated whether the virus had arrived on his farm through wild sparrows or smuggled eggs. Mr. Wong owned ninety thousand chickens—which were all destroyed—and his farm was put into quarantine for a month. However, he also owned a farm on the other side of the Chinese border, which allowed him to keep his business running, as the government gave little compensation for the culling.

I asked him if I could work on his farm. He accepted because, he said, as the head of the Poultry Workers Association, he had nothing to hide, and indeed his farm was described in the media as a "model farm" (*mofan nonchang*). It was more of a family enterprise than an industrial battery-style farm. Mr. Wong had four workers, three men and a woman, all of them migrant workers from China (*mingong*). My work for him involved feeding the chickens in the morning, with one of the men, and in the afternoon, feeding the baby chicks with the woman. The man, who knew I was studying avian flu, showed me the medicine the woman gave to the chicks, curious to know what disease it was curing. These workers were not anxious about avian flu, even though two of them had been put in quarantine in December: They followed their daily routine and were more annoyed by insects in the feedlots than by dead chickens in the cages. The proximity between feeding and medicating is interesting here, as the woman was giving drugs to the chicks every day through a big needle (*dazheng*) while I was giving them grains.

The woman who took care of the chicks also prepared meals for the three men. The meals were always the same: fish, pork, vegetables, and rice. When I saw her kill and prepare some poultry, I asked Ms. Wong if they ate chicken; she said that she kept some of the chickens for friends but didn't say she ate them herself. At one point during my stay, she gave one to the woman worker, who killed it and cooked it for the four men—which means that only women killed chickens during my stay. We didn't eat the chicken for lunch, however, but for dinner, after taking a shower and removing our working clothes. It was as if we needed to be cleaned of all the filth and feces we had gathered during the working day. But for us, eating chicken at the poultry farm was not a filthy experience, as it is for Mexican immigrants working in slaughterhouses at the U.S. border, as reported by Steve Striffler (2005). Rather, it was a joyful moment; for a while we were spared from the tiring work routine of the day, and looking forward to watching films about the People's Liberation Army on Chinese television.

On this occasion, I brought a bottle of French wine, and my co-workers stared at it with mistrust: Chinese wine is not red or white, as French wines are, but rather yellow. In the vicinity of the chickens, whose life had been taken for us to eat them, my French wine really looked like blood. But after refusing to drink the wine in their glass with the meal, my co-workers used the wine to clean their bowl, and drank it as a kind of soup.

Killing a chicken to eat it on the farm didn't appear all that violent to me, but I felt that the way they were taken out to the market *was* violent. Wholesale buyers came every Friday night, while the chickens were sleeping, and they would take between five hundred and one thousand chickens at a time. The farmer let them open the grey raising-cages and transfer the chickens, half asleep, to the red cages of the market. The chickens were so disoriented that they would not flee from the cages even if the doors remained opened, or if they slipped from the hands of the buyer. They were stuffed in these red cages, with beaks, crests, and feathers all pressed together, sorted according to their size. The buyer would flush the cages and the chickens inside them with water before heading out to the market where the auctions were starting.

In my conversations with the truck drivers, I was struck by the drivers' wealth compared with that of the workers on the farm: The drivers wanted to know how their sons could go study at a European university. These drivers were important intermediaries between the farm and the market, and avian flu had made them even more crucial to the live poultry economy, since it forbade buying direct at the farm.

The Retail Markets

I have followed a trajectory leading me from the wholesale market to the farm and back, from extraordinary public cullings to routine private killings. I have also followed the chickens on their way to the wholesale market and the farmhouse table. I now want to continue in the other direction, from the wholesale market to the ordinary consumers who buy their poultry in the retail markets. During my research, I conducted interviews with sellers of live poultry in the market of Tai Po. I liked this market, in a middle-class big town in the New Territories, because it had just been renovated, whereas the markets on the island of Hong Kong were often dull and old. On the third floor of Tai Po market there was a big restaurant that served the products of the market; on the second floor there were fruits and vegetables; and on the first floor there were fish (displayed in fish tanks), meat (cuts of pork and beef hung on hooks), and live poultry. The latter was in a separate part of the market, cordoned off by a wall. In the corridor leading to this part of the market, posters warned, "Don't carry live poultry," and "Beware of Avian Influenza." Half the shops here were closed, barred by a red banner. Entering this space felt like transgressing some dangerous barrier.

I spent most of my time with two merchants, each aged around fifty. The first was a woman who sold a Hong Kong breed of chicken (*Kamei*) for around 120 Hong Kong dollars. She complained about the measures the government had taken to combat avian flu. Whereas the wholesale market was controlled by the Agriculture Department, supposed to be more sensitive to the interests of the farmers and merchants, the retail market was controlled by the Food, Environment, and Hygiene Department, which protected the interests of modern consumers and took a more stringent approach to H5N1 contamination. Every evening, the controllers checked that the poultry that had not been sold were killed, so that no live poultry would spend the night on the market. Chicken meat from the birds killed the previous day was then sold next to the live poultry arriving in the morning and waiting to be killed, in a strange conjunction of the living and the dead. "If we don't kill the chickens at the end of the day," this woman said, "we will lose our license. We have no margin of toleration. That's why poultry merchants demonstrated against the government. Some of them even jumped into the sea." I was intrigued by the fact that "jumping into the sea" (*xiahai*), an act of protest in the context of a merchants' riot, also means smuggling, a frequent practice on the border to contravene governmental restrictions. "We are no robbers," she said. "Our job is to allow everyone to eat live poultry." Her son was working with her and told me he wanted to become a diving teacher.

The other merchant did not complain about the biosecurity measures. He said the inspectors were doing the cleaning job he previously had to do himself, and that this compensated for the increase in the price of live poultry. He sold poultry from China for around sixty Hong Kong dollars and showed me a poster declaring they had no melamine—a scandal had just broken on the presence of this toxic product in milk powder (Keck 2009). Whereas the woman remained in the front of the shop while her son killed the poultry at the back, this merchant did all the tasks himself: taking the live chicken out of the cage to display its bottom (a way to check that the bird is healthy), cutting the throat with a knife and dropping the chicken into a basket to let the blood drain, boiling the bird to take the feathers off, then cutting it into pieces. His son was working with him, but even so he told me he didn't think he would continue in this job. "Next time you come and visit me, all these shops will be closed. Don't forget avian flu was invented in Hong Kong!" He seemed like a nostalgic survival, a representative of a vanishing past, still doing his routine killing work.

The two merchants' customers were also quite different. The woman's clients asked for organic food because they preferred it to frozen chicken, which "tastes like wood." They stayed to chat with her while the dirty work was done by her son. The man's clients wanted cheap traditional food: "I've always done that" was their main motivation. They would take a ticket while the merchant was doing his dirty job under the eyes of the anthropologist, and then come back to pick up the dead chicken in a plastic bag. None of them would buy and drink the chicken blood, a current practice in China, now considered highly dangerous for avian flu transmission.

Buy and Release

During my research, I came in contact with a strange group of consumers, whose practices highlighted tensions in the live poultry markets that were previously hidden: They saw a contradiction in the fact that a chicken can be perceived alternatively as a living being and as a valuable product. I had heard of Buddhist groups who bought birds in order to release them in the wild, a traditional practice in China and Southeast Asia called *fangsheng* (Handlin Smith 1999). This practice had been criticized by environmental groups because the birds released were often found dead close to the site of release, generally because they had been displaced from their natural environment, but also because they had sometimes caught avian flu during transportation. Consequently, Buddhist organizations had called for a ban on bird release and asked believers to release sea creatures instead. This shift from birds to fish is interesting: It reveals that these two kinds of animals are perceived as similarly moving in an unbounded natural environment (air and water) and that their confinement in a market blocks these movements artificially. It would be impossible for Chinese people to think of releasing pigs, since pigs are conceived as the domestic animal *par excellence*. Cows raise a different problem: The consumption of beef was long forbidden in recognition of the agricultural work that cows performed (Goossaert 2005).

I connected with one of these Buddhist groups through the Internet and followed them in their release activities every Saturday. Members of this group went to the market of Tsuen Wan, a big middle-class city in the New Territories, to buy seafood—spending around one thousand Hong Kong dollars each time.

They were all active people, aged between thirty and fifty, and they found in this practice a respite from the tiring work of the week; some of them even bought fish every morning to release near their workplace. The group members weren't attached to any particular Buddhist temple, but they could ask a Buddhist monk who was passing by to join them for the ceremony. The group was flexible, open to all on the Internet who wanted to join, even anthropologists interested in live poultry markets.

Following them was a way for me to understand another aspect of how customers perceived live animals at the market. The fish shops were very close to the poultry stalls and displayed the same mix of liveliness and cruelty. Fish were regularly taken out of the large basins where they were kept in crowded conditions, cut open, and displayed on the stall with the heart still beating. One of my Buddhist friends stared at this beating heart and said: "I can feel the suffering of this fish. There is so much suffering here." But this language of compassion was still compatible with a rational calculation of the fluctuating cost of the animals that would be bought and released. When there had been a typhoon, the price of fish was very high, so members of the group bought clams and tortoises, bargaining hard to reduce the price of the basket of sea creatures that would be released.

I was intrigued by the fact that they appeared not to be bothered, as I was, by the arbitrary selection they were making between those animals that they bought and released and those animals that were left to be sold to actual consumers in the market. At one point they bought a basket of frogs to release them, then changed their mind and bought crabs instead, while the frogs that were temporarily destined to be released were taken back by the merchant and beheaded for another client. "People think we're fools because we give money to release animals. But all we can do is decrease the quantity of suffering in this market." They were aware of being just a part of the system, and not revolutionaries who would overturn the whole market for live food. Meanwhile, the merchants knew they could count on these strange but polite clients when the economy turned down.

After buying the seafood for release, under stressful conditions in a busy marketplace, the ceremony itself was quite serene and moving. The group sang prayers to the Buddha, dripped holy water (called "Guanyin water," after the name of a Buddhist goddess) on the creatures they had purchased, then released them in the waters of the harbor, or into a river in a park. After the release, they said prayers meant to cure the sick and to bless both the animals and humans in their future reincarnations. They said the release ceremony produced good "merit" (*gongde*) because the animals released were joyful and happy.

I was curious to see how these Buddhist practitioners took care of the animals they intended to release, since environmentalists had criticized them for their lack of ecological consciousness. Indeed, they were careful to have oxygen in the seafood pond while the animals waited for their release; they separated crabs from fish so the crustaceans would not cut the fish; they looked for rivers hidden by trees, to protect the released animals from the eyes of eagles who could catch them; and they dug holes in the mud of the shore or riverbank to bury the animals that died between the market and the release spot. Overall, the release ceremony was a brief moment when the animals were extracted from the market economy and introduced into a caring relationship.

But this moment, in contrast to the strange mix of killing and caring that constitutes the daily routine of a chicken farm, was short. After the release ceremony each Saturday, the Buddhist group went to a vegetarian restaurant where they listened to a Buddhist monk teaching about the Buddhist cosmology of reincarnations, or watched DVDs about live animal markets that included scary images of killing and suffering. Sharing these vegetarian meals with them was a joyful moment, contrasting with the painful moment at the market and the austere release ceremony. But I was struck by the fact that the live animals they sought to save were returning as virtual entities in these cosmological speculations or cautionary movies, while the actual live animals were trying to survive in an unknown environment, having passed through the human chain of the market economy.

Meeting these Buddhist groups was not, for me, only a way to think through the moral problems presented by eating animals but also a way to understand the role of consumption more generally in the market economy of live animals. These Buddhist groups refrained from killing and eating animals, in order to gain "merit," but they shared the view of ordinary consumers who also see animals as something to buy and consume. The only difference is that the Buddhists consumed animals in a virtual space, as spiritual entities who grant "merit," while ordinary consumers ate animals as material sustenance in the actual space of household economy. Both groups shared the view of live animals as "fresh" while not asking how this freshness was produced, and what the idea of a "live," "fresh" animal concealed. As Michèle de la Pradelle writes, "Freshness is the negation of the whole complex business chain leading from the producer to the packager, and on to the wholesale and then the retail market; it is a way to signify a direct relation of the product to nature; it is in itself a myth of origin" (de la Pradelle 1996: 174).

Conclusion

In this article, I have described Hong Kong as a place where live poultry is produced, exchanged, and consumed, or as a city where nature is at the same time controlled and proliferating (Cronon 1991). I have looked at the way avian flu reveals contradictory perceptions of live poultry as a "fresh" consumption good, by throwing light on conditions of production that are ordinarily hidden.

The need to kill poultry, whether routinely or during health crises, reminds us that poultry are live animals and not just exchangeable goods. The changing practices meant to deal with sick poultry are not only about making sure our food is good to eat, but also an occasion for thinking about how we come to eat what we eat.

Starting from the market, with its distinction between wholesale market (controlled by the Agriculture Department) and retail market (controlled by the Food and Environmental Hygiene Department), I have moved in two directions: toward the rural producers of live poultry, who can sometimes consume them, and toward the urban consumers, who tend to forget the ecological contexts in which animals live, although they take them briefly into account when assessing the health of the bird. I observed the perceptions and miscognitions of the live poultry economy not as the illusory deformation of an objective knowledge, but as a necessary result of its contradictory ontology. Therefore, I have not studied how live poultry becomes a valuable product, but how the intrinsic contradictions in the perceptions of that being—sick live poultry—produce different meanings as they are transformed in different contexts along the food chain: both fresh and diseased, mobile and contained.

While epidemiologists show the transmission path of the virus from birds to pigs to humans, I have followed the web of meanings that parallels and orients this flux of flesh, bugs, and money. Particularly striking, along the different steps of the food chain, was the recurrent analogy between poultry and fish. These animals, which must be bought live, are conceived as a "movement" that can be displayed or released. In this context, biosecurity measures introduce forms of control and confinement that tend to provisionally suspend this movement, because they try to prevent a definite suspension of movement: the specter of a pandemic. It is worth asking—even if it would ask for further studies, particularly through an investigation of artistic and cultural forms—if people in Hong Kong have not become frightened by live poultry because they convey an image of their own movement, and present it as something that tends to produce diseases. In the context of a pandemic disease transmitted from birds to humans, eating live poultry would not be only a risky act but also become a catastrophic form of identification (Descola 2005). Can eating live poultry be analogous to eating oneself?

Acknowledgements

I wish to thank Noelie Vialles for her intellectual support, the Fyssen Foundation for its financial support, and Leo Coleman for his work of collecting and revising texts.

–5–

Revisiting Lao Food: Pain and Commensality

Penny Van Esterik

My stories of the field, from the field are exotic, because they are about a very distant and different place: Lao People's Democratic Republic (Lao PDR), a mainland Southeast Asian communist country, until recently closed to researchers. Lao PDR is classified by the United Nations as a low-income, food-deficit country. One of the poorest and least developed countries in Asia, it has a per capita income around four hundred dollars a year. The Lao government recognizes sixty-five distinct ethnic groups, but stresses "unity in diversity" among all. Decades of war, including fighting for independence from French colonial control (1893–1954) and the American bombing during the secret war in Laos (1962–1975), left the country food insecure.

Lao PDR is a country of subsistence rice farmers, with some minority groups additionally growing maize and cassava. But a recent report on the national prevalence of critical food poverty indicated that nearly one in five people did not have enough money to buy the food necessary to meet daily minimum energy requirements. The upland peoples depend more on forest resources that they gather than on purchasing food, but these wild forest foods are increasingly threatened (Krahn 2005). Although the daily dietary energy supply per capita has been increasing over the last few years, almost 30 percent of the population remains below the minimal level of dietary energy consumption (according to a government report on food insecurity). According to UNICEF country profiles, 40 percent of children under five are underweight, 41 percent are stunted, and 15 percent are wasted. The Lao PDR government, along with United Nations partners, is working towards reducing the infant mortality rate (62/1000 in 2005), the under-five mortality rate (79/1000 in 2005), and the high maternal mortality rates.

Food imports and exports are minimal, government controlled, and directed toward urban markets. Lao PDR is a closed, protected trading system—but one where informal and nonformal trade with China, Vietnam, and Thailand thrives.

There are few stores of rice or other staples available at the national or local levels. Most households do not produce enough rice to meet their needs and have to purchase it. About half the provinces of Lao PDR fail to reach rice self-sufficiency because of drought, flooding, or underproduction related to irrigation problems. In short, for some households in some communities in some seasons, food itself is a scarce commodity.

The Food and Agriculture Organization (FAO) defines food security as existing when all people, at all times, have physical and economic access to sufficient, safe, and nutritious food to meet their dietary needs and food preferences for an active and healthy lifestyle. The Lao government defines household food insecurity as the inability to provide twenty-one hundred calories per person per day.

As a nutritional anthropologist, I was drawn to study these nutritional problems and learn more about how the Lao food system deals with food insecurity. Naturally, that learning included eating Lao meals. But by sharing Lao meals, I inadvertently also shared the substances that regularly killed Lao infants, children, elderly, and vulnerable villagers, the subject that I came to the country to understand. My experiences with food-borne illnesses made me focus on food safety as an integral part of food security, but also to recognize the broad social contexts of these problems, nationally and globally. For instance, the villagers who occasionally became sick with gastrointestinal infections had limited access to medical care, antibiotics, intravenous fluids, and other emergency interventions. This paper raises ethical, methodological, and theoretical questions emerging from an examination of two personal experiences with food poisoning, painful aspects of food consumption.

Living and Eating in the Field

Whether the field is archives, library, university, or Lao PDR, fieldwork is a state of mind, a critical mode of inquiry. It is not necessary to travel long distances to do fieldwork. When your fieldwork site is in the country where you live, or grew up, you can eat the foods of home, familiar foods, even when you are in the field. Feeling at home in the field often means being able to eat your own food in your own meal sequence; when doing research somewhere else, it means learning to love the food and eating habits of the people you are living with. This process of turning the exotic food of people from distant lands into your own comfort food is part of adapting to the fieldwork experience. Researchers who happen to love the typical food eaten in their research site will probably be a great deal happier than researchers who hate the local food. But for some reason, this is seldom talked about before going to the field.

In ethnographic work, you are your own research instrument. Preparing to go into the field usually involves reading the work of other researchers who have worked in the same area in the past. But following academic practices that separate mind from body (mind/body dualisms), we do a better job at preparing our minds for fieldwork than our bodies. The very embodied experience of doing fieldwork far from home is only rarely addressed, and formal preparations are often limited to a set of instructions to make sure you have adequate inoculations and medications, wear comfortable shoes, and, as I learned from my student, buy a LeSportsac brand purse. (If the lid comes off your water bottle, or if the bag drops into the water tank of a Lao toilet, the waterproof compartments keep your notes and camera dry.) Is this an adequate way to prepare our research instrument? Fieldwork involves living with others, and living like others. It also encompasses embodied experiences such as eating with others, and eating like others. The following experiences of food poisoning in Lao PDR reveal several dimensions of eating with and like the Lao in Lao PDR. But to make sense of the stories, first they need to be placed in the context of the Lao food system.

The Lao Food System

Poverty and food shortages may be recent experiences for the Lao, precipitated by disruptions to the subsistence agriculture caused by war and resettlement. Perhaps this is why many Lao retain a strong self-identity around concepts of hospitality and food sharing: to eat Lao meals is to participate in communally prepared and communally eaten meals, often very festive events.

As elsewhere in mainland Southeast Asia, meals feature rice as the central source of calories (between 70 and 80 percent of the total number of calories people eat in a day come from rice). In Lao PDR, glutinous or sticky rice is an important part of the collective identity of lowland Lao (*Lao lum)*, who make up the majority of the population. Glutinous rice is by far the preferred rice for the lowland Lao. The Lao appreciate the qualities of glutinous rice, and believe it is tastier, more nutritious, and aromatic than any other kind of rice. Glutinous rice absorbs little cooking water and is therefore usually soaked and steamed, not boiled. It is eaten by hand, formed into small balls and dipped into a variety of side dishes and sauces. At meals, glutinous rice is usually served from large shared baskets, with side dishes presented simultaneously. Accompanying most rice meals are sauces or pastes made from fermented local fish or shell fish. The fish are salted, dried, pounded, and packed with toasted rice and rice husk in jars for a month or more. This fish sauce (*nam pa*) is a crucial ingredient in most Lao dishes. In its thicker form (*padek*), it is served as a separate side dish with rice. The strong-smelling product is not appealing to many Westerners, who have little tolerance for fermented, fishy foods. But Lao who are overseas speak longingly of the local versions of *padek* recalled nostalgically from their homeland.

Fresh greens and herbs are gathered wild, collected from household gardens, or purchased in local markets. They are served in soups, stir fried with onion, garlic, meat, or fish, or served raw with fermented fish products as dipping sauces. In Lao PDR, as elsewhere in Southeast Asia, dipping sauces add zest to bland rice, stimulating appetites and tempting eaters to consume more rice. The Lao call these spicy sauces *jeaw*. Made from ingredients such as chili peppers (originally from Central America), garlic, lime, sugar, fish sauce, onions, and coriander, each recipe is unique to a region, community, or household. Some dry *jeaw* consist primarily of salt and chili peppers, and are not given to children.

Meat and fish are valued parts of Lao diets. Animals such as squirrels, deer, and wild pigs are hunted; snakes, frogs, crickets, and insects also supply protein, along with freshwater fish. Lao with cash purchase meat such as chicken, pork, duck, and beef. Small amounts of fish or meats are mixed with herbs and spices in stews and soups; larger amounts of meat or fish are grilled, mainly for communal festive meals. Soups are particularly valued as they allow cooks to stretch ingredients, make use of bones, and generally expand the meal to serve more people.

Household members and their guests eat together. Generous food sharing is important insurance against food shortages. However, the means of sharing food, which includes shared bowls, utensils, and the direct use of hands for feeding self and others, presents certain risks. Nevertheless, the social risks of not sharing food are equally important and commensality is a key part of the pleasure of food and eating (cf. Janowski and Kerlogue, eds. 2007).

Royal Food from Luang Prabang

My first story is set in the context of researching the structure of Lao meals, how they vary by region and ethnicity. I am not Lao, but I thought I loved Lao food. I particularly enjoy the pleasure of molding balls of glutinous sticky rice and dipping it in things. I seldom think of my colleagues' warnings about the risk of hepatitis as I dip my fingers into shared dishes of rice and then put the rice in my mouth. But after six weeks in Lao PDR thinking and writing and talking about Lao food, one night I threw up Lao food.

My research brought me to the old royal capital of Luang Prabang to learn more about the specialties of palace cooking (cf. Sing 1981). I wanted to know what happened to palace food that marked royalty and aristocratic, elite status, after the arrival of the communist regime in 1975. Dining alone in an upscale French restaurant, I found dishes called *mok gai* and *jeaw bong* reputed to be prepared in the most authentic royal style. I ordered the dishes and they arrived at the table with a basket of warm sticky rice; they were beautifully folded banana leaf triangular packets of minced steamed chicken (*mok gai*) and a small dish of red lumpy sauce (*jeaw bong*). I was set to take notes. I unwrapped the steamy bundle and turned over a slimy mound of minced chicken in a coconut-and-egg-custard gel strongly spiced with hot chilies and herbs. Taking a small ball of rice, I placed a mound of steamed chicken on it and popped the morsel in my mouth. It smelled and felt different, unfamiliar all the way down. The tastes were recognizable but the textures were not. I took notes. A few more mouthfuls and I had to admit I didn't enjoy the experience of tasting and swallowing the food, even though I enjoyed the thought of enjoying these dishes I had read about. I spooned some of the famous sauce, *jeaw bong,* onto my plate. Taking another ball of sticky rice, I dipped it expectantly into the vibrant sauce. Something glistened in the tomato-garlic mixture—something translucent and yellowish and hard. I popped the tasty morsel in my mouth, although it didn't stick easily to the rice ball. To my inexperienced palate, it tasted like many other *jeaw*, a rich and spicy flavorful sauce, appealing enough to tempt even the poorest peasant into consuming ample amounts of sticky rice. As an appetite stimulant to brighten up a monotonous bland diet, *jeaw* is an important culinary adaptation. But maybe what was unique about *jeaw bong* resided in the glistening morsels that kept slithering off my rice ball on the last mouth trip. I took more notes. Taking a spoon, I served myself a generous mouthful of *jeaw* and included several of the unknown bits. I felt like I had just ingested a mouthful of hot, hard elastics, impossible to chew and difficult to spit out as they were slippery.

For the rest of the meal, my mind propelled me toward my research questions about the Lao food system—how palace food compared to peasant food, the importance of using all parts of the animal, the likelihood of these food items being used as a suitable complementary food for toddlers, whether the recipes were made using iodized salt. But my stomach responded to the strange textures with great rumbles of pain and gurgles of disgust. These two Lao creatures were unfamiliar to my stomach, and they were clearly not constitutive of my sense of self. It quickly became clear that my digestive system was going to treat these two intruders as unwelcome strangers, food of the exotic other, not destined to become embodied as "self," and I was likely to upchuck in the resort hotel dining room. I reminded myself that these were all ingredients I liked (with the possible exception of what turned out to be sun dried slivers of water buffalo cartilage), and that there was no reason to reject the foods just because of their unfamiliar texture. My response to these tastes and textures was visceral, painful, and immediate. Even their appearance repulsed me. Back in my room, while writing more notes on the unique features of royal Lao cuisine, as if answering, these food elements returned to their Lao environment where they belonged, expelled and not embodied, remaining "other" and not "self," with no lasting consequences (except to my pride).

My attempt to discern the flavors and boundaries of Lao cuisine, including its colonial and royal forms, resulted instead in an unbidden experience of disgust evoked by unfamiliar tastes and textures, complicated by possible food poisoning. This solitary meal, consumed in a rich urban environment, contrasts with the more serious food problems encountered later in rural village settings.

Village Meals

The second story concerns meals consumed in isolated, food-insecure villages. In January 2005, I was in Lao PDR accompanying an Australian student study tour to Southeast Asia; I was also there to study food security. Until I was hospitalized for a week in Thailand, under treatment for bacterial infections resulting from food poisoning, I never considered food safety as an important element of food security. The only part of the FAO definition of food security I considered was food sufficiency; how much rice was available to feed the household, and for how many months? I was developing a parallel argument about cuisine in the context of chronic food insecurity, suggesting that what Westerners call cuisine does not develop in the face of food insecurity. But until I collapsed with septic shock, with a system full of bugs acquired by eating Lao food in Lao villages, I did not consider the importance of food safety.

During fieldwork in the villages, we often brought food to share with the community—treats such as a chicken or a slab of pork. I never felt unwelcome or exploitative as I asked women about their meals. Instead, the hospitality, the generous sharing of food was as genuine an emotion as I have ever felt in the field. Often the villagers expressed their desire that we see their situation, examine it, and share ideas about how to improve their food security and life chances. Most important was that we all ate together, ate with them and like them.

Anthropologists and food researchers often have access to an augmented diet, one that allows them to use their knowledge of nutrition and access to cash to add a few extra eggs or chicken legs to the communal dishes, while at the same time studying those meals—and still feel somewhat proud that they shared a peasant diet, experiencing, surviving, and enjoying meals as a Lao person might. In addition, I came prepared with multivitamins and a few granola bars for emergencies—a necessary boost, I thought, to a diet that might be lacking in some nutrients. I ate them in secret, whenever I could find privacy, because I did not have enough to share, and not to share is reprehensible in a Lao household.

I was not at all prepared when I found that after a month of eating happily in Lao villages, with no adverse reaction to any food and even supplementing my diet, I had accumulated a near-fatal bacterial soup of infectious agents including E. coli and salmonella. I was also not prepared for the speed with which the infections and dehydration caused other organ systems to shut down, triggered by an extreme loss of potassium. (So much for my emergency supply of multivitamins!) My white blood cells were not able to cope with the range of infective agents in my gut. I was evacuated out of the country into a Thai hospital, and healed by antibiotics and intravenous fluids unavailable in Lao PDR.

The emergency intervention and removal to an international hospital cost nearly eight hundred dollars U.S. After four days of twenty-four-hour saline solution and two kinds of antibiotics, my fever dropped and whatever was inside passed through me. I left the hospital the day after I was considered cured—too soon, perhaps, but I knew what I was missing by lying in a Thai hospital while the food that I had come to study was on the other side of the border.

After leaving the hospital and spending a few hours in a Thai shopping mall, with KFC, Burger King, Dunkin Donuts, and noodle shops on every corner serving real meat, it was difficult to take the bus back across the border into Lao PDR. The hammer-and-sickle flag flying in the capital, Vientiane, now signaled to me that I couldn't trust Lao food, that the food available to me was not safe, and that I (myself as both researcher and eater) should reject Lao food. I loved the taste of Lao food, but if I couldn't eat it, could I study it? That bus trip back to Lao PDR was the hardest, most painful trip I have made in the field, and I knew that if I didn't do it immediately, I could never go back to the field.

Lessons Learned

I have never been careless about eating in Southeast Asia. I am used to getting the odd stomach ailment, but also recovering from it in twenty-four hours, with the help of a little ginger ale, and an electrolyte drink if necessary. I enjoy street foods but consider both the appearance of the cart and the vendor, and the popularity of the place, before eating from it. Like the Thais, I wipe off the spoon before eating soup, and keep an eye on the newest hygiene techniques that urban regulators insist upon in order to monitor the food vendors on the streets, such as access to hot water and soap, and use of plastic gloves for handling ingredients. I should avoid ice, but usually enjoy it and can trust that it was made with clean water. Even mobile vendors in Lao PDR provided bottled water for their customers—although only tourists and westerners can afford it—or they offer tea (Du Pont De Bie 2004).

What have I learned from these painful experiences? At a very philosophical level, I have faced the problem of the futility and danger of separating the food researcher from the eating subject. I was not just studying Lao meals; I was eating them with my informants. I tried to eat like the Lao. But we do not simply become like each other by eating each other's food.

My stories are entangled in dualisms that oppose food quality and food quantity, self and other, biology and culture, and, as mentioned above, the untenable opposition between objective researcher and subjective eater. It is important not to get caught up in these binary oppositions. Eating, for example, is a biocultural experience. Eating food contaminated with E. coli is linked to the high infant and child mortality rates in the country. But it is equally important to understand how the local regimens of eating, including valued Lao patterns of food sharing, affect both food insecurity and food safety. United Nations agencies and epidemiologists count infant and child deaths from gastroenteritis, malnutrition, and toxic shock in Lao PDR, as I related at the beginning of this paper. But numbers provide a poor basis for interventions unless they are accompanied by information about local food systems, including knowing about how food items are combined into recipes, how dishes are combined into meals (e.g. meal formats), and the daily, weekly, and seasonal cycles of meals.

Consider the local regimes of Lao food consumption. In Southeast Asia, systems of sharing food are even more valued than the properties and taste of the food itself (cf. Janowski and Kerlogue, eds. 2007). Food is collected, produced, and prepared in order to be shared in feasts to celebrate personal and community rituals. In food insecure households, sharing food strengthens social relations and helps compensate for food shortages and the poverty of kitchens where few staples may be on hand. But this makes food safety problems particularly difficult to address because they challenge culturally defined ways of preparing and serving meals, and systems of sharing that are highly valued. A public health perspective on food safety might note the following practices:

- Rice is shared from baskets that are hard to clean.
- Rice-based dishes are eaten from common bowls, served with common utensils.
- Drinks are often shared from one glass and are difficult to refuse.
- Friends pick out the best pieces of foods by hand to give to others.
- Much of the food is eaten by hand—sticky rice, baguettes, fresh salad greens, grilled meats.

In spite of the fact that the Lao are scrupulous about washing their hands before eating, these valued food-sharing practices make food safety rules difficult to implement. By sharing food as I did, I inadvertently also shared the bugs which killed Lao children, elderly, and vulnerable villagers who didn't have access to antibiotics, intravenous fluids, emergency intervention, and removal to a sterile environment, as I did. In addition, I had excellent insurance coverage that eventually covered nearly every expense, including the drugs I took back with me across the border, into a country where neither the drugs, the medical testing facilities, nor the health professionals I had access to were available to most Lao citizens.

If the Lao villagers who shared those meals with me collected the same range of bugs, perhaps they would not have become ill because they had been exposed to them since birth and their systems were used to them. But if this acquired immunity did not protect them, and they did get sick, they might have only had access to a local monk who knows where herbal medicines could be obtained—that is if the villagers still had access to a productive forest containing medicinal plants. Upland villagers might have used opium to reduce the symptoms of stomach pain. There might be an elder who could offer a sip from a bottle containing a cobra pickled in whiskey, if other herbal mixtures were not effective. Such therapies would cost a great deal of money, but the family and the community would share the cost. If that were not enough, they might borrow money for travel and medicines at the usual 300 percent interest from a local moneylender. Children with serious gastrointestinal infections would need to have someone take them across trails and washed-out roads on a motorbike or a logging truck, if one came by. And they might well die on the way, as thousands do every day. That was exactly what I was supposed to be studying in Lao PDR—infant and child malnutrition. The severity of the problem, and the difficulty of treating the chronic infections that often underlie malnutrition, are underscored by my experiences with food poisoning. I am also reminded not to romanticize traditional medicine in villages without access to antibiotics.

Conclusion

I don't tell these stories often. When I tell others, the response is, "What did you expect? These countries are different and have no hygienic standards," or, "The food is only suitable for the Lao." If I agree with them, knowing that they are responding sympathetically to my painful experience, I am interpreting my experiences through a tropical medicine model of the infected exotic other, who lives in a place filled with diseases that present a danger to white visitors—anthropologists or tourists, it makes no difference. I want to avoid evoking these racist images about the dangers of the contaminated food of the other. But how do you talk about matter out of place, bacteria and parasites in food and in water, without resorting to a tropical medicine model? My gut did not know about the differential impact of bacteria and parasites on different bodies. Food security and insecurity can only be understood in the broader context of culturally shaped and highly valued rules for sharing food and extending meager food supplies.

Colonial and postcolonial writings make us sensitive to the powerful effects of stories in which Westerners always disparage the food of the other as disgusting or contaminating. Is it any better, when I tell these stories, to ignore the context—cut out the nasty bits—and present the stories as tales about the exotic meals of a food adventurer (cf. Heldke 2003)?

There are few contexts where these stories might be acceptable. After all, who wants to read about an anthropologist vomiting up Southeast Asian food when we have elevated food from this region as the newest chic cuisine in North

America (cf. Van Esterik 2008)? But they are true stories about eating in a very food insecure country. I hope by sharing these stories about food and pain, food analysts and anthropologists can develop a reflexivity of the palate to give us insights into how to integrate our subjective experiences as eaters with the tools necessary to understand and reduce the problems of hunger, malnutrition, and food insecurity existing in many parts of the world.

Acknowledgement

An earlier version of this paper was presented at the meetings of the Association for the Study of Food and Society in 2006.

–6–

In Search of the Elusive Heirloom Tomato: Farms and Farmers' Markets, Fields and Fieldwork

Jennifer A. Jordan

One summer day I went to the Naschmarkt in Vienna in search of heirloom tomatoes, for the dual purpose of research and dinner. I had a surprisingly difficult time finding any. The Naschmarkt is an old open-air market not far from the opera house near the center of Vienna. It is very bountiful, but there are vegetable battles afoot. The market itself has a long tradition, but the goods circulating through it hint at the changes taking place in what many people mistakenly see as stable European food cultures. Many vendors sell almost exactly the same thing. What initially looks like an incredible variety begins repeating itself a few stalls into the market. By and large these are not farmers' stands offering the particular crops planted on a given patch of land by a given farmer. Instead, many of the stands are one link in a basically global chain of the production and distribution of fruits and vegetables.

For decades, Americans have looked to European food culture as a source of inspiration and pleasure, as something to both admire and emulate. Julia Child and Judith Jones[1] fell rapturously in love with French food, and romantic tales of Americans encountering Italian food populate the travel sections of our bookstores. Michael Pollan's critique of American food systems draws heavily on a particular notion of stable (and European) food culture as one possible antidote to a society based so heavily on corn syrup and the processed foods in which it lurks (Pollan 2006). But much of this picture of European food culture ignores the fact, for example, that France is the second most profitable market for McDonald's (the United States is, not surprisingly, the most profitable market).[2] One of the paragons of stable food culture is also home to more than a thousand McDonald's restaurants. Food cultures are changing in Europe for many of the same reasons they are changing in the United States: globalization and the consolidation of food production and distribution, and also the ways that young people's culinary tastes differ profoundly from those of their parents. The growing number of women in the workforce has also contributed to significant changes in cooking, shopping, and eating. Additionally, lengthening commutes disrupt the often traditional family midday meal in many European regions. European food cultures today are in varying degrees of transition.

What this means, in part, is that there is nothing inevitable about the particular arrangements of vegetables we might find when heading out to the market. A complex political, economic, geographic, and cultural story lies behind those piles of tomatoes or jackfruit. After writing an article about heirloom tomatoes in the United States, I made a point of looking for heirloom tomatoes wherever I could. This included Vienna (where I came up nearly empty-handed), Paris, and Rome, cities certainly known (to varying degrees) for being inhabited by great lovers of food. I had assumed that the foods considered "heirlooms" in the United States would be ubiquitous in Europe, and set out to chart their presence in these three metropolises.

My difficulty tracking down heirloom tomatoes in Vienna—and, later, in Paris—speaks not only to a particular culinary challenge, but also to a far more complex understanding of the relationship between food and culture than that conventionally used by the many food writers who look to Europe as a source *and* a site of what Pollan refers to as "stable food culture." But the process of searching for these tomatoes also reveals the value of a quiet but highly mobile ethnographic method, applicable far beyond the relatively rarified margins of many Parisian and Viennese markets, and also applicable in everyday life, beyond the toolkit of the ethnographer. The observant, and at times conversant, visitor to such markets can look, observe, compare and also ask and wonder—micro-level approaches to an understanding of the politics and practices of food distribution.

Where, then, are the heirloom tomatoes? More importantly, what does their absence (or uneven presence) reveal, or at least suggest, about transformations and continuities in European food cultures? I set out on foot in two food-friendly cities, Paris and Vienna, using two slightly different ethnographic approaches. In Vienna, the rhythm of daily life informed my search, weekly forays to very different markets. In Paris, a frenetic but thorough and highly visual (and olfactory) series of pedestrian journeys yielded surprising details about the Parisian food supply and patterns of daily life. It is helpful to think about one representative object, which in each city/market, in different ways, represents new tastes that have emerged for "local" (or *ancienne* or *alte*) produce (with complex sociological causes). The tomato offers a unique nexus for this kind of analysis, showing both the robust presence of these "local" markets, which gives the impression of stable daily habits, but when actually sought out also shows how much of everyday food habit demands the regularity and supply of an industrial food chain. With a sociological eye, and a commitment to wandering and seeking, I don't make ironclad conclusions here, but offer this as notes on different ways in which to search and see.

Vienna: Naschmarkt

Even if the Naschmarkt is a sign of some changes in the landscape of European produce, heirloom and otherwise, it is still a treat for the senses. There are stalls packed to overflowing with boxes of nuts and dried fruit, tightly wrapped bags of ground spices, refrigerator cases displaying stacks of pure white feta, heaps of stuffed grape leaves, and wheels of gouda. Even in the dead of winter, people perch at the high tables of the cafés scattered throughout the market, bundled up against the chill as they drink champagne. All around the champagne drinkers, in winter and summer alike, the nuts, spices, fruit, and vegetables nearly spill out into the already narrow aisles. Prices are scratched in chalk on little pieces of blackboard tucked among the fruits and vegetables—sometimes, but rarely, the origins of the produce are indicated as well. The first day I visited in search of heirloom tomatoes, there were heaps of tropical jackfruit and dragon fruit (neither of which grows particularly well in Austria), in addition to piles of broccoli, leeks, apples, and more pedestrian produce. Many tropical fruits were once only available to the wealthy (in the colder parts of Europe and the United States), grown in meticulously engineered hothouses as barons and earls and emperors and kings competed to have the most out-of-season and out-of-latitude produce served to their guests—pineapples in Dublin, coffee beans at Versailles, oranges in Berlin. As I walked through the Naschmarkt that summer, I found enough exotic fruits to satisfy the most extravagant of baroque tastes, affordable to a much broader swathe of the population.

But when it came to heirloom tomatoes, I wasn't having much luck. I walked up and down the crowded aisles of the Naschmarkt, and in stand after stand I found three or four varieties of tomatoes in great abundance. They were slightly different from what I found in the Viennese supermarket, but not *so* different. There were "egg" tomatoes from Italy, for example, in great abundance. Coming from the United States, I certainly consider Italian tomatoes to be comparatively local—the Italian border is not so far away from Vienna, after all. There were also cherry tomatoes, and romas that were redder and pointier than the cellophane-wrapped romas in the supermarket. I found the usual perfect, round tomatoes on the stem as well. But in stall after stall, it was just variations on a theme, with the same narrow genetic range of tomatoes appearing over and over in the same lovely piles.

Near the far end of the market, where the food stalls start to give way to a few stands selling incense burners, hippie skirts, and wooden toys, I found a stall with a pile of "Fleisch" tomatoes amidst other produce, much like that found in the rest of the market. I talked to the saleswoman, and she said she had grown them herself from family seeds. They were mottled and fleshy, with cracks and crevices, heavy and dense. I bought a big one, crammed it into my bag with my camera and cell phone and keys (not the best way to treat a tomato, heirloom or otherwise), and continued my search. Finally, at the very edge of the market, out of the corner of my eye, I saw large yellow squash, haphazard celery—produce that was less opulent and glossy than what I found at the other stands, but also more varied. And then I spotted a little assortment of heirloom tomatoes. There were black plums, red and yellow currant tomatoes, and others whose names I don't know. A handwritten piece of paper tucked into the tomatoes read *alte Sorten*, old varieties, which is as close as the German language comes to the phrase "heirloom tomato." I asked the saleswoman (who turned out to also be the grower) if I could take a picture, then mentioned that I was writing a book about old vegetables. We talked for a while about how, for her, the heirlooms are a way to offer something that's not in the supermarket, to take advantage of a niche, and to be part of a very local food supply. The tomatoes were lovely, and I bought a little basket of tiny red ones, later wishing I had bought up armfuls of the rest of her produce, so different was it from everything else I came across in the rest of the Naschmarkt, not to mention the neighborhood supermarkets.

Tomatoes, heirloom and otherwise, are neither abstract nor theoretical. These tomatoes come from fields and greenhouses, destined for plates and bellies. Walking through food markets, anywhere in the world, is an act with methodological implications. Looking at markets is a way to understand practice, what people are actually doing each day. Looking for heirloom tomatoes also requires moving through space, on streetcars, subways, or on foot, moving through the city. Moreover, to understand the Naschmarkt, and its produce, I had to think about other markets, other places where I have wandered to buy food.

How could it be that the most popular market in a city full of people devoted to good food had just a handful of heirloom tomatoes for sale? In the United States today, it would be very difficult to find such a large-scale and popular open-air market with so few heirloom tomatoes, especially at the height of summer. This seems like a contradiction. Vienna is a city of food lovers, a city whose stable food culture even shows up on postcards (mostly of fancy coffee, cake, and Wienerschnitzel, but still). Indeed, spending time in Austria has permanently changed how I look at food. This may be because, as I grow older, I pay more attention than I did when I was younger and lived in other places, but Austria is also a country of people who love food. This is a place where people talk about food like they talk about soccer, mulling over the qualities of a piece of meat or a sauce, recounting great meals to each other as if recalling a fine soccer play. On a flight from the German capital to the Austrian capital, a German friend of mine sat near two Austrians (recognizable by their strong Austrian accents) who spent the entire flight talking about food the way other people might talk about sports or politics—recounting the details of meals (both recent and long-ago), listing recipes and ingredients, and comparing notes. There was none of the false Puritanism that plagues so many Americans (and Germans), the, "Oh, I couldn't eat another bite" attitude, the insistence on being good and modest—a deep anxiety we seem to have about expressing pleasure when it comes to food. The people on the plane were experiencing outright pleasure in the memory and anticipation of good food, and had a systematic layman's attention to detail. Once at a fancy boiled beef restaurant (boiled beef is a Viennese delicacy), I overheard the group at the next table discussing in elaborate detail another meal they had eaten, while simultaneously polishing off copper pots full of beef broth, fried potatoes, creamed spinach, and horseradish stuffing.

Yet despite a widespread devotion to the fruits of the culinary arts, Vienna is a city that has far less heirloom produce than I can get every Wednesday and Saturday of the growing season in the middle of Chicago—an incredible variety of apples, potatoes, and other good things to eat, in the shadow of high-rise condos in one of the biggest cities in the country. During my stay in Vienna, I found that I could get heirloom tomatoes if I looked very hard for them, but often only outside of the city—in the lush seed-saver gardens of the group Arche Noah, tucked into the walls of an old convent, or in the flat expanse of fields planted by the "Tomato King," Erich Stekovics, in Burgenland. More recently, little trays of heirloom tomatoes, packed in cellophane, became available in one of the supermarket chains for a brief period in the summer. But in the open-air markets, I found nothing to compare with the wealth of tomatoes available in the big urban farmers' markets in the United States. I also sought them out at a market I visited more regularly than the Naschmarkt, closer to my apartment and more integrated into my daily life (and the daily lives of many of Vienna's residents).

Vienna: Brunnenmarkt

The Naschmarkt is certainly not the only market in Vienna, and it is the one that caters most to tourists and champagne drinkers. The city is checkered with other markets, catering to very different neighborhoods and consumers. Most of the markets are much less opulent than the Naschmarkt, and geared more toward home cooking than tourism. One market that combines everyday produce with a bit of champagne drinking is the Brunnenmarkt. At one end of Brunnenmarkt, several worlds meet: a predominantly Turkish and ex-Yugoslavian market, with the stalls piled high with very serviceable fruits and vegetables; a collection of farmers' stands at the far end of the market; and a square full of ex-students in advanced states of relaxation. Walking through the market behind, rather than in front of, the stalls, you pass towers of waxy cardboard boxes and gritty plastic crates either already empty or waiting to be emptied onto the slanted boards where customers pick through the vegetables. These generous stalls, with enormous piles of pale red tomatoes, curly spinach leaves (in the right season), cabbage, onions, squash, spring onions, and eggplant are clearly serving a different kind of kitchen than the meticulously stacked stalls of the Naschmarkt, an impression that is reinforced by the adjoining butcher shops that sell whole goats or lambs, and clean white trailers that advertise all imaginable organ meats.

In recent years, the champagne drinkers and other bourgeois bohemians have found their way to the edges of this market as well, parking themselves (ourselves?) at coveted tables catching the first sun of the spring or the last rays of summer, sipping small glasses of beer as a tonic against the excesses of the previous night, picking at plates of falafel or fried eggs, keeping one eye on a son or daughter running wild with the pack of children playing in the square, the other eye on the newspaper or the attractive crowd of grown-ups.

At the farmers' end of the Brunnenmarkt, just up the street from the crowded café tables, if you snooze, you lose. These vendors have no endless supply of wholesale refrigerated produce from which to continuously replenish their stocks, but rather only have whatever dusty herbs and multi-colored apples they were able to harvest in the previous twenty-four hours. When the watercress or the red peppers run out, that's it for the day. For years I seemed incapable of making it to the market in time to score a small paper parcel of handmade Kärntner Kasnudeln: a delicious dumpling stuffed with mint and Topfen, somewhere between ricotta and a very dry cottage cheese, difficult for the uninitiated to make at home. The dumpling maker always ran out of dumplings well before I had gotten anywhere near her stall.

Thus, one telling index at any market is whether or not the stalls are sold out at the end of the market day. In Vienna, the main stalls at the Naschmarkt maintain a stunning opulence from early in the morning until late in the day, constantly replenished from stacks of cardboard boxes and plastic crates. At the back end of both the Naschmarkt and the Brunnenmarkt, however, are stalls from farmers rather than wholesale distributors, and their tables start to empty out as the day progresses, to the point that only a few tired spring onions or wrinkled cooking apples might be left in the afternoon. It is at these back-end stalls where one can find a few handfuls of heirloom tomatoes at the very height of summer.

As my trip through the Naschmarkt revealed, heirloom produce is not necessarily easy to come by. Indeed, sometimes it is much more difficult to find in European cities than in U.S. cities. The scene is very different in other parts of Europe, and even other parts of Austria. But the scarcity of heirlooms in Vienna's biggest produce market hints at the instability of European food cultures themselves, and at the importance of everything from globalization, to transnational government (like the European Union), to personal memories in shaping the availability of particular fruits and vegetables, and agricultural biodiversity more broadly. Looking for heirloom tomatoes took me through milieux of tourists and locals, and Turkish grandmothers and Viennese bourgeois bohemians; it encouraged me to consider very different ways of being in the city. The relative scarcity of heirloom tomatoes was something I continued to encounter in all the European cities I visited, albeit with notable exceptions.

Paris: Focused Fieldwork

My hunt for heirloom tomatoes in Paris took a very different form from the relaxed exploration of daily life that I used for understanding Vienna. In Paris, the brief nature of my stay combined with my determination to get the lay of the heirloom-tomato land meant that I moved through the city at a very unnatural speed with a mix of stacks of metro tickets, camera, and notebooks at the ready in my pockets. A map and a list of markets completed the ethnographic toolkit. It is possible that I violated a tenet of participant observation by visiting the markets in a pretty unnatural way—zipping across the city on foot and on the metro, visiting as many as five markets in a given morning, and above all without a kitchen, so that I was mostly looking rather than buying. In the farmers' markets of Paris, my systematic hunt for heirloom tomatoes, or *tomates anciennes*, left me nearly empty-handed, but also with a few surprises. First, the *tomates anciennes* have certainly made their way into popular Parisian consciousness, but not in a particularly diverse way. Judging by its ubiquity, the *coeur du boeuf* or beefheart (or oxheart) tomato has gained quite a foothold. I found it in every market I visited, displayed in carefully stacked piles or in flat boxes bearing the clear label that these were *tomates anciennes*, or traditional tomatoes, commercially produced and distributed at the wholesale market that supplies most of the Parisian "farmers'" markets. A black variety also showed up from time to time, equally shiny and packed in similarly professional boxes.

One of the few exceptions to the surprising tomato homogeneity in Paris was at the stand of Joël Thiébault at the Alma-Merceau market, on Avenue du President Wilson in the 16th Arrondissement, just up the street from the spot on the Seine where Princess Diana died. This is a gorgeous market on a quiet bourgeois and elegant street, a long narrow avenue lined with white trucks and vans, many beat up and seemingly held together with duct tape, which provide the backdrop to the brightly colored stalls, aglow with electric lights in the gloom of the canopies. Thiébault is the purported heirloom vegetable king of Paris, and a vegetable activist in France, who sells out of his stand at Alma-Merceau some seventeen hundred varieties of vegetables, grown on twenty-two hectares in Carrières-sur-Seine, just seven kilometers from the Eiffel Tower. Thiébault also offers a vegetable box, by subscription.

This market was full of overflowing flower stands, so well stocked that the buckets of flowers threatened to block the narrow path through the market. Stalls abounded with clothes—the frilly little-girl dresses and the oversized linen shirts so popular that summer—pots and pans, household textiles, gleaming piles of fish on ice, and runny cheeses and stacks of fresh eggs in cardboard flats. But at eight thirty in the morning, the market was still surprisingly sleepy. There were butchers' stands with halves of baby pigs lying on a table, fowl with head and feet still attached, and freshly skinned rabbits stretched out behind glass. Thiébault's heirloom tomatoes outshone anything else I saw in Paris in terms of quantity and diversity. His stall was stunning—a wall of red and white radishes, a great mountain of ruffled lettuces, a cascade of huge bunches of herbs—so fragrant I just stood and sniffed for as long as I could—and, finally, a great pile of heirloom tomatoes, "this year's collection," seven euros per kilo. I bought a few tiny ones for my breakfast—some were good, some not so good.

The powerful, heady scent of the mountains of fresh herbs for sale at this stand tells a story about the uses and habits of this market—fresh herbs (particularly when sold like this, in massive piles, and not, like flowers, with their stems perched in buckets of water) are a very transient good. That aroma of dill, basil, mint, and everything else green and fresh indicates that the leaves have been bruised here and there, and that the process of decay has already begun. These are not herbs that can easily be boxed up at the end of the day and sold again tomorrow or the next day, but rather, they must be sold quickly (especially on hot summer days), while their leaves are still full of life and their essential oils still present.

Later that day and in the following days, I visited a dizzying collection of markets (taking notes after each in order to keep them apart) and took hundreds of pictures. By the time I had been to five or six more markets, I realized I was seeing some very similar produce from one market to the next. Even in the off-the-beaten path market-hall across from my down-at-heel hotel, in a decidedly less upscale neighborhood than Alma-Merceau, the hall was full of lovely fish stands with crackling piles of ice and carefully arranged palm fronds and piles of produce as well as very nice and down-to-earth meat stands. I found the St. Quentin market totally charming; inside a traditional market hall, it was a little dingy and not very big, but it had plenty of great fruit and veg just like in any other market, great meat and sausage and fish, and a well-stocked hardware store. Still, nothing quite matched Thiébault's stand in terms of diversity and being direct from the farmer.

Judging by the amount of French being spoken, and the fact that people like me (with cameras) were completely outnumbered by locals with heavy shopping bags, most of the markets I visited seemed to be places where residents tend to shop, with far fewer tourists than at the Campo de Fiori in Rome or the Naschmarkt in Vienna. There was, and is, no question that some of the market attendance involved a certain amount of posing, buying well-chosen food in a very public way.

Shopping at an open-air market, indeed, can be about much more than provisions, or eating and drinking. Carlo Petrini, a major figure in the origins of the Slow Food movement, got in trouble for describing the patrons of the Ferry Building Farmers' Market in San Francisco as actress-like, carrying their produce around like a fashion accessory, but there is inevitably some element of seeing and being seen; this is public space after all, and whether your goal is to cut a good figure with a well chosen *coeur du boeuf* tomato placed in your handwoven shopping basket at the Boulevard Raspail in Paris, or to catch up with your friends and vital neighborhood gossip, it is a stage and a performance of the everyday.

Some of the Parisian markets were very effete, and even the guidebook points out that the organic market at Boulevard Raspail, for example, is a place for celebrity spotting. Much of what's available is organic, and there is some very expensive meat (forty euros per kilo for sausage!). There were all kinds of dairy products—organic liters of milk, thick crème fraîche, cheeses of all kinds. Stalls selling soap and herbs gave off strong scents, and there were other stalls selling organic bread and whole grains, with bulk bins similar to those at Whole Foods. There was definitely gorgeous produce, and some heirloom tomatoes, as well as many things I could not get in Chicago. But every market I went to in Paris seemed shiny and polished, with perfect displays, much less haphazard and ramshackle than Monterey or Chicago Green City, and very few stalls sold straight from the farmer.

Of course, this means that the supply is reliable, maybe more affordable, and possibly more efficient. This is one of the many conundrums of supplying food to urban populations. When you are trying to feed a city, I think it can be important not to ignore the advantages of economies of scale, but also to take a critical approach to such economies of scale. How do these things develop? What are the habits and the habitus they foster? One of the most striking things to me was the relative lack of variation from market to market, and the relative absence of farmers. Most of the gorgeous fruit, vegetables, greens, herbs, fish, and flowers come from the wholesale market built on the outskirts of town when Les Halles (the old massive market in the center of Paris) was shut down. The tomatoes (and everything else—mangoes and watercress, springtime ramps and under-ripe papayas) are shipped or trucked in from places near and, more often, far.

Method and Shopping

Shopping at these markets is clearly a part of daily life, a ritual, forming part of what people do pretty automatically without thinking twice. This accretion of decisions and actions over seasons, months, years, and decades, has consequences for bodies and landscapes, communities, and neighborhoods. An open-air market in a European city (indeed, anywhere) is not generally the result of a whim or coincidence. Instead, such markets result from and embody a dense web of habits and inclinations, appetites and regulations, animosity and corruption, pleasure and necessity. The observation of people's comings and goings, the contents of the stalls, the fullness or emptiness of customers' shopping bags all yield details that can tell us of daily life and broader structures.[3] Markets have to do with habits and appetites, but also with laws and regulations, technology and even corruption. In these markets, we encounter cultural habit, but also webs of regulation and, in many cases, mild corruption as well, ranging from the money-laundering potential of such cash-based markets to the importance of good connections and possibly small bribes in securing the best locations.

Habitus can be read out of the ebb and flow at these markets; it presents itself in the presence or absence of bodies as well as the types of those bodies: women in headscarves with rolling shopping carts full of spinach and onions (spinach that would take hours to properly prepare, since springtime spinach is notoriously muddy and gritty), slim young Austrian mothers with expensive shopping bags, or tourists curiously inspecting the produce but proceeding largely empty-handed. When the markets are full of people, it means something—a behavior that comes relatively naturally or automatically to enough people (and in Paris, unlike at the Naschmarkt, the locals often outnumber the tourists). What comes naturally, automatically? What do people decide to do when they get up in the morning, what do they have and make time for, where do their feet take them in the city?

This is a distinctly visual, and sensory, approach. Are the tomatoes waxed or not, stiff and under-ripe, prematurely rushed to market? Or are they hours away from decay, fit for today's lunch but not tonight's dinner? This is definitely exemplary of how I go about my ethnographic (albeit broadly/loosely understood) research—making my way through gardens, farmers' markets, and supermarkets, talking to farmers and tomato fanatics and shopkeepers and chefs, getting the lay of the land in a pretty experiential and sensory way. These markets also very much function as public, urban spaces where I can observe interaction.

Are there heirloom fruits and vegetables in Paris? Yes, but less than I expected. I visited many markets and supermarkets, as well as historical vegetable gardens. I also poked around in culinary bookstores, and later in archives of newspaper articles and Web sites. Paris is, of course, unique, but the method can be applied to any city. What's in the supermarket? What can we find in the farmers' markets? What's being sold on the street? What do people seek out and actually consume? I went in search of heirloom vegetables, and while I also found freezer cases full of Weight Watchers entrées and people in line in the supermarket buying bright orange soda by the liter, I also found a stunning array of fruits and vegetables in the markets. Where is the stable food culture?

I think it's safe to say that heirloom tomatoes have come to Paris. (Did they ever leave?) I found them, although not in excessive numbers, in the markets of Paris, and also found evidence in books at the culinary bookstores. A clear perception in the literature on gardens and on food is that these traditional things made a comeback in the 1990s.[4] It is striking that there really seems to be a parallel turn to all sorts of "ancient" vegetables, at least judging by the publication dates of various books on the topic. Phrases like *grand-mère* are invoked repeatedly in the titles, as are *legumes oubliés* and *tomates anciennes*.

While heirloom tomatoes speak to tradition, many who seek them out are actually in search of new physical sensations (taste, color, shape) rather than the tomatoes of our childhoods.[5] Thus the search for such tomatoes and other "old-fashioned" food may be propelled by personal recollection, but also by a search for novelty in the form of fruits and vegetables long forgotten by industrial agriculture and supermarket produce buyers.

In contrast to a city like Chicago, where heirloom tomatoes are available (in season) in an incredible Technicolor array, Vienna and Paris don't make it easy to find much beyond mainstream tomatoes, which also tells us something about political structures behind markets and food cultures, and about the uniquely American provenance of the "heirloom" concept.

In the end, my search for heirloom tomatoes in European cities—cities that pride themselves on their devotion to good food—yielded surprising results. While Michael Pollan and others look to Europe as a bastion of stable food culture, these markets reveal something far more complex. These markets reveal, or at least hint at, a degree of instability in places where Pollan and others see stable food cultures. Searching for heirloom tomatoes in Vienna and Paris yields different perspectives on the place of these tomatoes (and heirloom produce more broadly) in daily urban life, and reveals tremendous variation—from places with deep cultural and agricultural traditions, to places where there is far less available at a farmers' market than I might find in Chicago's Green City Market or the weekly box of vegetables my mother receives from a local farmer in California. Furthermore, the act of observing these places yields some possibilities for more broad ethnographic inquiry.

Europe faced incredible upheaval over the course of the twentieth century, socially and politically, and also in terms of agriculture and the food supply. Some of the patterns we see today in Europe may seem stable or whole compared to our fast-paced and fragmented dietary habits in the United States, but they are by no means simply unchanged for centuries, delivered straight from the thirteenth to the twenty-first century. Instead, they are the result of a particular historical moment, a very much post–World War II culinary era with highs and lows, strengths and weaknesses. This complicates the idea of stable food culture—these things are not automatic but intentional. Arguing for stable food culture as the antidote to health problems is absurd, for many reasons, but in part because it employs a fundamentally inaccurate understanding of culture itself.

We need to treat the notion of stable food culture carefully, and to pay attention both to the threats to stable food culture in Europe, and to the remarkable possibilities presented by the diversity of food cultures in the United States. Watching and listening (and tasting, smelling, and touching as well) in these markets yielded unexpected results, and an important correction to my own assumptions about heirlooms on both sides of the Atlantic.

So, the call for a stable food culture can, in some ways, be either an excuse or an unreachable expectation. Any stable food culture must be understood as a kind of nexus of recipes and habits, the structures of workdays and labor markets, tastes and channels of distribution. European food cultures are very much in flux, and I think we should be cautious about posing such assumed stable food cultures as an antidote to the various things we can find wrong with the current system of producing and consuming food in the United States. Some critiques also rely on an overly simplified idea of culture as an unbroken chain of habits, practices, and meanings reaching back into the past. But a more complex notion of culture—as something contested, as a shifting rather than a stable set of meanings and practices—is more helpful in examining both European and U.S. food cultures, as well as food cultures around the world.

Lamenting the lack of a stable food culture in the United States might (in some cases) be less advisable than simply embracing the culinary and botanical patchwork that we have today, here and now, and seeking it out amidst the genetically uniform landscape of corn-based products and industrialized meat production. We cannot ignore the bigger structural factors—the changes in income structures that lead to dual-income households; the changing expectations for women; the physical structures of superstores and once-a-week shopping where we load up the back of the station wagon—this as opposed to a pedestrian shopping culture where it's easy to pick up a few things for dinner in a storefront supermarket on the way home from work. But we also have unprecedented access in the United States to a range of ingredients both fresh and packaged (including fresh market ingredients from Hmong farmers in Wisconsin, the foods available in Mexican grocery stores, or from the items overflowing in produce stands in Chinatowns across the country).

Walking through markets, watching and tasting, offers a methodological approach potentially useful in supermarkets as well as markets profoundly different from those in Vienna or Paris. For example, if we are concerned to understand recent efforts in the United States to offer access to fresh produce to residents of so-called food deserts (through establishing small local markets or urban agriculture like Growing Power in Milwaukee and Chicago, or lobbying to have food stamps accepted at farmers' markets). This approach is also potentially fruitful in places such as the scores of African markets that convulsed with the dramatic escalation of rice prices in 2008, the markets offering a front-row seat to the global and micro-level repercussions of price fixing and weather patterns, politics and economics.[6] Public markets around the world bear the imprint of habits of daily life, but in ever-changing ways; they're not inherently sites of stable food culture, but rather places where individuals and merchants and corporations and governments actively produce food landscapes, where food culture is negotiated and practiced and created. And the ethnographer, as well as the tourist and the home cook, can walk through such markets with a shopping basket in one hand and also the mindfulness of these investigative techniques, which can illuminate change and continuity, constraint and possibility.

Acknowledgements

Research for this chapter was conducted in part on a Lise Meitner/Austrian Science Fund grant at the Institute for Culture Studies and Theater History at the Austrian Academy of Sciences in Vienna, Austria. Many thanks are due to my colleagues at the Institute, to my colleagues at the University of Wisconsin-Milwaukee, and to Leo Coleman for his extremely helpful comments on several drafts of this chapter.

Notes

1. Child and Prud'homme 2007; Jones 2008.
2. Audi, Nadim, "France, Land of Epicures, Gets Taste for McDonald's," *New York Times,* October 26, 2009.
3. See Dave Lebovitz's great discussion of markets in Paris versus the United States: http://www.davidlebovitz.com/archives/2007/06/is_american_foo.html.
4. See, for example, Evelyn Bloch-Dano, *La Fabuleuse Histoire des Légumes* (Grasset 2008); Béatrice Vigot-Lagandré, *Les Légumes de nos Grand-mères* (Nouvel Angle 2009); Michel Viard, *Légumes d'autrefois* (Éditions Flammarion 2005); and Elizabeth Lemoine, *Les Légumes d'Hier et d'Aujourd'hui* (Éditions Molière 2003).
5. See Jordan 2007.
6. "Krieg um den Reis," http://www.arte.tv/de/suche/3107666.html.

–7–

Keeping out of the Kitchen: Cooking and Power in a Moroccan Household

Claire Nicholas

It was lunchtime, finally. I tore off a hunk of soft bread from the triangular portion of the household's round loaf, which was placed in front of me at the low wooden table. The communal dish of turnip and potato *ṭājīn*, the fourth of its kind we had eaten this week, sat waiting in the center of the table. I tried to be thankful for the meal, even as I groaned inwardly at the monotony of flavors. We waited for *bismillah* (in the name of God), usually uttered by Nezha[1] and repeated by each of us, before beginning to eat. Soaking up the warm juices with the bread, I corralled a chunk of potato and pulled it back towards the edge of the dish, using the bread and my right thumb like forceps, and popped it into my mouth. Nezha, Hafsa, and Khadija were doing the same. We worked through the turnips and potatoes in the space of ten minutes, leaving the chicken thigh and leg quarter exposed squarely in the middle of the dish. No one touched it, until Nezha reached over with both hands, divided the meat into four small portions, and placed them toward the edges of the dish, one in front of each woman. When we had all finished, everyone sat back from the table on the rugs lining the floor of the room. I complemented the chef, Nezha's eighteen-year-old daughter, Hafsa, since she had spent the better part of the morning preparing *lfṭur* (breakfast) and baking the bread for the day, followed by housework and another hour or two preparing our *lghiddā'* (lunch). Before getting up to wash her hands in the open-air courtyard of the house, Nezha casually asked me if I ever cooked at home, in *Amrīka* (America). When I joked that I was useless in the kitchen and mentioned that my husband was a better cook than I everyone laughed. She pushed the point further: "Why don't you ever cook for us?" I paused, then answered that I didn't know how to prepare Moroccan dishes, the spices were unfamiliar, and the ingredients I would need to make one of "my" dishes weren't available at the *sūq* (the weekly open-air market).

We had been building up to this conversation for some time. This meal took place well into four years of visits to, and stays at, Nezha's home in the village of Zaouiya. I went there to study a recently formed women's weaving cooperative, an initiative led by the Ministry of Tourism and Handicrafts and a local association dedicated to regional social development. A charitable characterization of Zaouiya, located in the heart of *l'arobīya* (a sometimes derogatory term for the countryside), would describe the village as peaceful. Less diplomatically, it might be called a borderline ghost town. Services are limited to two small *ḥānūt*, the Moroccan version of a convenience store, and only one intermittently functioning pay phone. There are, however, residues of a more glorious past, including the ill-kept tombs of the towns' five founding saints and the continuing vibrancy of its weaving practices. The women of the village, working at home, have, for at least four centuries, produced the *jellaba saissīya*, a high-quality textile typically used in the fabrication of men's *jellabas* (hooded tunics) and worn on formal occasions by the elite (e.g. the royal family).

In 2008, the cooperative headquarters finally opened after three years of sporadic construction, funded through a partnership between the Ministry of Tourism and Handicrafts and a regional development association, on land donated by the rural municipality. The cooperative locale includes workshop space for six looms. Given that the cooperative membership exceeds forty women, the co-op board and manager were obliged to draw up a rotation list, whereby pairs of weavers take turns producing two lengths of cloth in-house at the locale (this amounts to about two months of weaving time). Many women simultaneously maintain weaving projects on their home looms, and during their time out of rotation continue to weave exclusively at home. While the construction of a separate work setting outside the home amplifies the differentiation of weaving from other household work, the limited time spent at the locale attenuates this effect to a certain extent. There are, however, some implications of this tentative formalization of weaving "work." Namely, that the burden of domestic chores seems to fall heavily on nonweaving or younger female household members, a point to which I will return later.

During my first few visits to the village, I was treated to the famed Moroccan hospitality, and welcomed as a privileged guest. Afternoons were spent sipping tea as Nezha and I made the rounds to various weavers' homes. Lunch invitations were plentiful, and I sampled the local couscous on more than one occasion. This period was, in many ways, the honeymoon phase of fieldwork. The Moroccan phrase for honeymoon, *shhar el-'asal*, translates as "month of honey," but people sometimes joke that it would be more accurate to say *shhar el-bṣel*, or "month of tears" (literally, "month of onions"). Indeed, signs of tension arose from the beginning, as my host and other women of the cooperative struggled to figure out exactly what I was doing there. How might my presence alter the existing balance of power and feminine alliances that shaped sociability and the commercialization of cloth?

Inverting the anthropologist's stereotypical territoriality ("my village," "my tribe"), Nezha clearly felt I was "her anthropologist," and her possessiveness was at times stifling. Indeed, during my first visit to Zaouiya, I was originally a guest in the home of the cooperative's president, Fatima. Since Fatima, in accordance with her husband's wishes, never visited the market, Nezha introduced me to the *sūq* and proceeded to hijack the rest of my visit, insisting that I share the noontime meal with her family and spend the night. This commandeering of the foreign anthropologist caused an explosive argument between the two women and Fatima's husband later that day, since Fatima and her family had been waiting for me with a heaping dish of couscous. Nonetheless, this first visit set the tone (and my place of residence) for later stays, and I tolerated Nezha's possessive friendship in part because her relative freedom of movement and far-flung connections were interesting to follow. But managing our relationship while trying to build others turned out to be a delicate affair. I quickly realized the need to balance an openness to the haphazard (which usually entailed conforming to Nezha's plans), while asserting some autonomy to follow my own agenda. Part of this negotiation centered on time management and, by extension, on what constituted my obligations as a quasi-household member.

The Culinary Division of Labor and Household Hierarchy

The household in Morocco is both a locus of affective attachments and an economic unit composed primarily but not exclusively of family ties. Crawford's (2008) analysis of rural Moroccan households calls attention to the gerontocratic and patriarchal hierarchy ordering relations within the household, but also emphasizes the temporal mutability of inequalities within and between them. In other words, the changing demographic composition of particular households contributes to shifting divisions of labor between different members over their lifetimes. The specific period in which my path crossed into Nezha's household testifies to the precarious nature of these arrangements and the difficulties of constituting a household as a female provider. Nezha, the divorced mother of two teenage daughters, was the de facto head of household. Her ex-husband had little contact with his daughters and provided no financial support for their upbringing. Thus, earnings from the sale of her *jellaba* fabric served as the primary household revenue. This was supplemented by the rent paid by two boarders: local middle school teachers in their early to mid-twenties, Khadija and Malika. My contribution to the household economy included room and board money, calculated to match the rate paid by Peace Corps to local hosts.

At an early point in my village sojourns, it became clear that the hierarchy in Nezha's all-female household mapped onto the division of domestic duties, including cooking, tea preparation, dishwashing, cleaning, and shopping. As main provider and the eldest female, Nezha was essentially exempt from household chores and cooking duties, which allowed her to weave throughout the day and evening. Her usual workday began at six thirty in the morning and ended around eight thirty at night. During this time, she sat weaving at her loom, anchored to one wall of the house's central living and sleeping room, pausing to eat breakfast, lunch, and afternoon tea. Her work rhythm allowed for maximum flexibility: There was always time for a short nap after lunch, visits to neighbors or the homes of sick residents, or a quick errand at *Dār El-Ma'allma*, the cooperative's headquarters.

The tasks of cleaning and meal preparation usually fell to her two daughters, and especially to the elder, Hafsa, who had recently dropped out of high school to help out around the house. Her younger sister, Dunia, who boarded at the high school in the nearest town during the week, was essentially exempt from cleaning and cooking duties. Even during her weekend visits, she managed to avoid domestic responsibilities in favor of watching television and visiting village friends, much to the frustration of her older sister. Khadija, one of the young teachers, alternated with Hafsa in cooking and shared all her meals with the family. Close in age, Khadija and Hafsa were each other's confidantes. Yet when tensions arose, Hafsa usually sided with her mother, going so far as to spy on Khadija while the latter "chatted" on MSN, and to keep track of her computer usage to justify Nezha's claim for a larger electric-bill contribution. For the most part, Khadija deferred to Nezha, accepted her criticism without comment, and avoided open conflict, behavior that I interpreted as an effort to maintain friendly relations with her host family. The English teacher, Malika, was more of an outlier, and preferred to prepare her own meals and eat by herself. She had her own small butane gas tank and grill for this purpose, and claimed a vaguely described stomach ailment that prevented her from eating with the rest of the household. Her self-sufficiency caused some suspicion among the other women and girls: Gossip centered on her strangeness (*f-shi shkl*) and the validity of her supposed health problem, which was taken to be an impolite rejection of household sociability.

I observed a similar patterning of cooking, cleaning, and related duties in two other Zaouiya households. One young woman, Houda, lived with her husband, her two young children, and her mother-in-law (who was also a maternal aunt). She balanced child-rearing responsibilities for her infant daughter and three-year-old son while accomplishing the bulk of meal preparation, dishwashing, and laundry for the entire household, with only occasional assistance from her mother-in-law. In the home of Fatima, the cooperative president, almost all of the cooking, tea preparation, child rearing, and laundry fell to Hind, the younger wife of Fatima's husband's brother. Fatima's was one of the wealthier households in Zaouiya, and the household (composed of two families) occupied two adjacent homes. This division of labor gave Fatima the freedom to travel to neighboring cities for meetings and other cooperative business, as well as ample time to make house calls to other weavers in order to keep up with the *akhbār* (news). While domestic work and food production was divided exclusively, but unequally, between the female members of these households, their husbands assumed responsibility for food shopping and provisioning.

Home to Market: The Fine Art of Shopping

Nezha, as *mulat ed-dār* (house owner/head of household) and provider, took on the role that typically falls to the male head of household. Every Saturday, she trekked the three kilometers to the local *sūq* to stock up on food and household staples. From the very beginning, I established the habit of accompanying her on these trips, in part to help with carrying heavy bags of vegetables and fruit around the *sūq*, in part because the market also housed wool and textile products, which gave me the opportunity to observe Nezha selecting wool yarn. Market day therefore combined shopping for both work and household provisions, which points to the interpenetration of these two domains (work and home life or private life) in the relational and organizational structuring of the female weavers' lives.

Until 2008, weaving in Zaouiya was an exclusively domestic activity, meaning that in practice it blended seamlessly with the rhythm of household chores, childcare, and social calls. This is not to say that weaving the *jellaba* cloth bore the same value as cooking or cleaning. Indeed, as far back as the weavers remember, the *jellaba saissīya* has enjoyed both national and local prestige as a luxury commodity. Thus, weaving stands apart from other domestic work, both as a remunerative activity and because of the symbolic value of the type of cloth produced. In the past, the *sūq* served as the beginning and endpoint for woven cloth: Weavers or their husbands purchased the loose wool or hand-spun yarn to start production, and sold the finished cloth to local merchants. Some weavers maintained relations with private clients on the side, which usually guaranteed higher profits. The prominence of the *sūq* as primary commercialization channel for both raw materials and final product has diminished in recent years, as weavers have begun using machine-spun wool yarn for the warp, thus sourcing yarn through the cooperative and purchasing silk or *sabra* (rayon in most cases) for the decorative woven elements through intermediaries who are *not* located at the *sūq*. Nonetheless, the *sūq* remains the principal source for food and the hand-spun wool yarns used in the weft.

The typical *sūq* shopping trip involved rushing out of the house around seven thirty in the morning with no breakfast, followed by a long walk down the poorly paved road between the village and the market. If we were lucky, a kind Samaritan passing by on a *karossa* (a donkey- or mule-drawn cart) would let us hitch a ride. The first stop was always at the wool and textile section of the *sūq*, where women from the neighboring countryside, seated around the perimeter of the stands, sold bags of loose, carded wool and hand-spun wool yarn. We frequently ran into other female weavers from Zaouiya, all there to carefully select the wool or yarn they needed to complete or begin their weaving projects.

I tagged along as Nezha circled through the women selling their yarn, watching over her shoulder as she eyeballed the skeins and occasionally asked to take a closer look. Taking each skein into her hands, she would untwist the bundle and carefully isolate a yarn strand, looking for the consistency and fineness of the spun wool. Once, stopping in front of a woman selling loose washed wool, she pulled out a chunk of the fibers and slowly tugged them apart, twisting and pulling in a gesture mimicking the action of spinning. In most instances, I saw her turn away from the female vendors without a word, or silently return a skein and walk away without comment. The interactions between weavers and sellers were of the most businesslike nature. Everyone was there to strike a hard bargain, and it was definitely a buyers' market. But amidst the buying and selling, there remained a fair bit of time for socializing and exchanging news. At the communal scales near the corner of one of the stands, the weavers of Zaouiya clustered together and chatted, sometimes about "work," but mostly they recounted the comings and goings of various villagers or their families. Nezha was one of the five or so women who served as a sort of commercial intermediary for those who had no customers of their own (on commission, of course), so it paid to get updates on who was working on what sort of fabric and whether they might be looking to sell it through her.

By the time we moved to the vegetable and fruit area of the market, I was usually starving. But we never stopped at one of the numerous stands selling hard-boiled eggs and bread or *harira*, a hot tomato and chickpea-based soup. Instead, Nezha always made a beeline for the vegetable and fruit stands, which, in the summer, were overflowing with piles of glossy, ripe produce, and, in the winter, were dismally stocked with turnips, potatoes, carrots, onions, tomatoes, and some wilted green beans. In our first few trips together, I tried to assist with the vegetable selection: We'd squat together in front of the vegetables piled on worn plastic tarps, while the salesman, seated in the center near the scales, spent his time tossing out beat-up hubcaps for customers to fill, weighing kilos of produce, calling out prices to curious passers-by, and making change. I'd look over at other customers, both men and women, grabbing one or two carrots at a time and tossing them onto their hubcap with a perfunctory glance to be sure nothing was obviously rotten or insect-ravaged. By contrast, Nezha took her time, rummaging through the pile of carrots to extract a likely candidate, carefully inspecting it for deformities or blemishes, and, if it passed muster, putting it onto the hubcap. I noticed her preference for medium-sized, uniformly shaped carrots. Abnormalities, like a crooked form or an irregularly tapered root, were quickly rejected. When I attempted to participate in the selection process, my choices were frequently deemed unacceptable. After the third market visit, I was instructed to wait near the stand of her preferred spice dealer to "guard" our bags.

Standing on the outskirts of the produce market, watching Nezha inspect the meager winter offerings one Saturday, it occurred to me that the agonizing care with which she selected vegetables paralleled the attention she gave to her yarn purchases, and also reminded me of her almost obsessive concern with folding the *jellaba* material once it was cut off the loom. On several occasions, I observed her enlist Hafsa's help in folding the cloth lengthwise, once, twice, three times, until it was stretched taut between them in a three-meter-long rectangular column. Mistakes were met with curt reprimands of, "*Jibdi mziyen!*" ("Pull it firmly!") and, "*Shddi mziyen*" ("Grasp it tightly"). A cheap piece of black synthetic cloth spread out on the floor protected the fabric from dirt as Hafsa kneeled on one end of the column and Nezha slowly moved toward her, folding the cloth. Before each fold, she smoothed out any wrinkles, inspected the fabric for stray yarns, cutting them with a razor blade, and brushed off bits of loose fibers. The final product was a sort-of squared off roll, which Nezha wrapped in a woman's square foulard (headscarf) and packed away in a locked suitcase. Her vigilance over the smallest details—with respect to food, wool, and finished cloth—was part of what made her one of the best weavers in the village.

Concocting a Role: Kitchen Incompetency and Supplemental Shopping

After the first few trips to the market in Zaouiya, I started to feel a bit guilty about not helping out around the house or with meal preparation. However, I didn't want to be integrated into the cooking rotation with Hafsa and Khadija, in part because of the time they spent preparing meals (especially Hafsa), time which I preferred to spend hanging out at the weaving cooperative, watching the women work and trying my hand at spinning and carding wool. Part of the problem was the silence maintained between Nezha and me when it came to the terms of my residence with her, and what exactly my room and board money covered. It was impossible to address this openly, for fear of an awkward or shame-inducing conversation. Nezha accepted all my money as if it were a gift, not a payment calculated on the number of days I spent there. And we both played along with this face-saving fiction, though the ambiguity of the arrangement engendered substantial angst on my part.

My solution was piecemeal. In trying to assert my independence to come and go freely, and to spend time with other members of the cooperative (including some of Nezha's avowed "enemies"), it seemed crucial to avoid being lumped in with the "subordinate" women and to forge some sort of a role as a secondary provider. Nezha exercised near absolute control over the outings of her elder daughter and, to a certain extent, those of Khadija, who had no other friends in the village and therefore followed Nezha's program and visiting schedule. Hafsa rarely left the house, only occasionally to share a meal with the neighbors or walk out into the nearby fields with her mother, sister, and myself. She never went to the market. This virtual confinement reflected the generally conservative Zaouiya views of appropriate visibility and exposure in public spaces for marriage-age girls. My status as an engaged, and later married, woman in the household clearly didn't put me into the same category as Hafsa, a protection-needing female, but my dependency on Nezha for introductions, social guidance, and information (especially early on) undermined any possibility of being treated as her peer.

My strategy emerged somewhat haphazardly, never really cementing into a policy, *per se*, and was characterized by inconsistency and contradiction in the face of unfolding situations. Nevertheless, in retrospect it boiled down to a dual approach: On the one hand, I styled myself as a cooking ignoramus, and on the other, created a role as the "supplemental" shopper. Thus, when pressured to cook, I claimed ignorance of how to blend Moroccan spices, said that the ingredients to make "my" dishes were not available, or that I was useless without all my usual kitchen gear. This incompetence was not entirely feigned.

In the early days, when I was still working out my participation in household chores, I occasionally wandered into the kitchen to offer assistance. The kitchen was located in a concrete storage space separate from the rest of the house. Most of the dried provisions were stacked up in various plastic barrels and bags at one end of the room, barricaded by two large pieces of cardboard. Spices and oil sat atop one of the plastic barrels in a corner, placed in jars, small plastic Tupperware containers, and plastic bags. Hafsa seemed to be the only person who knew where ingredients and spices might be at any particular moment. The oven was basically a steel cabinet hooked up to a butane tank, with one door that insisted on falling open at inopportune moments. Nearby were two burners, one formed out of an iron frame made to fit over a small butane tank, the other a weighty iron burner that was connected to another butane tank with a poorly fitting rubber hose.

When I offered to help cut up vegetables for one lunchtime meal preparation, Hafsa handed me an onion and one of her dull, all-purpose "made in China" knives with a plastic handle. She watched, curious, as I sorted through the clutter of dishes in the plastic drying rack for a suitable plate on which to cut the onion. After the first two cuts, severing the ends from the bulb, I ran the knife down the arc of the onion, making a shallow incision, and removed the skin. Apparently, my technique was slowing down the whole process. Hafsa took the onion from me, saying she would handle it, and deftly cupped it in one hand, while she worked around the top with forceful, shallow, staccato cuts. Holding it over the pressure cooker, she made a horizontal slice and the small pieces from the first round of cuts dropped into the pot. This process was repeated and in the space of about one minute she had finished mincing the onion. On another occasion, Hafsa asked me to light the large iron burner while she attended to another cooking task. I fumbled with the knob of the gas tank and held a lighter just above the center of the burner. There was a whooshing popping noise and a flash near the joint connecting the hose to the burner. Then a flame leaped up in my face. I recoiled instinctively, narrowly avoiding a serious burn, and became very wary of the burner/gas-tank rigs in the future.

At the collective table, I proved to be equally worthless in peeling certain fruits. This was especially true of apples. The communal setting of fruit consumption after lunchtime meals meant that I had an audience of at least three women observing my fumbling attempts at paring. Usually, Nezha, Hafsa, or Khadija would intervene, offering to peel it for me or handing me a portion of her own. My awkwardness with a knife clearly demonstrated inexperience and unfamiliarity with food preparation tasks in general, confirming my claims to being a poor cook. At a certain point, cultivating this impression of incompetence seemed like an effective way of exempting myself from time-consuming and labor-intensive tasks.

But I didn't want anyone to think that I was unwilling to "get my hands dirty," so I opted, albeit sporadically, to assist with cleaning, especially with the dishwashing—a painstaking procedure given the lack of running water. The first step was to draw water from the underground cistern in the center of the courtyard, about fifteen meters from the dishwashing station. The trick was to fill the two black plastic basins with just enough water to do the job, and not a drop more. If Nezha spotted over-full basins, a reprimand for wastefulness inevitably followed. After Hafsa scrubbed the dishes with a piece of netting and the minimum amount of *tīd* (Tide), she handed them off for rinsing in the second basin. They were then placed in a plastic mesh bin, and the excess dishes were balanced carefully between a rock and the side of the kitchen wall.

Informal conversations with Hafsa during these dishwashing sessions gave me a chance to explore her feelings about being pulled out of high school, whether or not she wanted to become a weaver like her mother, and her thoughts on what proved to be a temporary engagement with a young man in El Jadida, the regional capital. She was ambivalent about leaving school, but defended her mother's decision, saying that the cost of books was a heavy financial burden and the money would be needed to prepare for her then upcoming wedding. She mentioned her mother's recent pressure on her to get serious about learning to weave, but also told me that she would rather become a doctor, teacher, or nurse (occupations that were well out of her reach as a high school dropout). Dishwashing was also the backdrop for my social education, and Hafsa admonished me on several occasions, saying that I should be wary of other people's questions. She brushed aside my protests that I had nothing to hide as if they weren't relevant: "It's none of their business, they're just being *fiḍulī(a)* (nosy)." She directed especially hard words toward one young village woman, a person I thought was a family friend and who later became one of my closest friends, calling her a *brgāga* (gossip-monger) with loose lips. Our conversations highlighted the weight of village "talk" and its potential to damage one's reputation, and pointed to the value of information management in women's social relations.

Equal but Different? Apportioning Supplemental Goods and Weaving Cooperation

To further offset my ineptitude in the kitchen, I carved out a niche as the buyer of supplemental or luxury food items, mostly packaged food or snacks that accompany breakfast, tea, and dinner. In this sense, I became a provider of sorts, albeit a nonessential one. As the indulgent shopper, I bought sweet and salty treats that enriched our meals together. As it developed, my shopping list came to include a host of goods identified by Arabicized versions of their French names: *carwassa* (croissant), *frumāj* (fromage, mostly *La Vache qui Rit*, a spreadable cheese), *konfitūr* (confiture, in most cases apricot jam), *danūn* (from Danone, and now the generic term for any brand of packaged yoghurt), *limunada* (lemonade, also a generic term for any soft drink, such as Coke or Fanta), and *cowcow* (cacahuète or peanuts). I also bought a few products that fall outside this rubric, namely *zitūn* (olives), muesli (this was an utterly foreign addition to our breakfast regime, which I will return to later), and the Moroccan *ḥallāl* (non-pork) version of mortadella, which Nezha always referred to as *kāsher*. With the exception of the olives and peanuts, all these goods were sold at one of the two village *ḥānūt* (similar to a convenience store or a limited-selection grocery store). The weekly combined costs of my shopping excursions amounted to some sixty dirhams (about eight dollars), about what Nezha spent on vegetables and provisions at the weekly *sūq*.

Though these supplemental items came into the household cupboards via a secondary source (myself), their integration into meals was still monitored and controlled to a large extent by Nezha. For instance, our *danūn* consumption involved the careful parceling of individual cups; each person in the house was allotted one serving after dinner or in the morning. If someone ate a yoghurt out of turn, or on their own, as I sometimes did, this was subtracted from her overall yoghurt quota. When it came down to the final three or four cups, we all knew whose was whose. However, snacking or eating by oneself was generally frowned upon, as if individual appetites should be regulated according to the household's eating schedule and the common menu. This accords with the more general prohibition on eating by oneself in public or in a group: the notion being that one should always share with one's entourage. Although eating according to one's own cravings went against communal ideals, we all indulged our preferences for particular flavors and serving styles within the context of the common meal. While I liked the pudding-like consistency of normally refrigerated yoghurt, Nezha and Hafsa put their portions in the freezer, until the yoghurt was transformed into a frozen treat.

The carefully calculated equality in consumption also determined how we divided up the spreadable cheese for breakfast and dinner. Conveniently, *La Vache qui Rit* comes packaged in small, triangular, individual aluminum-wrapped portions. But somewhere along the way, Nezha had decided that the portion deemed appropriate for one person was too generous. So each of us followed her practice of taking one half-portion, thus leaving the other half for another woman at the breakfast or dinner table. But again, each woman combined the cheese with the apricot *konfitūr* and olive oil in the way she saw fit. Nezha preferred to pour a tablespoon or two of olive oil into a small clay saucer and mash together the cheese and oil with a hunk of bread. Hafsa sometimes followed suit, and I was partial to spreading the cheese by itself or with a dollop of jam onto my triangle of bread, making a sort of sandwich.

This delicate interplay between equity of collective consumption and individual expression carried over into the realm of the weaving cooperative. In theory, the horizontal structure of the cooperative emphasized the democratic ideals of one producer, one voice, while simultaneously uniting the weavers in pursuit of the group's collective gain. In practice, these ideals manifested in the rotation of weaver pairs in and out of the locale's workspace, giving all members equal chance to work in house. Furthermore, to ensure a fair and random selection of members for trade-show participation, the cooperative conducted a lottery, performed in a meeting attended by interested weavers.[2]

On the days I practiced my wool carding or spinning, the weavers took turns bringing large loaves of round bread or *msimmen* (a buttery, layered, crepe-like pastry) to be shared with tea in the afternoons. At the same time, I noticed a certain competitive cast to the weavers' interactions. Despite fairly obvious differences in quality (which were rarely discussed in the open), each pair of weavers asserted to me that their work was *première qualité* (the highest level of quality in a vaguely defined ranking of first, second, and third tiers). In one particular incident, as I questioned a young weaver on the strength of hand-spun warp yarns, another, older weaver inserted herself into our conversation and implied that the younger weaver's yarn had been thickly spun, thus rendering it stronger. The younger weaver took this as an insult and immediately denied that the thickness had anything to do with the strength, but rather that it was the dexterity and skill of the spinner (who happened to be her mother) that made all the difference. Houda, the young mother of two who became a close friend, commented to me that for all the supposed solidarity of the cooperative, whenever government officials came to visit, each weaver wanted to shine, or to stand out as the best: *bghāt tbān* (she wants to appear—to show herself). Thus, while the structure of the cooperative imposed an equal playing field amongst its members, daily weaving practices and relations among members demonstrated a fair bit of individual maneuvering. In this sense, it paralleled food consumption in the home.

Furthermore, work at the cooperative's locale linked up in complicated ways with the household division of labor. When questioned as to which work setting she preferred, one weaver proclaimed that weaving at the cooperative was better because it exempted her from housework, which then fell to the younger or subordinate women in the household. Another remarked that working at the locale was like being a *muwaẓẓafa* (an employee, with the added nuance of belonging to the formal work sector, with time-regulated work hours and job security). In one case, a weaver mentioned withdrawing her younger daughter from school in order to help out around the house. Indeed, the cooperative seemed to be exacerbating certain inequalities in the household division of labor especially vis-à-vis nonweaving females, even while it promised greater economic autonomy and security for its members. In Nezha's household, these inequalities were already firmly entrenched, in part because its survival depended primarily on the weaving income provided by Nezha. But in other households, the burgeoning success of the cooperative suggested a further differentiation of women's work, where those who weave concentrated increasingly on only that, and other female household members performed the cooking, cleaning, and childcare.

The Bitter Pill: Ambivalence in Fieldwork Relations

My struggles to maintain my autonomy, while sharing food and contributing to the household economy, relate more broadly to the difficulty of defining reciprocal obligations as an American anthropologist in a Moroccan household. In some sense, these struggles were attempts to resolve the ambivalence characterizing most fieldwork relationships, where economic, social, educational, and cultural differences inevitably color interactions. The mutual ambivalence shaping my relationship with Nezha plays out clearly in the negotiation of muesli consumption. Following two or three previous occasions when I had fallen violently ill while visiting Zaouiya, a friend suggested I bring my own breakfast with a high dose of fiber to strengthen and regularize my digestive system. Muesli can only be purchased in Morocco at some of the larger supermarket chains, such as Acima or Marjane, located in most major cities. It's a fairly high-cost item: thirty to forty dirhams (four to five dollars) buys a small plastic pouch containing between five and six portions. Since the local *ḥānūt* in Zaouiya only infrequently carried fresh milk, I bought a large box of Nido (powdered milk for children) to go with the muesli. My friend had suggested I explain to Nezha that I was eating the muesli for health reasons, thus avoiding the usual obligation to share. However, when I arrived at Nezha's home and unloaded the muesli and Nido, along with some gifts of scarves and jewelry for Nezha and her daughters, she was so curious about this completely new breakfast option that it felt impolite not to include it in the communal food stock. We sat together in the weaving/TV room, and I read the ingredients listed on the package in Arabic to her. She quizzed me on the price, the possibility of acquiring the ingredients at the *sūq*, and its supposed health benefits. The next three or four mornings we replaced the usual breakfast of bread, *La Vache qui Rit*, *konfitūr*, and olive oil with reconstituted Nido (mine was mixed with bottled water) and packaged muesli. Almost immediately, Khadija decided the flavor and texture were distasteful and she refused future servings. Hafsa was ambivalent about it, but Nezha seemed to enjoy consuming the unfamiliar concoction of oat and wheat flakes, almond slivers, raisins, and, on one occasion, freeze-dried strawberries. After the first bite, she announced it was too crunchy and left the muesli to soften in the bowl of milk, where the freeze-dried strawberries disintegrated and stained the Nido a faint pink. The muesli didn't last long, and after three trips watching the overpriced cereal disappear quickly, it didn't seem worth the trouble of lugging it on the bus ride from Marrakech to Zaouiya just to eat "healthy" for three days.

Nezha's gleeful savoring of the novelty food item paralleled a similar openness to new experiences and the world outside of Zaouiya that I observed over the course of our relationship. As one of the primary commercial intermediaries of the village, Nezha maintained relationships with several out-of-town clients around Morocco. She traveled frequently to *foires* (trade shows) in Casablanca, Marrakech, and El Jadida, both as a representative of the cooperative and as a *femme entrepreneur* (female entrepreneur) and member of associations such as Femmes Artisanes (a national network of female artisans with boutiques in Azemmour and Marrakech and royal patronage that guaranteed exposure at national trade shows) and Fondation Zakoura (a nationwide micro-credit organization). Despite complaints of the poor sales at these trade shows, Nezha always spoke favorably of the connections and friends she made at the events, relationships that sometimes led to new clients. Beyond the economic benefits of an ever-expanding network, she seemed to genuinely value developing relationships outside the village: enriching her *tajriba* (experience) was an end in itself. This, I believe, was her initial interest in welcoming me into her home.

The reasons why Nezha continued to tolerate my presence and research activities, on the other hand, remain ambiguous to me. Over the four years of our relationship, she became increasingly resistant to my constant questioning and photographing of the weaving process, and suspicious of my widening circle of female friends in the village. Whereas I started out as an unknown factor in her existence, and thus a potential catalyst for a better life (through some imagined commercial expansion by way of the "wealthy" foreigner or assistance in helping her leave the village permanently), toward the end of my fieldwork, it became clear that this wasn't going to happen. Despite numerous careful explanations of my research and that it would eventually result in a dissertation and book, I heard from another woman that Nezha didn't believe this was my true purpose, and she also felt I wasn't giving her enough money. This was the ultimate disappointment. After four years of struggling to locate myself in her household as a friend, a near "structural equivalent," as helpless in the kitchen but useful in "enriching" the productive foundation she provided, I'd never really bridged the fundamental inequalities separating us. I remain, for her, a wealthy (but stingy) and *qārīa* (educated) American academic with a culturally unintelligible research project. Nezha, for me, is a woman struggling with difficult circumstances, trying to cobble together an existence for herself and her daughters by any means necessary. Though Nezha seemed to relish the novel flavor of the muesli, along with the possibilities our relationship opened up, in the end, commensality on the tenuous and ambiguous terms we had negotiated did not make us equals.

Indeed, during my time in Zaouiya, I learned that the division of labor that makes sharing a meal possible enacts household hierarchies that predominantly favor the authority of elder, female weavers. This translates to the disproportionate execution of meal preparation, dishwashing, and housecleaning by younger, subordinate women, and/or nonweaving females. As weaving "work" moves partially into the cooperative locale and out of the home, the differentiation between the tasks falling under the category of "women's work," including weaving, threatens to further intensify. The extent to which this exacerbates generational tensions remains to be seen. It most certainly required delicate negotiation as an anthropologist trying to find her place somewhere between the kitchen, the *sūq*, and the *ḥānūt*.

Notes

1. I have used pseudonyms for the people and places in this essay, with the exception of El Jadida and Marrakech, two large cities peripheral to the scope of my discussion.
2. However, in the days following the lottery, the two women who had "won" decided they didn't want to make the journey to the trade show, and conferred their spots to the co-op's president, who typically makes these journeys and had the money to pay for travel and lodging.

"Do You Know How to Eat . . . ?" Edible Expertise in Ho Chi Minh City

Nina Hien

"Nina giỏi," announced Chi Chinh as she breezed into my room one afternoon and handed me a cold glass of freshly squeezed fruit juice. What had I done to make her believe I was so *clever*, so *skillful*, so *good*? This kind of praise was usually given to someone who had shown mastery over something complex. What had I done to deserve such high approval from the head cook of the household? Chi Chinh prepared the daily meals for my friends, a well-to-do professional couple living on a long-term basis in Ho Chi Minh City: Phuong, a Vietnamese-Canadian woman and Peter, an American man from New York City. They owned several businesses here. This was the summer of 2010, and they had invited me to stay with them in their home in the central District 1.

I was baffled and wondered about this comment. At the same time, I was curious about what kind of juice I was holding. Taking a sip of the rosy liquid, I discovered that it was refreshingly tart pomegranate. This was the first time I had seen or been served this fruit in Vietnam. Apparently, in late 2007, following a global surge of reports about its health benefits, a sharp spike in its import into the country from China had occurred.

Even though Chi Chinh had a slight frame, she had a way of waddling around, her thin body moving from side to side instead of in a straightforward motion. This unlikely carriage gave her an air of authority and seemed to assert her ethnic Chinese origins, of which she was clearly proud.[1] Many of the dishes she made reflected this background through the use of Chinese spices, ingredients, and cooking techniques. A few times, Chi Chinh mentioned her experience of living abroad during a period when she had been the cook for a family in Singapore. She learned then how to make dishes from different Asian cuisines. Indeed, a few days after I arrived in Vietnam, she made Japanese maki for my friends' children. This feat was then memorialized by a photograph of the show-stopping rolls that ended up taped to the door of the children's closet amid the mass of pink Barbie-doll stickers.

Chi Chinh was clearly eager to show off her cooking prowess and experiment with new and different ingredients, styles, and tastes. Her way of thinking and ambition was striking because cooks who were able to or who would cook non-Vietnamese food and break from standard fare were not all that common. Just ten years earlier, even though other types of cuisine were beginning to be known in the market, Vietnamese cuisine was the main food served in family homes, often even ones with non-Vietnamese backgrounds. Indeed, a few days before the pomegranate juice incident, Chi Chinh had offered me a glass of golden-hued passion-fruit juice. This had triggered memories of hunting for this intensely tropical-tasting fruit in the market a decade earlier. Its flavor and texture had first captivated me after I discovered it in a container of Australian yogurt, which I found on the shelves in a supermarket for foreigners in Ho Chi Minh City. But then, when I looked for the fresh version, I came up empty-handed, even though my Vietnamese dictionary has a word for passion fruit—*chanh dây*—which indicates that it was at least known in Vietnam. Only a year later, it appeared in market bins at a ridiculously low price. Unfortunately, I bought and ate so much of it then that I completely lost my passion for it for a while.

Long known or not, passion fruit was identified by my Vietnamese relatives as something odd, not even food for humans. When I brought a large bag of it to dinner at their house one night as an offering, one of them said that some people considered it livestock feed. No one seemed to know what to do with it yet. Indeed, I sensed that my food contributions (as well as the other gifts I gave) were perceived as strange. I often felt that I was making some sort of a social blunder, which made me feel awkward about the practice of gift-giving altogether. But perhaps it was my sense that no matter how much I attempted to blend in, it was very likely that I would always be considered a stranger (the term for foreigner being *người lạ*, literally a "strange person") and a novice to the highly complex and elusive Vietnamese ways.[2] But perhaps, like any alien food that could eventually become integrated into daily diets, people from the outside could eventually be included? Accompanying the entrance of so many newcomers and commodities, which is creating profound shifts in the sociocultural structures in contemporary Vietnam, are many related changes underway in its food culture.

So how exactly does something strange become adopted in or adapted to the local "menu"? How does it become part of the repertoire of acceptable and agreeable flavors and tastes, possibly even cherished? Does something ever stop being foreign? If so, how does it become an object of common consumption? And furthermore, what does not make the cut onto the plate and the palate, and why not?

Here, what first gets marked as odd has the capacity to become familiar and even inscribed in the country's articulated gastronomy, which has had a long existence. Historically, in writings about food culture in this context, the expression *"học ăn học nói,"* literally "to study to eat, to study to speak," frequently appears. The latest place where I noticed this maxim is in the introduction to a recent collection of old and new scholarly and popular pieces about Vietnamese ways of eating, the philosophy of its cuisine, and concrete musings about specific national and regional dishes (Xuân 2000: v). The saying indicates that both of these activities are primary to existence, but must be acquired in forms that have pronounced rules—and a strong relationship with each other, as "cultured" activities.

Learning how to eat comes before learning how to speak. Eating is the primary faculty. But these activities of the mouth are intimately connected and coalesce in the meal, making the act of eating inherently social. This being the case, it is worth mentioning that photographs of people with their mouths open at feasts are often hidden because of the presumed vulgarity, so eating for its own sake (as animals do) is not the main goal, or at least not one that should be represented. Furthermore, one of the chapters in this book, written by reputed Vietnamese cultural scholar Trần Ngọc Thêm, emphasizes the communality of the act of eating and conversing in Vietnam—in contrast with Western dining encounters, during which conversation is supposedly avoided (Trân 2000: 40).

This general (mis)conception of Western eating practices, however, does not inhibit anyone from engaging non-Vietnamese newcomers in conversation. One of the most basic, conventional tools used to facilitate discussion and gauge the guest/outsider is the posing of a couple of common, but curious, questions that reveal how the meal operates as a space for evaluating belonging, difference, and position. It seems clear that by actively learning the techniques and rules of how to deal with food and the meal, cultural fluency and mastery is possible, which may then create a sense of belonging.[3] This involves both familiarity and intimacy with distinctive local flavors (on the sensual side) and the acquisition of knowledge about (on the rational and intellectual side) particular edible substances and dishes. And, as is often the case in the course of such cultural training, some pretty humiliating lessons can arise (as we will see).

The Familiar, the Exotic, and the Gross

One day when I was scoping out the cookbook titles at a bookshop on the central Nguyễn Huệ Boulevard, I almost tripped over two little Vietnamese girls who were camped out on the floor in front of a full section of books devoted to decorative food arts. They were engrossed by a book from a nearby shelf featuring specialties from different regions around Vietnam. This book boasted dishes using snake and eel, uncommon fish, assorted rodents, and the controversial "pet" meats of dog and cat. These local Vietnamese dishes from unfamiliar provinces were clearly very exotic and exciting to the girls. From the squeals they made, it was also evident that they were incredibly (and happily) grossed out by the dishes.

Unusual Vietnamese cuisines are not the only sign of a new interest in the exotic. That day, I also spotted a few book titles combining European cuisine with Asian cuisine. One of them, *100 Món Ăn Á-Âu Ngon Miệng* (*100 European-Asian Delicious Dishes*), hinted that a deliberate fusion cuisine might be arising.[4] This fusion, however, did not actually indicate any blending of dishes. Within the book, the ideologies expressed and the way the dishes were characterized maintained clear national classifications. And for the most part, there was little concern with recipes. The text eagerly constructed equivalences between cuisines and offered justifications as to why certain foods are consumed, offering a pre-emptive defense against a feared non-Vietnamese perception that Vietnamese cuisine is barbaric, or at least, repugnant. So for instance, regarding cat meat, the author points out that cat is also eaten in daily Peruvian meals as well as in specific rural areas of Switzerland and northern Italy (Thu 2010: 96–7). Apparently, pet-meat eating is happening in the West, too!

All this is to say that, clearly, an investment, a fascination, and an engagement in noticing and determining edible differences, including indulging in the exotically gross, are now prevalent in Vietnam. And not only does this indicate a burgeoning openness and curiosity toward new food and tastes (as one view of globalization would have it), but it also produces new anxieties and attempts to normalize certain substances and establish even the most unusual (and possibly repulsive) items of Vietnamese cuisine as equivalent to, and on par with, the foods of other nations.

The rhetoric of political *normalization* has indeed entered this culinary realm, which is key to the success of this process of creating smooth relations between the inside and the outside, the native and the foreign. In Vietnamese host talk, "*Quen chửa?*" ("Are you familiar/accustomed yet?"), is often one of the first questions posed to people who are not just tourists visiting the country for a brief stay. The answer is a way of determining how to be a better host, but also gauging the degree of investment and commitment that the respondent has towards being in the country.

I have been asked this question with regard to the climate, the water, my health and well-being, and the general and basic daily ways of existing in and navigating around the city. The "yet" implies that there is an inevitable and assumed outcome of acclimation and perhaps even of assimilation—that it *will* surely happen with time and experience: "Vietnamization," with the Vietnamese term itself denoting a sort of chemical transformation and commodification, will occur. (The "yet" also frequently comes attached to inquiries regarding marriage and childbearing, which helps to peg the situation, position, and status of the stranger.)

But asking about a sense of familiarity with foods serves most specifically to locate the subjects of the question in terms of their inclusion and belonging—their proximity to being Vietnamese. One test, for instance, is whether a person is affected by the local bacteria in water. If unaffected, a sense of relief and comfort is registered on several levels. First, no one can be held responsible for bad hosting. And with that, the guest will be less of a disruption to order and possible loss of face. Second, an "accustomed" guest also wards off, on a larger scale, a national embarrassment that both the people and the Vietnamese state feel concerning issues of hygiene and modernization, based in the conviction that good services and infrastructure would indicate that Vietnam is no longer a backward (and filthy) third-world outpost that will be threatening to and contaminate anyone entering.

Being able to drink the local water is thus a fluid marker of defining who is Vietnamese. People are gauged as being Vietnamese, or at least fluent with Vietnamese ways, when they are able to drink the local water and become part of the same pool of life. *Nước*, water, after all, is the word for country. And water, especially with all the droughts and blights in Vietnamese history, is highly valued. (The state, incidentally, is *nhà nước* (house of water), which is that which structures and contains the country). "*Quen chưa?*" is even frequently posed to overseas Vietnamese when they come visit. In some instances, it can be used in an implicit way to criticize them for forgetting their source and origin—their roots.

Another substance used as this kind of test for how Vietnamese a person is, happens to be much more specific and potent with immediately visible consequences, in contrast to the generality of water. *Nước mắm* (fish sauce or "water of pickled fish paste") is one of Vietnam's most treasured products. Compared to water's hidden qualities and dangers, *nước mắm* is more definitive of how localized one is with regards to common sensibilities. Not everyone is able to appreciate the taste (and stench) of fish sauce.

"Do You Know How to Eat *Nước Mắm*?"

In the year 2000 at a fashion/variety show in Ho Chi Minh City, Huong Lan, a singer who had been extremely popular in Vietnam before 1975, had returned to Vietnam to visit and perform. Before she began to sing, she had a short interchange with the MC of the show. He questioned her about why she returned.

She replied that her grandmother still lived here, but that she also loved all of the different varieties of fish sauce. On that definitive note, the show resumed.

Nước mắm is considered liquid gold here. Like water, it is also used to test the authenticity and degree of Vietnameseness. Fish sauce stinks intensely, but has a deep and complex flavor of what seems like many generations of dead fish. It is like a good bottle of wine, but it doesn't taste anything like it smells. This is its deceptive magic. And unlike wine, one only needs a drop to be dazzled. It is also considered one of those rare daily delicacies with which no one ever gets bored. So cherished and sacred, it is one of the most common bottles to be carried home in the suitcase of anyone who has been to Vietnam for the first time.

As a young child, although I had never been to Vietnam, I would open the bottle of *nước mắm* in the kitchen condiment cabinet simply to gross myself out. This was during the U.S.-Vietnam war and this potent blast of rottenness was what I imagined to be the scent of the country (and because of that, I really had no pressing desire to go there). But later, when I started tasting it in sauces, its paradoxical qualities made me curious as to what kind of a place could have produced such a potion.

In the early days of fieldwork, when I would first sit down to a meal in Vietnam with someone new, I was typically asked something that always struck me as funny: "Biết ăn không nước mắm?" ("Do you know *how* to eat fish sauce?"). Although the substance or dish has changed over time and place, the structure of the question remains the same. Before going to Vietnam, when I was doing research in a Vietnamese community in the Bronx, I remember being asked if I knew how to eat *chả giò* (fried spring rolls). But now that these rolls are familiar to foreigners, the item in question seems to have changed. Indeed, with time, the "delicacies" I was confronted with increased in intensity and included things like furry and crunchy duck embryos.

Perhaps the overall question seems strange because how one eats something has never seemed *that* complex or *that* prescribed to me. I just put whatever it is in my mouth, and try to mimic other people at the table. I often experience serendipitous pleasure when I discover an unlikely combination of sauces or flavors. Eating (and cooking) can be a laissez-faire activity with few rules. But in a place and time where hierarchies and categories are more significant (and positions are destabilizing with the dramatic shifts toward a capitalistic economy), ways of eating can be fraught with serious intentions and implications that go well beyond my simplistic and practical approach. This odd question reveals some of these intricacies, these complexities in the ordering of the senses and behaviors at the Vietnamese table. It immediately makes me self-conscious about how exactly I am eating, and then brings out my anxiety of eating something the wrong way. Dining becomes much more conscious, deliberate, and exacting—and may seem, in some respects, less enjoyable. In fact, I have learned that eating something the right way, with the right dipping sauce, combination of ingredients, and in the right sequence, makes the eater an active part of the creative (or productive) experience. Done right, this does maximize the pleasure derived from the whole meal. In Vietnamese cuisine, it seems that heightening sensual pleasure is a deliberate activity, as is getting the most from the smallest piece—maximizing each morsel.

This question of knowing how to eat something arose in an especially significant way on my first trip to Hà Nội in 2002, the country's political capital, in the north. I had been invited for dinner at the home of a journalist, and on the way there I was informed that we were going to eat a special soup called *bún thang*. An exquisite and rare ingredient is the finishing touch of the broth—the pheromone (a hormone emitted to attract mates) of a water bug called *cà cuống* (*Belostomatidae*). I was told that a tiny (and expensive) drop of this ingredient produces an enticing flavor and aroma. We had to stop at a special shop in a small dark alley to obtain a vial of this precious liquid. The whole enterprise felt a little illicit. When asked if I *"biết ăn không cà cuống?"* I was not only being asked if I had ever eaten this soup before, but was also being clued in to how special the meal was to be. The addition of a precious drop of *cà cuống* emphasized its value and also celebrated my presence as a special guest. Oddly enough, this experience may have been one of the most gracious acts of hosting and welcoming me that I have experienced throughout the many times I have been in Vietnam. And it is only now, as I am writing about it, that I fully realize the honor.

But there are many other nuances in and possible reactions to the seemingly simple query, *"Biết ăn không* (a particular food)?" The question can be used for other strategic purposes and interpreted in different ways. What could seem just an idiom, on closer inspection reveals a specific and expected way to approach and understand a particular kind of food—the question reveals that there are strict techniques of dining, which are methods of establishing authority and asserting cultural expertise, coexisting with polite ways to subvert the etiquette and avoid eating something that one doesn't like.

Idiomatically, the question could simply replace other formulas of politeness. It could stand in for the query: *"Ăn được không?"* ("Can you eat this?"). But the response to *this* question, *"Không ăn được đâu"* ("No, I can't"), in its negativity, could appear impolite and would run the risk of cutting off or damaging the relationship with the host. It would also require an explanation as to why you cannot eat what has been offered, and you might have to reveal an allergy or some other weakness, which is something to be avoided at all costs. So everyone can save face by turning the question into one about knowledge and skill. A response phrased as, "I don't *know how* to eat that" creates much more ambiguity than a simple, "No, I don't want to eat that." But of course, with this vagueness comes the potential for things to backfire; the person asking could enter the role of the expert and start giving lessons, showing you the best way to eat the food, ultimately coercing you to eat food you do not want to eat.

It needs to be noted that this question is not only posed to non-Vietnamese foreigners. Vietnamese "foreigners" visiting different localities in the country often have to respond to it as well. As one of my friends recently explained, "To taste the local [dishes] is to know the local." He said that he frequently gets asked this question on visits to the countryside. Sometimes he outright refuses the food offered by saying it is *lạ qúa* (very strange), but then he has to bear the accusation of being an "industrialized person" who is less authentically Vietnamese. Depending on the social circumstances and the food involved, he may even be chided for being less than manly. But then, how else can one politely refuse? Sometimes the only way to do so is to cover the bowl with your hand, to prevent it from being filled. If that, too, becomes a battle, though, the words *từ từ* (later, later, I'm eating slowly) can be used.

Thus, the question of knowing seems to have salience because it is assumed that there is clearly a proper way of eating Vietnamese dishes, and that these are set in form and non-malleable. At this point in time, recipes do not change very much. Most dishes are highly standardized, and Vietnamese cooks see little sense in adding random ingredients to them, for these could potentially destroy the taste of the dish, and such innovation could expose the cook to criticism. It is assumed that the dishes and how their recipes have been formulated are already perfect and need no change. This strict adherence to the recipe was clearly not the case in the past, even the recent past: Ironically, two of the most iconic Vietnamese dishes, *phở* and *bánh mì*, are a product of culinary integration of French ingredients during colonial rule (the first using beef in rice noodle soup and the second being a baguette sandwich with pâté). Within the current national scheme, in which it is important to maintain Vietnamese identity, the integrity and purity of Vietnamese dishes seems to be the first order of the day. Clearly that which has not already been influenced by certain kinds of global tastes and brands is considered intact and pure.

The foods that most convey intimacy, enjoyment of which are definitive of belonging (proof of Vietnamese status), also happen to be some of the smelliest items on the Vietnamese "menu"—*nước mắm* (fish sauce), *mắm tôm* (shrimp sauce), and last but not least, *sô riêng* (durian fruit). In these cases, knowing how to eat something also implies liking to eat it. This again echoes the idea that the ingestion of questionable substances, or distinctive ones, such as water or fish sauce, can be used to gauge and determine familiarity and belonging. We might think that if a person can accept (and love) the smelliest foods of a place, then that person has earned entry and intimacy. But, water aside, these three foods are also simply misunderstood by outsiders; they are the hardest to know "how to eat." But it is worth the effort; all three have delicious and complex flavors obscured behind their odors, which often scare people away who do not know their hidden value.

Through these encounters with food, we can see that skills—in the kitchen and simply in the "eating"—learned the hard way, with some pain, and perseverance, finally offer some insight beyond their "exotic" face value. But this process of learning takes time, and, as already mentioned, sometimes requires humiliating lessons.

Having No Know-How

Back in 1998 when I arrived for my first language training and fieldwork in Vietnam, I was clueless about the technicalities of taste and the overall meal modus operandi here in the city. I was staying at the home of my father's younger brother in the Bình Thạnh district of Ho Chi Minh City. Before I left the United States, I had planned to contribute to the household chores as a way of returning their hospitality. At that point, I was unaware of the almost feudal upstairs-downstairs hierarchies of the Vietnamese "middle-class" household, where everyone seems to have at least one maid and a cook and a nanny. Denied the chance to do more substantive tasks, I helped by setting the napkins on the table before dinnertime, and I rotated with one of my cousins the duty of wiping off the table after the meal. In my life in the States, I maintained a house, tended a garden, and was about to open up a restaurant, all while studying in graduate school. Prior to that, I had worked in the restaurant business for almost twenty years bussing tables, running food, and waiting tables. I felt quite comfortable with the cook and the maid, and to be allowed to help only in these limited ways seemed somewhat ludicrous.

For dinner each night, we sat at an oval dining-room table that my uncle and auntie had received as a wedding present in the 1960s. My spot was always next to my uncle (who sat at the head), and directly across from my aunt, who always served me the choicest pieces of fish or meat and showed me how to eat them, and in what sauce or substance to dip them. It seemed to be her role to size up my tastes, "distastes," and, of course, mistakes. Meanwhile, my uncle was on a kick of eating red rice with sesame and salt, and he had decided that we would do this together at the start of each meal. He was intent (sometimes it seemed to the point of being obsessive) on keeping me healthy while in his "custody," safe from the bacteria (and diseases) that could undermine his care. His protectiveness may have seemed a little bit paranoid to an outsider, but he had survived for ten years in jungle "reeducation" camps after the war (having been a high official in the South Vietnamese air force) and had watched many of his friends die from illness and malnutrition. He wanted to honor his older brother (my father) and make sure that I didn't die in his care or return home ill. Unfortunately, his attempts at keeping me healthy did not work.

For several weeks during my stay, I suffered from different feverish and intestinal maladies and dropped many kilos, which didn't reappear until well after I returned home—to a healthy diet of pasta and potato chips.

Before heading off to Vietnam on this first trip, I had also decided to make a special meal to thank the family for hosting me. So I carefully selected a dish that I knew I could pull off well with the ingredients that would be available at the local market. It was a chilled shrimp dish, a recipe from the *New Basics Cookbook*, with a simple sauce of olive oil, lemon, and fresh chili with chopped tomatoes, bell peppers, and fresh herbs. It was to be served over *nui* (linguine noodle/wheat pasta).

I really thought this dish would go over well. Many of my family members had eaten Italian food before (my cousins had worked as tour guides escorting American and European foreigners around the country, and my uncle had been a pilot who traveled around the world). Indeed, pizza was probably the earliest Western food to be accepted and enjoyed by contemporary Vietnamese people, and the first non-Vietnamese restaurants that one of my cousins took me to was a pizza place called Mãy-Nhà-Tân—a.k.a. Manhattan. (It took me a few minutes to figure out the name correlation. Needless to say, the pizza there was nothing like a delicious greasy New York City slice.)

The first misunderstanding, however, came well before the cooking even commenced. My aunt sent the cook out to buy shrimp, while I went to pick up all the other ingredients. The cook came back with some extra-colossal lobsters, which were very expensive (not the modest U20s—the restaurant lingo for medium shrimp—or smaller ones, which I had expected to use). I hadn't told anyone (and was never asked) what size I needed, but to me "shrimp" meant "small," literally. I was completely unaware of how many different sizes and types of crustacean fell under the Vietnamese term *tôm*. My aunt assumed that I would make a dish that the wealthiest of families would be serving.

During the meal, my cousin's husband repeatedly complained about the taste of my special dish, or rather its lack of taste. Most everyone else just looked glum. So out came the chili-garlic sauce to drench it with added flavor. This did not offend me. I just wanted them to enjoy the meal. The Vietnamese word for taste is *gu* which is derived from the French word *goût*. Should I have made a French *plat* that evening instead?

The next day, one by one, everyone reported to me that they had slept poorly, and had spent most of the night on the toilet—everyone except for my uncle, who kindly told me that the meal had been delicious. But this dramatic physical reaction to my cooking stopped me from ever wanting to cook in that house again. At that time, I had not known enough to ask ahead of time if they *knew how* to eat this dish. I had not offered them any polite way of begging out. If I had, I could have saved myself from experiencing this humiliation (and perhaps their bowels as well).

Conclusion: Edible Expertise

Because of my lingering sense of ineptitude, specifically with regards to food, and generally in terms of my positioning in the Vietnamese scheme of things, a decade later Chi Chinh's random and sudden compliment puzzled and delighted me. In the past, I had only been called *giỏi* with respect to my achievements as a student. So finally, I asked her what had I done to make her consider me so *clever*, so *skillful*, so *good*?

She explained that it was so because in her assessment, I *"biết ăn"* ("knew how to eat") all Vietnamese dishes. What was usually a question was now a declaration. And there was more. She had also noticed that I knew how to eat other kinds of food because, on the nights when I ate dinner away from the house, I often went to different ethnic restaurants—both Asian and non-Asian. It became clear that she had been keeping tabs on the eating patterns of the people in this house.

In the next breath, she mentioned that my Vietnamese friend Phuong—her boss, who worked out the daily household menu with her—did not eat certain types of foods. By contrast, in her view, Phuong's American husband, Peter, knew how to eat everything, just like me.[5] Chi Chinh's judgment of her employers' tastes was truly questionable. Food-wise, Phuong is one of the most adventuresome people I know. One day the caretaker of one of her properties discovered a wild porcupine trolling the land, and he killed it with a rock and gave it to Chi Chinh to cook up. When it turned up on the table during lunch one day, Phuong was the only one who took a bite. Peter and I didn't dare. (I am usually game to try new things, but frankly, intending no insult to the cook, the porcupine dish looked terribly unappetizing—repulsive, in fact. It was served in a bowl and looked like a few dark shit-brown logs covered in green sauce.)

When speaking about her boss's limited gustatory range, Chi Chinh also insinuated that Vietnamese palates have a narrow capacity for taste, an assessment I had commonly heard before (but never agreed with), mostly from other non-Vietnamese familiar with Vietnamese cuisine. In comparison, she said that her own sense of taste and knowledge of different cuisines (which she implied was much more expansive) originated from her being Chinese and again, because she had lived in Singapore and had been exposed to Malaysian and Thai cuisines, among others. Chi Chinh seemed very eager to establish herself as more worldly and less local than other Vietnamese (even if they were cosmopolitan ones like Phuong). Keen on flaunting her culinary exposure and expertise, she attempted to one-up what she presented as the provincial tastes of her employer. Besides being an authority on food and a holder of international experience, she created in this way a form of distinction and difference, circumscribing and delineating Vietnamese national/ethnic taste through her assertive commentary and criticism.

By making these kinds of assessments and innovating with her own dishes, Chi Chinh allotted the highest status and cultural capital to the ability to consume different kinds of food, which involved valuing culinary curiosity and a sense of daring, as well as the acquisition of knowledge and the technical know-how to handle different cuisines—broadly, an omnivorous way of eating. And this allowed people who were not Vietnamese to be perceived as an authority of both Vietnamese and non-Vietnamese food, as determined by experience and experimentation, not by a more static form based on essentialized claims of authenticity and insider knowledge.

By comparing these experiences and encounters a decade apart, it seems to me that, at least in contemporary Ho Chi Minh City, a new way of evaluating difference of status by practices of consumption is developing. Just ten years ago, the landscape and impulses and performances of status were much more dogmatically interior to Vietnam. This interaction with Chi Chinh and her claim to be the household culinary expert because of her conscious sense of cosmopolitanism were loaded with implications: offering ways of seeing status reformulations enacted through the knowledge of food, heightened international sensibilities and entrepreneurial and adventuresome spirits. All of this stands in contrast with a more rigid sense of communal Vietnamese tastes and food preferences associated with a different era, an era in which knowledge and its authority was unquestionably in the hands of specialists and people in powerful positions rather than consumers and amateurs. Chi Chinh clearly availed herself of the opportunities that the expanding global market presented. She could do this now because of the enhanced options and discussions about diverse foods accompanying the growing market and interest for foreign commodities. She was taking part in a food revolution. And in her attempt to form an alliance with a fellow outsider, oddly, I became acknowledged as an edible expert of any and all cuisines—at least by her.

Notes

1. After the U.S.-Vietnam War in the late 1970s, the Sino-Vietnamese community was heavily persecuted by the new socialist state and forced to assimilate or leave the country. These policies caused a huge exodus from the country via boat by the majority of the Chinese-Vietnamese.
2. This was despite the fact that my own father was born and grew up in this Vietnamese city. Theoretically, an individual's nationality and "homeland" are determined by where one's father was born. However, in reality, because my mother is European, and I was born in the United States, I will probably never be considered fully Vietnamese.

3. This parallels French colonial ideologies of assimilation and the notion that the Indochinese could become French through education.
4. At the end of the 1990s, the cooking section had been limited to generalized traditional Vietnamese dishes. A few elegant and very expensive (beyond the reach of most Vietnamese at that time) hardcover books with recipes for international cuisine, from such countries as Mexico, France, Italy, and Spain, started to appear, but predominantly only in the international bookstores in the city.
5. On another occasion, Chi Chinh had commented on how similar he and I looked! On different occasions, I have oddly been told that I resemble former supermodel Claudia Schiffer, despite the fact that she is strikingly blond and curvaceous, and I am dark-haired and part Vietnamese, with somewhat noticeable Asian features and a slight body structure.

–9–

Learning to Exchange Words for Food in the Marquesas

Kathleen C. Riley

Often enough after mentioning to some new acquaintance in America that I spent a year doing doctoral research on an island in the middle of the Pacific Ocean, I get a response along these lines: "Poor thing, it must have been so tough eating bananas and drinking coconuts on the coral beaches!" Normally I just look away or say somewhat incoherently: "Well, it's not exactly what you imagine . . . not totally easy . . . but yes, the islands are beautiful." Let's admit right off: I'm not talented at cocktail banter.

But now and again, someone will take note of my wavering and express some genuine interest in hearing the "real" story, in which case I've been known to go on a bit. I'll explain that coconuts are a subsidized cash crop, not just refreshing drinks growing with straws sticking out for anyone's enjoyment; that bananas ripen slowly on their stalks, are chopped and hung from someone's rafters, and are not for sale; that the Marquesas are volcanic islands that lift straight up out of the ocean, lack coral reefs, and have narrow, black sand beaches; and that these tiny beaches abut jungles infested with a biting fly called the *nono,*[1] along with mosquitoes bearing dengue fever and elephantiasis, and people's homes have no screens on the windows.

But this is just the tip of the iceberg (or, more appropriately, volcanic peak). It would take hours and more than words to describe, much less explain, the real moments of both romance and difficulty of my first year of fieldwork. For instance, what it was like to fish from a rock at night with a bamboo pole, line, and hook accompanied by my best friend, Mo'i, trading stories about men and childhood, only to be struck dumb by the sight in the moonlight of two rays swimming by. Or how it felt to beg Tehina to show me where watercress was growing wild in a corner of the jungle (once inhabited by someone who had planted the watercress there), an adventure during which I almost lost my precious Teva sandals to the two-foot-deep mud, and subsequently lost Tehina's respect because I wept about it all. That both of these recollections are about food and friendship is no coincidence. In fact, the heart of this story that I have such trouble telling is how hard it was to find both food to eat and friends to talk to and how I finally learned to do both by realizing that the two are inextricably meshed in the Marquesas— as they may be to a certain degree everywhere in the world.

But to tell my particular story, I need to begin by explaining that I went to the Marquesas to study something called language socialization. Language socialization is the process by which people learn to communicate effectively within the particular sociocultural contexts they are thrown into by birth or, later, happenstance. When we are children, language socialization involves, first of all, learning how to exchange sounds for food and food for words, and this primal learning occurs differently in different cultures via different languages all around the world. For instance, in the Marquesas, children acquire their communicative skills in two languages and within the context of two cultures: indigenous Polynesian and colonial French.

Anthropologists who research language socialization frequently become aware that in the process of studying how children learn the language(s) and culture(s) to which they are first exposed, so too are we, adults plunged into a strange new world, being socialized to do the same for ourselves. In particular, we learn, as quickly as possible, how to be invited back for one more meal and for one more conversation, because without access to both of these, our work would be made impossible.[2]

This chapter then is both a tale and an analysis of how one anthropologist learned from her Marquesan hosts—especially the children who were also still learning—how to procure food (when hungry), negotiate food preparation tasks (when attempting to fit into the social order), and eat with etiquette (when local tastes were still something of a mystery). But I begin here with a little historical background in order to explain why food was not only a preoccupation of mine but also of my Marquesan hosts—something worth thinking and talking about a lot.

Foodways and Food Discourse in the Marquesas

Prior to European contact, Marquesans subsisted primarily on breadfruit and fish. They prized pork above all other foods, and relied on and valued a wide number of other foodstuffs. Their social structures were shaped by the means of production, conservation, and exchange of these staples: productive land and trees belonged to powerful families, while men were added to the family through polyandrous relations to provide labor for agriculture and pig husbandry. Meanwhile, valley-based chiefs or **haka'iki** acquired the allegiance of warriors and ritual specialists through their ability to marshal the labor for food production. Thanks to the organizational powers of these chiefs, huge pits were dug, breadfruit was collected for fermentation in these pits, and the fermented paste (**mā**) from the pits was redistributed in times of drought to those connected by social obligation and kinship.[3]

In such a social world, family membership is defined less by "blood" relations and more by the exchange of food—a point illustrated by the fact that the word for adoption in Marquesian is **hakai**, a word whose direct translation is "cause to eat" (Kirkpatrick 1983: 42–3). In fact, the word for eat (**kai**) is omnipresent in the Marquesan lexicon as a part of words that do not, on the surface, appear to have anything to do with food: for instance, "miserly" is **kaikino** and "childish rage" is **kai pipi'o**. Additionally, many sexual expressions make reference to eating, much as they do in English (Suggs 1966). The significance of food is found as well in several other key expressions and cultural domains that have been maintained, though transformed, throughout two centuries of contact with Westerners.

The notion of **tapu** (borrowed into English as "taboo"), around which much of social life revolved prior to European contact, regulated who could produce and consume food when, where, and how. For instance, women could not garden (i.e., produce food) while menstruating, and men of the more powerful classes ate in **tapu** houses food prepared in ways governed by **tapu**. Even at present, owners may carve this term into the trunks of prized fruit-bearing trees which they wish to guard from theft. I have myself experienced the efficacy of this practice when I climbed a tree to harvest just one orange and descended with an inflamed thorn gash in my palm—a scar I still carry as a reminder of the potency of **tapu**.

Similarly, eating plays a significant ethnopsychological role in Marquesan culture. The intestines (**koekoe**), not the head or heart, are considered the seat of feelings and thought for Marquesans. And although debates persist as to whether cannibalism was ever a habitual practice in the Marquesas, eating the flesh of a human sacrifice (**heana**) was, according to local lore, a way to appropriate an enemy's power, but may as well have played a nutritional role in times of extreme drought (Handy 1923: 218–21).

Beginning in the late eighteenth century, the introduction of European trading habits, weapons, and diseases catapulted Marquesans into a desolate period of depopulation, displacement, and social anomie. Their natural resources (such as sandalwood) were exhausted, new land-depleting livestock (goats and cattle) were introduced, and cash crops (coffee, cotton, and coconut palms) were encouraged at the expense of sustaining breadfruit groves and taro swamps. Although the population began to recover in the 1920s, the subsistence labor that had once created social relations was siphoned off by the allure of wage labor and export crop production. With the money Marquesans learned to make, they also learned to buy flour, sugar, oil, and canned beef, and later baguettes, frozen chicken thighs, and processed snack foods. From this transformed diet, Marquesans developed diabetes and rotten teeth. Meanwhile, though the population as a whole grew fatter, fat lost its status as a sign of prestige as French ideologies of beauty were imported along with high-fat cheese and high-carb beer and wine.

As of the twenty-first century, copra production is still the primary source of income for many Marquesan men, although by now, the oil from dried coconut has lost its value on the world market, and the French state subsidizes its production. Women's collectives are being formed to engage in replanting subsistence crops, and children are acquiring degrees in culinary arts in order to become chefs in the tourism industry. Diet pills are now among the things people ask me to send them from the States.

In other words, the global market is having an impact on Marquesan foodways in complex and contradictory ways. And yet, while some ingredients and recipes, buying patterns and agricultural practices, eating etiquette and culinary ideologies have changed, life in the Marquesas does not feel at all like life in France. In fact, the very categories of production, distribution, and consumption cannot be clearly distinguished in Marquesan culture as they are in French culture. Today, as in precontact times, one is apt to eat fish raw while fishing or spend a couple of days finishing an avocado collected and left open on a kitchen table. There are still no regular mealtimes except those prescribed by the French school system, and copra laborers tend to work in the coconut groves from early morning until mid-afternoon without food, only to return home and eat a bowl of rice and chicken or whatever else they find left over in the *garde-manger*—the wood and wire-mesh lockers on legs that sit in bowls of water to keep the ants and flies out of the food kept within.

When meals are prepared, they are put together out of pieces of frozen fish and baguettes ferreted from one's own or an extended family member's freezer. And where families sit down to meals together, they begin with two French discourse rituals: saying grace or *prière* (**pure**) and a *bon appétit* or eat well (**kaikai meita'i**)—direct translations from the French and without indigenous precursors. Yet those who dine together still eat off of one another's plates, using primarily fingers for utensils, but perhaps with less etiquette than was once displayed by their ancestors who carefully fingered a mouthful of breadfruit paste out of a large central bowl with a precise twirl of the wrist.

Now, as in the past, feasts (**ko'ika**) demand and allow for extended periods of collection, redistribution, preparation, and consumption of foodstuffs (as well as social and linguistic stuff). However, in this case, rather than blending the acts of making and eating food, at present, Marquesans sunder the two, and rather than reveling in the art of mixing food and talk as do the French, Marquesans find it far better to do one and then the other. Thus, at most feasts both hosts and guests hang back long after the **kaikai** is prepared and set out on tables for consumption; they joke and gossip, drink and observe, but they do not actually eat. Apparently the display of plenty is more significant than the taste because by the time they do commence eating (and they consume a lot once they begin, quickly and without a word), the pork and bananas and **poe** from the earth oven are usually cold and gluey.

According to my older informants, pan-Oceanic traditions of hospitality were once so strong that any passing stranger would be invited to "come in and eat!" ("**memai, kaikai!**"). Although they claimed that this discourse routine has died away since the advent of money, I still heard the call frequently enough, if only to train a child in how to call in a friend to chat. Nonetheless, it also informed the packaged rituals of hospitality—tourists, visiting dignitaries, and new administrators who were greeted in the village with flowers, dances, and chants of welcome ("**mave mai!**"), as well as feasts of river shrimp and lobsters, earth-oven roasted pig with mountain bananas and mango **poe**.

In other words, one finds today in the Marquesas, as elsewhere in the Pacific (Pollock 1992), a curious interweaving of European and indigenous communicative routines and foodways that are learned by both visiting anthropologists and children through the means of language socialization. In the following sections, I look first at how I learned to find food by learning to engage in local social interactions, and then proffer in the final section some preliminary conclusions about how children not only learn, but also negotiate and transform the foodways of their community.

The Anthropologist Learns to Manage Food Insecurity

Not being part of any kin- or family-exchange network, I experienced food insecurity in the Marquesas first hand. No welcome party called out to me: "**Mave mai!** Come feast!" as happens for the monthly tour groups. And at first, no families were willing to risk inviting me in, as I wandered along the village paths, in the traditional way: "**Memai, kaikai!**" At first, there was mostly suspicion: What was I there for, what did I want, and what did I have to offer in return? As I've intimated, I'm not good at small talk or easy explanations.

But even the French nurse and Tahitian teachers with whom I first took up residence in the village seemed inordinately preoccupied with the issue of procuring food. Though they had been there for half a year or more, and were better funded than I (on my National Science Foundation and Wenner-Gren doctoral grants), they discussed at length the fact that it was not always clear to them how to exchange money for nutrients. Some packaged foods could be bought at high prices from the village store owned by the **haka'iki** (chief, now turned mayor) though beer, wine, and soda were her primary stock. Of the other foods available in the village, there was little that didn't require cooking or proper storage facilities. I had neither, once I separated from my tiny expat community and rented one of the **haka'iki**'s tourist bungalows, which consisted of four walls, a bed, sink, toilet, and porch. For the first month or so after moving into the bungalow, I subsisted largely on Sao crackers, Kraft cheese (a kind that required no refrigeration), and canned fish. Later, I discovered that I could stock up on these same staples (at a cheaper price) by going directly to the cargo boats that came through every few weeks.

Another shock to my naïve Western attitudes about finding food was the fact that the **haka'iki**'s "restaurant" had no menu or regular hours. If you wanted to eat there, you needed to order a day in advance and pay top prices for the sorts of mini-feasts consumed by the French, who came from the administrative center on the other side of the island to play tourist on weekends. Further, the village nurse and teachers could only eat there when invited by the French administrator, because the nurse and teachers had ruptured their good relations with the **haka'iki**. Even after I distanced myself from them, the **haka'iki** still was not interested in feeding me on a regular basis.

There were a number of other sources of purchasable foodstuffs, but access to these depended on knowing someone who would provide either information or transportation (or both). The **haka'iki**'s jeep went weekly on a reasonably regular schedule to the administrative center (where food could be bought from slightly larger stores, especially a *boulangerie*—baguettes having taken over from breadfruit as the staple throughout French Polynesia). A seat in this jeep could be had for a reasonable rate, but only if all the seats had not already sold out, which was usually the case unless one had an inside track with the **haka'iki**. There were also gardeners in the neighboring valley of Anaho who came through the village on their way to sell their carrots and cabbages in town—but one had to have ties and/or be quick and on hand to make a purchase from the back of their trucks. It was the same with the fishermen-turned-tuna-vendors; they would drive through when they had a catch, usually headed for the homes of their extended family and friends, and might give up a half or whole fish for a reasonable price—but this amount of fresh fish was useless to me until I had friends with freezers, which fortunately I finally found.

That is, finally I began to understand how people managed to avoid feeling insecure about where their next nutrients were coming from: They had trees of their own producing breadfruit, bananas, limes, avocado, papaya; land on which to plant taro, sweet potato, manioc, or pineapples; space in which to fatten their pigs; machetes and guns (and a few necessary bullets) to go out after the semi-wild goats or wholly wild cows that roamed the island; speedboats, nets, harpoons, and hooks to fish for tuna, sharks, rays, and smaller ocean fare; a rope and flashlight for gathering wild chickens from the trees at night; or simply a bucket for gathering river shrimp and shellfish on the rocks. Nobody had all of these, but every person had relations with others through which they could get access to land and tools for raising or procuring food. Everyone managed by working for others, praying for them, having sex with them, or offering them a place to sleep, a place to plant, or a way to connect to others with connections.

All of this I lacked at first. But I finally got caught up in some local networks of relationships—a result, perhaps, of curiosity, compassion, or strategic self-interest by those in them; it's impossible by now to disentangle the motivations or to what degree they played a part. Enmeshment began with joking **keu**, a typical testing and socializing genre in these villages: Villagers would comment, out of the blue, about my scrawny build (I am not "scrawny" by U.S. standards), and my assistants would snicker sympathetically over my breakfasts of cheese and crackers. However, this stage was quickly followed by gifts of papaya and shrimp, and invitations to meals with my adopted families. The final stage of my integration into village ties of subsistence and exchange was the feast held in my honor at the end of my first period of fieldwork; several years later another was held for my daughter's fifth birthday. And in thoroughly Western fashion, I still worry that I have not yet sufficiently "repaid" my friends for these efforts. Repayment is not the issue, relationship is.

Meanwhile, being in this web of relations gave me access not only to food but also to discourse. As a linguistic anthropologist, of course, such access to talk was the primary objective of my study, but without food (and the understanding of how to negotiate access to it), I would have been incapable of carrying out my research. And as I've mentioned, much of what I learned about how to do this I learned from children, in the context of studying how they were learning to develop the communicative competence to manage their food (in)securities and their social relationships.

Learning Food, Learning Language, Learning Society

Over many months of fieldwork in the Marquesas, I spent time with children engaged in a wide variety of food-related activities. We planted pineapples and manioc together and cooked rainbow-colored Thai wafers in boiling oil. I helped them collect shellfish from wave-swept volcanic rocks and lay out halved bananas to dry on wooden copra racks. I listened as they said grace (**pure**) in unison and fought over the last packet of Sao crackers on the shelf. I shared a plate of papaya and goat in coconut milk with a two-year-old and allowed my daughter to watch as a twelve-year-old butchered (ineptly) a piglet for her birthday feast. I received mangos and grapefruit left on my bungalow porch by the children as they passed in the morning on their way to school and served Petit-Écolier cookies on that same porch when they returned in the afternoon to draw pictures of sharks and coconut trees with the crayons and paper I provided. We have chattered over many meals that involved bowls of Nescafé and rubbery old baguettes.

Many of these interactions I have audio- and videotaped. With the assistance of the adults in the children's extended families, I have methodically transcribed every word and **mea** (literally "thing" or "do"; this word functions much like the turn-holder "like" in English). And using the intuitions of the assistant at my side, I have interpreted the covert intentions and evident impact of each speech act and glance and attended to the underlying story beneath the apparent talk.[5]

The transcript provided at the end of this chapter is the sort of data that results from this research process. Utterances are in boldface and their translations are in plain type. French utterances (and their translations) are also italicized whereas utterances in Marquesan (and their translations) are not. Text in parentheses provides contextual information or interpretations. The specific linguistic resources discussed below are underlined. Three dots indicate short pauses or omitted interactions. Analysis of this sort of socializing discourse can reveal a lot about the way individuals acquire linguistic competence, cultural knowledge, and social practices, and especially in the transcript under discussion here, how children (and anthropologists) learn to engage in the give-and-take of food.[4]

As mentioned above, the production, distribution, preparation, and consumption of food are not rigidly defined spatially or temporally in Marquesan society. Thus, children are engaged from early on, and throughout the village, in rich and convoluted talk about how food is acquired, cooked, and eaten. This occurs in a wide array of contexts—from fishing boats and gardens to the **haka'iki**'s store—but the social interactions I use here to illustrate my points are taken from a Sunday meal at home with one of the four families I worked with most closely. This conversation involves two adults—the mother, Tapu, and the father, Po'ea—and their three children: nine-year old daughter Vaetui, three-year-old son Poutini, and thirteen-month-old son A'ere.[5]

Post-church Sunday meals are by far the most formal—if any meals can be said to be formal in the Marquesas—and "traditional"—meaning that local foods are preferred for these meals. This one consisted of grilled fish and breadfruit (**me'i**), raw fish with lime (**ika te'e**), and boiled mountain bananas (**me'ika mouna**) covered with coconut milk (**ko'ehi**). None of the ingredients were store-bought, but Tapu mentioned that she procured the **me'i** from the tree at the teachers' house. Elaborate as this meal was, and though everyone was aware that I wanted to record as many of the children as possible, two of the children (Pio, the five-year-old boy, and Vaite, the eight-year-old girl) never showed up for the meal. I recorded anyway, and we ate without them.

Interest in food—the ingredients, their preparation, and the cooking tools needed—who possessed it, and who could therefore offer it to whom was evident throughout the taping session. Though clearly affected by my presence that afternoon (this was early on in my fieldwork and so my attendance was still something of a novelty), this conversation turned out to be typical of those

I experienced in all of the households where I have done research, even after I became much more like "family." For instance, in addition to the fragment reproduced here, there were: discussions about how much fish was available, accompanied by extensive searching in the freezer to find additional fish; serious negotiations over how to prepare which kinds of fish (raw or grilled), since there were limited supplies; an extended negotiation about a missing knife that was needed to prepare the fish; and a search for a mango that Vaetui had claimed for hers.

At one point, a neighboring adolescent came over to request the stone used to pound breadfruit that the two families shared and was teased on several fronts. First, Tapu questioned her use of the wrong Marquesan word for the tool (the girl called it a **tukituki** rather than a **tuki popo'i**—the former would be for pounding small materials such as herbs for medicines rather than breadfruit into **popo'i**). Second, Po'ea mockingly quizzed her about what was on the menu at her house: "You're eating breadfruit with what else . . . a grain of salt?" She responded with: "No, with fish!" Finally, they jointly warned her not to drop her uncle's stone as there were no other **tukituki** if that one broke; she responded with mock exaggeration that she would fall rather than let his **tuki** fall. (These stones are carved into explicitly phallic forms, and I presume that all three were variously aware of some sexual innuendo in this exchange.) This brief but rich interaction demonstrates the concern that Marquesans feel with socializing not only their own children, but also other children, using the typical teasing genre that I explained above, which was also used with me.

Nor was my education ignored during this taping session; Tapu and Po'ea took pains to teach me the names of various fish and the difference between green and ripe coconuts. They also began to play or **keu** with me over the topic of grating the coconut, a practice rich in sexual connotation because of the way one sits astride a wooden block and grates the coconut against a jagged metal bar that projects from the block, spewing white shavings from this protuberance between one's legs. Po'ea wondered whether I must think them "strange" for engaging in this practice. And seconds later, he queried Tapu as to how I was managing without my husband here, the common assumption in the Marquesas being that one really should not go without sex for more than a few days, and certainly not for several months. The associations drawn between sex and food abound in many cultures, but are particularly explicit in the Marquesas, both being implicated as material practices and symbolic resources in the construction of social relationships.

The extract of discourse presented here for microanalysis is taken from the extended period during which all of us are focused to varying degrees on preparing the meal (though the children are also engaged in consuming bits of it long before the meal as a whole is fully prepared). In addition to preparing the meal, Tapu has her eye on the baby, is trying to get Poutini out of his wet clothes, and is directing Vaetui to put other clean clothes away; however, most of these speech acts have been omitted from the transcript in order to focus on the discourse that winds its way in and around the food. Inside the kitchen, bananas are boiling on the stove and crab meat is being extracted from its shells. Just outside the kitchen door, breadfruit and small fish are cooking on an open fire and coconuts are being grated to make coconut milk.

Specific anxiety over the quantity and availability of food is manifest in the transcription in several places. First of all, on line 1, Tapu asks Vaetui, then outside the house, whether she has found any lemons (i.e., a necessary food-gathering task Vaetui has been asked to complete). Although we cannot hear Vaetui's response, it is apparently not polite, as Tapu scolds her rhetorically: "What was that you just said to me?" Then on line 3, Vaetui returns triumphant with the requisite lemons and is rewarded with a line of recognition from her mother: "There's the lemons!" Later (beyond the limits of this transcript), Tapu complains that Vaetui found only three lemons and that one is rotten, which reminds her to scold Vaetui again for throwing out some meat that Vaetui claimed was rotten. Meanwhile, still at the start of our transcript, Tapu is asking Poea what else they have to eat for this meal besides breadfruit. Po'ea points out on line 2 that they do have the crab. This concern over whether there's enough fish for the meal returns in much more detail later on. Finally, Tapu spends a good deal of breath in this segment teaching Vaetui the importance of removing all of the crab meat from the shell.

Interestingly, no one criticizes Vaetui for eating some of the crab meat while extracting it for the meal; in fact, Vaetui freely announces (1ine 20) that she's being a little slow in her task because she's too busy eating. Instead, the principal critique is that Vaetui did not learn to remove crabmeat quickly and efficiently by watching Tapu do this same task the day before. In other words, within a family, food insecurity is not so great that every mouthful is measured and meted out. Rather than negotiating access to and ownership of the foodstuff itself, emphasis is more apt to be put on the possession and transmission of knowledge about the actions of producing the food.

Also evident in this transcript are the means by which social roles and obligations involved in preparing a meal are negotiated. For instance, one sees relatively polite negotiations between relative equals: for example, Tapu and Po'ea discuss who "owns" (i.e., is responsible for) which preparation tasks: husking the crabmeat versus grating the coconut (lines 6–11). Elsewhere, one sees more pointed critiques, commands, submissions, and rebuttals between unequal interlocutors: for example, the give-and-take between the parents and Vaetui concerning the tasks of finding lemons (lines 1, 3) and removing meat from the crabs (lines 5, 13–23).

The social relations negotiated via these interactions are indexed by linguistic elements, many of which have no real semantic content but which carry an evident socio-emotional meaning. The use of these linguistic resources with and around children not only socializes the appropriate use of the linguistic elements, but also teaches the social assumptions implicit in their usage. For instance, Tapu uses the particle **a'e** with Po'ea (lines 9, 11). When I asked my assistants what this particle meant, they would shrug and say it meant nothing much, maybe something to soften a request. When I insisted on some kind of French translation, they offered *un peu* (a little), and when speaking French, I began to hear them saying *un peu* (a little like saying please) as a politeness marker, something that Francophones from France don't really do. By contrast, Tapu and Vaetui use irritated paralinguistic growls (lines 1, 27, 31) and mocking terms such as **e ho** (line 21), or defensive particles such as **ho'i** (lines 14, 17, 18) with each other. **Ho'i** was another word my assistants had trouble translating. The best we came up with was the sarcastic French *bien sûr* (of course).

However, in families such as this, status is not set in linguistic stone. For instance, Tapu (line 9) initiates her negotiation of processing tasks with Po'ea using the defensive particle **ho'i** before switching to the conciliatory **a'e**. Gender hierarchy (with males on top) was never clear-cut in the Marquesas even prior to European contact, and since the adoption of certain French, Catholic, and even more modern ideologies such as feminism, the negotiation of dominance and subservience between husbands and wives can fluctuate from utterance to utterance in everyday conversation. And these ambiguities are not ignored by children. Thus, one finds that immediately following this interaction, Vaetui (line 14) adopts the **ho'i** particle in her own attempt to defend her competence as a food processor. As in all of the Marquesan families with which I worked, the older girls operated as sous chefs and secondary caregivers for their younger siblings. As a result, they sometimes adopted their mothers' pragmatic ploys in order to challenge their mothers' dominance in the family.

Another linguistic resource used by family members to negotiate social relations is that of code-switching—that is, switching between the languages at their disposal within a given conversation. Women and girls in particular used a shift from French to Marquesan or back again to index a shift in tone. For instance, Tapu switches to French to applaud Vaetui's achievement of the lemon-gathering task (line 3), and Vaetui switches to French to make a plea for having completed her crab-processing task as well as she was able (line 22).

One other linguistic resource worth tracking in this transcript is the usage of possessive particles. All Polynesian languages use two types of possessive particles—alienable and inalienable[6]—to mark the possession of both actions and objects. For instance, throughout the transcript the alienable possessive particles **a, ta,** and **na** (lines 1, 6, 7, 9, 11, 13, 19) are used when discussing foodstuffs as well as the actions involved in producing and consuming food. By contrast, French and English use possessive particles to "possess" only nominatives, including social relations. Following suit, Marquesans use French possessives to discuss relationships, as is manifested here in the exchange between Tapu and Vaetui, who use *ta* (line 25) and *ma* (line 28) to mark Vaetui's relationship to her godmother. However, in Marquesan, they use their own possessive system not only to mark the ownership of relationships and objects but also the actions with which objects are used to forge relationships. This was illustrated above in Tapu and Po'ea's debate over their respective tasks: "mine to work" (line 6), "mine to do" (line 7), "mine to remove . . . yours to grate . . . mine to grate or yours?" (line 9).

In other words, Marquesans discuss not only who possesses food (and therefore has the right to cook it, or eat it, or give it away) but also who possesses (or is responsible for) the actions by which food is made and eaten and exchanged. In all of these cases, "possession" should be understood to mean not only a "claim to," but also a "responsibility for" and "responsibility to." For instance, Vaetui clearly feels a responsibility to protect her godmother from her mother's deprecations (lines 24–31). Additionally, this bit of mother-daughter gossip shows us how Marquesan women, when talking about beauty, overtly value thinness now and disparage those who are *grosse*.

As is evidenced by just this small transcript, a range of communicative resources, from specific morphemes to pragmatic stances, both signal and socialize local understandings of how foods and the (sometimes emotional) speech acts surrounding them play a role in social life. What is clear is that children learn through socializing interactions not only how to deal with food and how to talk about it, but also how to use it to negotiate social relationships within a society in which one's access to food depends primarily on one's social relations. That is, they learn to use talk to secure food and to understand food as the matrix for engaging in social interaction.

In the course of my engagement in interactions of this sort, as well as through the process of analyzing the discourse after the fact with the aid of my Marquesan assistants, I came to understand some of the intricacies of how Marquesans in particular weave together food and talk and community. And in the course of doing research on social interaction, I managed to become not only a semi-competent but also a thoroughly well-nourished member of the community that had adopted me.

Conclusion

As elsewhere in the world, food was and remains a fundamental idiom in Marquesan culture at a number of levels, both economic and psychosocial. Issues of food (in)security, the aesthetics of fat, and the reputation of generosity or stinginess pervade everyday life and discourse. Children learn to engage in this discourse for the sake of access to both food and social relations. In doing so, they not only guard against food insecurity and social excommunication, they also learn to insert their own twists into what they learn, and over time these minor negotiations become the stuff that drives the engine of cultural and linguistic transformation. For instance, in a multilingual and multicultural environment such as the Marquesas, children are the means by which newly hybrid foodway patterns and food discourses are mixed and baked.

Anthropologists are bound in principle to study objectively, to cause no harm, and to contribute as little as possible to change. Yet, as is well known, we do intrude in a thousand ways, demanding a lot and leaving detritus in our wake. We plunge into our hosts' social lives in order to stave off hunger as well as to decipher the local codes of social interaction. As anyone who has done this knows, our best attempts to practice our discipline ethically are inevitably flawed.

Nonetheless, this hapless anthropologist, with perseverance, did learn a bit about being a community member: how to lend a hand in food preparation (catching and cleaning octopus; collecting and squeezing limes); how to stay out of the way when I would have been useless or dangerous to others (for instance, hunting wild cattle with just a machete); how to consume food properly (with fingers off a plate shared with someone else); and how to use pragmatic markers in all the right places (the particle *a'e* for please; the proper possessives for food and tasks; and the like). I also finally learned to quit worrying about where my next meal would be coming from, to trust instead that it would indeed arrive along with tidbits of local news that would fill me up as much as the meal itself. That is, I learned that hunger for "small talk" is as real as hunger for food and that the strength of my **koekoe** would depend less on extracting nutrients from the natural world and more on attaching myself by way of an inalienable web of words that has extended across the hemispheres without Facebook or common prayer or the chance to break off bananas and eat together for years and years and years at a time.

Acknowledgements

As I hope I've made abundantly clear here, this chapter could not have been written without the sustenance of my friends in the Marquesas, for which I wish to thank all of them: *Kou ta'u tatou*! And for this bit of writing I am in particular grateful for the food, talk, and transcription assistance offered by Tapu and Po'ea Poihipapu. My fieldwork in French Polynesia was also made possible by doctoral and post-doctoral grants from Wenner-Gren and the National Science Foundation. And I am deeply grateful for the intellectual guidance and moral support of many colleagues and friends: Bambi Schieffelin, Vincent Crapanzano, Christine Jourdan, Neil Shepard, Heidy Baumgarten—to name only a few, but these at least cannot go unnamed—along with members of the New York

Linguistic Anthropology Working Group, who kindly critiqued a draft of this paper. Finally, I wish to thank Leo Coleman for his wise editing and patience. Of course, any errors of fact or judgment rest on my shoulders alone.

Notes

1. In this chapter, in order to distinguish some of the linguistic resources used, Marquesan words are set in bold, while French words are set in bold italic.
2. For an overview of language socialization as a discipline, see Ochs and Schieffelin 1986; Garrett and Baquedano-López 2002; Ochs and Schieffelin 2010. For my own work on language socialization in the Marquesas, see Riley 2001, 2007. The intersection of food and language socialization has been analyzed in several studies: Schieffelin 1990; Ochs et al. 1996; Paugh and Izquierda 2009; Riley 2009.
3. See Dening 1980 and Thomas 1990 for ethnohistories of precontact and early contact times.
4. My language socialization discourse data were collected in 1993, 2000, and 2003. The transcript used in this section is the result of my initial ethnographic study conducted in 1993.
5. That babies contribute to conversations is an assumption shared by both psycholinguists and many parents. However, beliefs about how babies contribute to conversation vary from culture to culture. In the Marquesas, babies are addressed as creatures whose behavior can be controlled through words and tone but without expectation of any real social comprehension; as a result, babies' vocalizations and gestures are read as signals, but only of their primal needs. An instance of this can be found in the transcript (between lines 12 and 13) when A'ere cries after falling off the bench and is comforted by his mother with physical ministrations and French baby talk. Another interesting baby talk phenomenon to be noted in this transcript is how both Po'ea and Tapu have adopted the French terms and the French practice of referring to themselves in the third person as *Papa* (line 5) and *Mama* (line 13) when speaking to their children. It is fairly certain that this practice did not occur in precolonial Oceania.
6. Somewhat like gender for speakers of French, this morphosyntactic distinction between alienable and inalienable possession is almost impossible to explain to someone who does not speak the language; those who do speak it say that they just feel the difference, like an instinct: breadfruit is alienable, tobacco is not; a photo in your wallet is alienable, the photo of you is not.

Appendix

TRANSCRIPT

Setting: Sunday afternoon in March (1993), kitchen of Tapu and Po'ea's house
Participants: Po'ea (father), Tapu (mother), Vaetui (nine-year-old daughter), Poutini (three-year-old son), A'ere (thirteen-month-old son), and Kate (researcher)

1. Tapu: (to Vaetui) **Koaka ta'oe hitoro?** Found <u>your</u> lemons? **Mm mm mm mm** (irritation) **E aha <u>ta'oe</u> mea 'i pe'au mai nei?** What is <u>your</u> thing that you just said to me? (to Poea) **Me'i, e aha?** Breadfruit, what (else are we having)?
2. Po'ea: **'A'o'e, mea.** No, (we have also) thing (crab).
3. Tapu: (to Po'ea) **E ava te'a meika?** Are those bananas (boiling on stove) cooked yet? (Vaetui arrives with the lemons) ***Voilà les citrons!*** *Here are the lemons!*
4. Po'ea: (to Tapu) **E tuku titahi me'i ma te kaokao.** Put the breadfruit next to the heat (fire). . . . (Tapu is telling Poitini to change out of his wet clothes and Vaetui is giving A'ere kisses) . . .
5. Po'ea: (to Vaetui) **Vaetui, a mai a hana me <u>Papa</u> tenei hana.** Come help <u>Papa</u> with this work (removing the meat from the crabs). **E? Memai**

   _____

6. Tapu: (to Po'ea) **A vaipu, <u>na'u</u> e hana.** Leave it, <u>mine</u> to work (removing the crab meat) . . . (Tapu and Po'ea both scold Poutini about changing his clothes; Vaetui tattles on her sister Vaite for having exchanged clothes with a friend)
7. Tapu: (to Po'ea) ***Papa*, vaipu <u>na'u</u> e mea.** *Papa*, leave it, <u>mine</u> to do.
8. Po'ea: **Heka te 'ehi?** (Yours) to grate the coco?
9. Tapu: **Na'u ho'i e ko mai. Na'oe e heka.** <u>Mine</u> of course to remove the crab, <u>yours</u> to grate. . . . **Na'u a'e heka, na'oe?** Aah? <u>Mine (politeness particle)</u> to grate, or <u>yours</u>? What (do you think)?
10. Po'ea: **E?** What (did you say)?
11. Tapu: **Na'u a'e heka?** <u>Mine (politeness particle)</u> to grate?
12. Po'ea: _____ . . . (A'ere falls off bench and cries loudly; Tapu takes him up, talks to him in French baby talk, and spreads coconut oil on his head and stomach)
13. Tapu: (to Vaetui) **E mea, takitaki ana 'oe me he mea 'a Mama 'i tinahi?** Hey whose-it, did you remove (the crab backs) as <u>Mama's</u> (doing) yesterday?
14. Vaetui: **E ho'i!** Yes, <u>of course</u>!
15. Tapu: **Eya?** What? (doubting Vaetui's claim)
16. Vaetui: **Tenei?** This (the crabs here)?
17. Tapu: **E ho'i tenā!** Yes <u>of course</u> that!
18. Vaetui: **E ho'i!** Yes, <u>of course</u>!
19. Tapu: **E aha a <u>ta'oe</u> ha'a manea ana.** What's with <u>your</u> taking so long there?
20. Vaetui: **Va'e nei au kai.** I'm in the middle of eating. (begins singing)
21. Tapu: **Vaeuti, mo'i ha'a manea.** Vaetui, don't take so long. **Mea'ia te tikaue tenā mea.** The flies are doing on that thing (crabs). (Vaetui singing) **Vaetui, aue ha'a manea e hoa!** Don't take so long <u>friend</u>! . . . (Tapu puts baby down, still scolding Vaeuti, comes over to work on removing the crab meat)
22. Vaetui: ***N'a plus, maman.*** No more (crab to be taken out), *Mama.*

23. Tapu: **A mea 'oe ha'a ko'i poniho'o poniho'o.** You do it, make it quick, quickly quickly. **Paotu! Ena me te' ā mea te' ā keke.** All! There's that thing that side. . . .(Tapu begins discussion about the new baby of Vaetui's godmother's daughter Tehina . . .)
24. Vaetui: ***Mais alors! Tehina, elle est <u>grosse</u>!*** *But really! Tehina is <u>fat</u>* (now).
25. Tapu: ***Oui, elle va être comme <u>ta</u> maraine, elle.*** *Yes, she's going to be like <u>your</u> godmother.*
26. Vaetui: ***Pas vrai!*** *Not true!* (doesn't like insults to her godmother)
27. Tapu: ***Pas vrai? Pas vrai? Te aha?*** *Not true? Not true?* What? **. . . . Mm?** (irritation)
28. Vaetui: **<u>Ma</u> *maraine, elle est un peu <u>grosse</u>.*** *My godmother, she's a little <u>fat</u>.*
29. Tapu: **Aia! *Un peu <u>grosse</u>, te aha?*** Huh! *A little <u>fat</u>,* what?
30. Vaetui: ***Comme toi.*** *Like you.*
31. Tapu: **<u>Ehn!</u>** (insulted growl)

–10–

Eating Vegetarian in Vietnam

Christophe Robert

I thought of calling this text about my encounters and experiences with vegetarianism in Vietnam, "How I became 'gay' in Saigon." Then I thought it would not work, not simply because I am not gay, but because I could just as well have titled it, "How I became Christ in Saigon" or, "How I became a Soviet in Saigon." This is a story about naming and about crossing borders and boundaries. This is a story about moving to Vietnam and finding my way around in a rowdy workers' neighborhood in a large, bustling metropolis, about struggling with the language and the intricacies of complex ritual and pilgrimage practices. It is about the process of forgetting faces and places, and suddenly remembering long-gone conversations and details of rituals as memories resurface in the wake of someone's death.

In January 1999, I rented a small, two-story house next to a much larger one in the neighborhood adjoining An Dong Market, the most important wholesale textile market in Saigon/Ho Chi Minh City (HCMC). I was embarking on eighteen months of ethnographic fieldwork in Saigon, and I had rented this house courtesy of one of the administrative assistants at the Institute of Social Sciences of HCMC, with which I was affiliated for my research. She acted as an intermediary for (and got a commission from) the landlady who had this small ochre house for rent. Quickly, I settled in a routine of eating lunch and dinner with the family of B., the woman who had helped me find and rent this house.

The house, nestled in the complex social world of a small urban lane, provided me an excellent position from which to begin my research on youth and debt in Saigon. The large avenue in front passed by a small park, originally built by Korean soldiers during the American War in Vietnam and renamed Peace Park after the liberation of Saigon in 1975. The view from Peace Park revealed prostitutes cruising on bicycles and scooters, nodding furtively at potential customers, and streetwalkers discreetly plying their trade in the park, discarded paper tissues marking these swift encounters.

The nearby market and massive grey concrete hull of an abandoned construction project formed the outer visual horizons of this small neighborhood, as seen from the fifth-floor rooftop terrace of my neighbors' house. Below us, the rumor of the rushing traffic rose up from the streets, reverberating in the labyrinth of tight alleys surrounding geometric blocks of large apartment buildings. The neighborhood straddled the administrative boundaries of Districts 5, 10, and 11—the boundary between Saigon and Cho Lon, between the Vietnamese and the ethnic Chinese parts of town. A few dozen paces away, the bulky, squat concrete frame of An Dong Market rose above the rooftops. From there, the wholesale textile and clothing trade extended all the way from Saigon and Cho Lon to the deepest reaches of the Western Region (*Mien Tay*) and the Cambodian border on the far side of the Mekong Delta.

* * * *

My ethnic Chinese neighbors live in a large multistory house. They laugh at me when I inquire about their beautiful new house. "Beautiful new house, uh?" the matriarch of the family laughs out loud, her dark, toothless, wrinkled face shrinking in laughter. "But this is our old house!" She then relates to me how their house had been seized from them after the war. "We helped the Revolution. We housed some VCs and messengers here at night. And this is how we got thanked." Their problem was that they were a wealthy Chinese family, a dangerous combination of ethnicity and class in the dark post-war years of Saigon in the late 1970s. The house was seized from them. Only through murky negotiations involving large cash payments under the table to local officials were they able to reclaim their house in the late 1990s.

I initially spend a lot of time with "Auntie" (*Bac*), as she inevitably refers to herself when speaking to me, her foreign "nephew" (*chau*). My first name, Christophe, is basically unpronounceable for a Vietnamese. American-style, I try to shorten it to "Chris," but that too leads to interesting semantics. I become "Christ," or "Mr. Christ" in polite conversation, usually pronounced roughly as "Quyt"—which incidentally means "mandarin orange" in Vietnamese. Clearly, something has to be done about my name. Bac likes the fact that I speak Vietnamese and study hard. I spend a lot of time in her household, talking with her daughters, who are roughly my age. This is a very devout Buddhist family. "Auntie is addicted to reading the [Buddhist] sutras!" She laughs and pokes a bit of fun at my scholarly concern for youth drug problems and addiction.

This is how, by reference to my studies, I get a new name: Minh Tam, which means bright mind, or bright soul. Bright, here with the connotation of light (enlightened) as opposed to dark and unenlightened. Given the context of this name being given by a devout Buddhist family, I quickly realize that it is a very Buddhist name, a very peculiar one. When I begin to use this name in everyday conversation, I get teased for having a girlie name. Why? Because in the late

1990s, a well-known male pop singer named Minh Tam had been outed as gay. This is in part "how I became gay" in late-1990s Saigon, but it is not the whole story. The ambiguities of my position in the fictive kinship structure I found myself placed in mattered, among people and in a neighborhood that had no experience of Westerners or ethnographers; it also mattered that I was not married with children nor seen with a girlfriend. Additionally, my practice of vegetarianism contributed a great deal to this situation in which people often—"jokingly," of course—assumed I was gay. Men in the neighborhood assumed I was wasting away by not eating meat, thus depleting my internal bodily heat and male sexual energy. This was compounded by the fact that, in their view, I was spending entirely too much time speaking with women. They chided me for not going out drinking with them, but the competitive displays of masculinity involved in male drinking bouts were not appealing to me. Hence, the jokes about my being gay. This was a joking reversal of the negative Vietnamese stereotype, prevalent in the 1990s, of oversexed, hard-drinking, whoring Western men—heavily propagated at the time by the Public Security police, and by television and press representations in an ongoing moral panic stemming from the "opening up" of Vietnam to foreign investment and trade.

* * * *

The neighborhood where I live is one of borders and boundaries. On the first morning after moving in to the house, I go out on foot to find a place to eat breakfast. I walk alone on bustling Su Van Hanh Street. I am wearing sandals, beige slacks, and a light blue shirt. Sidewalks on both sides of the street are packed with street sellers and their displays of candy, cigarettes, lottery tickets, and soft drinks. The mobile carts of noodle-soup sellers, with circles of customers sitting on tiny blue and red plastic stools, and the folding chairs of sidewalk cafés further block the sidewalks. One cannot walk on the sidewalks in these busy workers' neighborhoods. I make my way into the street, weaving slowly in and out of pedestrian and motorbike traffic, a few feet from the curb. The background noise is intense: motorbike engines and horns, the piercing grind of rusty brakes, music pulsing from the sidewalk cafés, calls from the food sellers, conversations and jokes fusing from all directions. I sense that I am disturbing things and attracting notice. And yet, from within this heavily layered soundscape, accompanying the noise, I also feel gazes on me, as if the street traffic opens up slowly in front of me as I pass, and, almost imperceptibly, a brief moment of surprised silence echoes, soon overcome and filled with words again. And I hear this strange word, following me, spoken in surprise by many mouths, "*Lien Xo, Lien Xo!*" In Vietnamese, *Lien Xo* means Soviet. That morning remains in my memory as the encounter in which I became Soviet.

In areas of the city where people are more used to the presence of Westerners, I often experience this strange aural phenomenon: a slow unfolding of the same repeated word in my wake, "*Tay! Tay! Tay!*" (Westerner) spoken by many different voices, accompanied sometimes by a nod in my direction or by a pointed finger. Children are nudged, and another wave of sounds rises up, completely strange to Vietnamese, "Hello, hello, hello!" The children laugh, unsure exactly of where their expectant greetings will lead—to silence, mostly, as I smile and walk on. This experience of the call and my inability to answer it became unnerving over time, but there was something exhilarating in having become *Lien Xo*. The interpretive possibilities that this opened up were almost limitless and intensely phantasmagoric. Why Soviet? Did I look and dress like a Soviet? (I certainly did not look like the tourists, who favor shorts and tee-shirts, sunglasses and small backpacks.) Had Russian engineers lived in this neighborhood? Had they built it? (The large, rectangular, communal apartment buildings in the neighborhood indeed had a Soviet feel to them.) Enchanted and slightly dizzied by the interpretive possibilities, I sit down at a café and order a bowl of beef noodle soup (*pho*) and a strong iced black coffee (*den da*). This is my first morning in the neighborhood.

Over time, as I spend more and more time with my neighbors and accompany them on their annual religious pilgrimages to Chau Doc and the Mekong Delta, my associations with Buddhism become stronger. Vegetarianism comes to occupy an important place in my experiences in the city. One peculiarity of my neighbors is their diet. Many Buddhist Vietnamese eat vegetarian (*an chay*) one or two days a month, on the first and the fifteenth of the ritual lunar calendar. This mild dietary form of religious penance—abstaining on those ritual days from eating meat and killing animals—marks their religious affiliation with Buddhism. My neighbors, however, are completely vegetarian and never eat meat, fish, eggs, or dairy products. This is no doubt linked to what Bac had referred to as her addiction to reading the Buddhist sutras. Her and her daughters' devotion is indeed profound. Unlike most people in the city, they attend evening prayers at the Buddhist temple daily. Every day at dusk, they don the light blue-grey robes of the lay practitioner and walk over to the nearby temple. Every morning, I am awoken around five by the rhythmic beating of the prayer stick on a wooden shell, punctuated at intervals by the deep, loud sound of the brass prayer bell. Bac is already up, praying in the Buddhist altar room on the top floor of the house.

This is only the beginning of an early morning routine. Before seven, after having cooked breakfast for her daughters who then leave for work in the center of the city, she walks to the nearby wet market to buy fresh fruits and vegetables, fresh tofu and soy milk. She comes back and begins cooking around ten. Lunch is eaten at eleven thirty, followed by a nap.

I love her food. It's always crisp, clear, and clean. The dishes are extremely simple, but vary almost endlessly. In the kitchen, she waves her large knives and chopper as she cooks and jokes. I am not supposed to be there, in the kitchen with her. She and her daughters chastise me when I tell them that I'd like to learn some of these incredible dishes, the stark simplicity of which is appealing to me.

They wave off my request, "This is women's work!" End of conversation, at least in this household.

* * * *

Perhaps the fact that my name—a common Buddhist name, popular for women, as well as the name of a gay pop singer—evoked images of effeminacy makes more sense when combined with popular imaginings of where strength and virility come from and manifest themselves, and how diet influences them.

In the popular Vietnamese imaginary, eating a vegetarian diet raises concerns of weakness and effeminacy, in part due to male concerns and anxieties about masculinity. Vegetarianism is associated with weakness, with deprivation. Since food and diet are still imagined in terms of humoral influences and the balance of "hot" and "cold" elements, the lack of meat is symbolically associated with femininity, coldness, and darkness—yin and yang being always already over-coded, and the feminine principle largely negative or threatening. Buddhist priests take vows of celibacy and eat vegetarian. Combined with the fact that nine-tenths of regular Buddhist practitioners are female, this leads by association to the widespread belief that vegetarianism saps strength and virility, and is thus a female realm and practice, from which men should abstain. In addition to daily prayer services, Buddhist monks are ritual specialists called upon for funerary rites and mourning practices. This furthers the association of vegetarianism with death and lack. But this is the negative and stereotypical view of those who observe cynically and from outside the practice of eating vegetarian.

* * * *

Eating vegetarian in Vietnam creates another map of the city. While eating out in Hanoi or Saigon is easy and routine, and involves almost endless choices of dishes, eating vegetarian is restrictive: The restaurant choices are fewer, the range of dishes narrower. My friend Lam, who knows all the good restaurants in Hanoi, struggles to find good vegetarian restaurants. She has to think about it. She limits her choices to two places in the city, places to which she returns.

These vegetarian restaurants are different from other Vietnamese eating places. The food and the atmosphere point to a realm away from that of the food, outside of itself. In the Bamboo Grove restaurant, the atmosphere is quiet, the walls lined with beige linen, the lights soft. The small speakers hanging from the ceiling pipe in meditative Buddhist, devotional music at low volume. One notices something odd about the menu: It addresses a nonexistent English-speaking clientele. The exercise is touching more than comical: Nonsensical literal translations point to the imaginary landscape where religion meets ideas about health-crazed foreign tourists, coalescing into a wish for a larger clientele.

In the Lotus vegetarian restaurant in Saigon, on the other hand, there are many Western diners. It is located one block from the infamous "Western quarter"—the backpacker district—and it was written up in the Lonely Planet tourist guide for Vietnam. These Western tourists are comical and a great source of amusement for Vietnamese who have never seen the inept chopstick technique of Westerners, and their strange eating habits. On a Vietnamese table, dishes are arranged in the center of the table and each diner picks up food from the many dishes and deposits it in a small, individual, rice bowl, before picking it up with rice and eating it. The food that sits in the center of the table is shared. Everyone picks up morsels from every dish. Everyone brings it first to the rice bowl and then to his or her mouth—the symmetry is what is essential here, the notion that the meal is shared food and that the meal symbolizes the connection between those sitting together at the table.

By contrast, the sweaty, puffing tourists occupy a lot of room on the small chairs and at the table. They hover uncomfortably in the room, placing the dish they ordered for themselves in front of them, where a plate would go in a Western table. They miss the point that these are dishes to be shared, not individual plates of food. They place the rice bowl further out in front of them, and, reversing the order, dump rice in dishes of vegetables and tofu, diluting the clumps of rice to individual grains which are impossible to grasp with chopsticks; this compounds the trouble they will have eating it. The reason why rice is packed in a small bowl is that it can then easily be picked up with chopsticks. What is striking, watching these Westerners, is that they seem never to have looked around themselves and noticed how one eats in Vietnam; granted, the scene may be overwhelming already, with the ambient noise, the loud clatter of traffic outside, and the high decibel conversations around them in Vietnamese. The Westerners' difficulties cause great amusement for some Vietnamese, but also curiosity. How is it possible that these people don't know how to *eat*? There is a ready answer: Well, they're Western. This doesn't answer much, but it answers enough.

These vegetarian restaurants are strange to Lam. She says that the food there is not as good as that served in Buddhist pagodas during religious festivals. The menus in these commercial enterprises are based on "normal" dishes: one can order vegetarian "chicken" and "barbecue pork," or "sour (fish) soup" and so forth, all prepared with tofu and gluten to mimic the look if not taste of "real" dishes. In Vietnamese, there is no phrase referring to eating "normal" food—one simply eats. The word "eating" here is unmarked, and means eating a diet that includes meat. But the language marks vegetarianism and codes it as different and potentially strange: one "eats vegetarian" (*an chay*). In Vietnamese colloquial speech and jokes, there is always a suggestion of lack, of something missing, of weakness, when discussing vegetarianism. This is balanced by the fact that the decision to eat vegetarian is a form of Buddhist penance and of mourning. But the penance is affirmative, not negative or inscribed in the flesh as deprivation. It is affirmative because it refrains in order to facilitate, not to mortify or punish. The idea is to refrain from killing, or as it is understood generally, to abstain from contact with death and dead matter in order to enable the safe passage of the deceased to the other world and the realm of spirits.

By eating vegetarian, one refrains from killing and eating meat, and one nourishes life, the continued afterlife of the deceased. It is life-affirming.

* * * *

My mind drifts: Ten years ago, during my first period of field research in Vietnam, I lived with a Buddhist family, ate vegetarian, and had to endure jokes about "eating vegetarian" and therefore being weak, effeminate, perhaps gay. Now, I am spending the seventh lunar month eating vegetarian. The seventh month is the time in the lunar religious calendar when the souls of the dead reappear and communicate with the living. The seventh lunar month is the time when those souls imprisoned in hell are temporarily released and can be attended to by their families, and "fed" by means of prayer, incense burning, and vegetarian ritual feasts.

Lam lost her mother in late winter. It is now mid-summer in Hanoi, and hotter and drier than usual. The dust whirls in the avenues at dusk; the acrid smell of smoke hangs over the small streets of the Old Quarter. Lam wants to eat vegetarian daily to pay her respects to her mother. It is a complicated process. It starts with ritual. She explains that she began to eat vegetarian (*an chay*) when her mother died and during the ensuing Buddhist mourning rituals. This was not really a conscious decision on her part: "It came naturally. I was surprised that after a few days I kept eating vegetarian, and I continued for the full forty-nine days of the mourning ritual. It felt very healthy, and I lost weight."

She explains the importance of the early period of mourning.

> I ate vegetarian for forty-nine days after my mother's death. The first forty-nine days are the most important period for the new life of the person who has passed away. They begin another life in the other world. You could say that I began to eat vegetarian when I thought that this would be good for my mother's soul. How? First, because I missed my mother terribly and secondly, because I wanted to help her soul. According to Buddhism, in the first forty-nine days the spirit of the deceased will be inspected by the Court of Hell. If the family of the deceased behaves right during these first forty-nine days—for instance, by not eating meat and fish, not lying, not arguing, not killing sentient beings—this will help the soul of the deceased pass the tough inspection of the Court of Hell. This is the doctrine of Buddhism. I think this doctrine is very humane, because besides helping the soul of the deceased to atone for their bad deeds (since according to Buddhism everyone has done bad deeds), it also helps those who eat vegetarian to feel healthier and lighter.

Eating vegetarian here is associated with Buddhism, with the precepts and practice of monks at Buddhist temples. After her mother's death, Lam seeks refuge and solace in temples. Racked by the guilt of the living, she seeks her mother. The presence of monks comforts her; they explain death to her; they translate it into the language and conceptual frame of Buddhism. She knew Buddhism, as everyone more or less does in Vietnam, in a distant manner: In the wake of death, it now becomes a way of making sense of what evades sense. Eating vegetarian is another form of devotion, and it affirms life, by placing itself on the side of living things, of peaceful life, of devotion and mindfulness. I am almost surprised when Lam notes that it felt healthy to eat vegetarian and that she lost weight; in the context of discussing her mother's death, it sounds almost inappropriate. But this can be analyzed differently, as a reaffirmation of life through the idiom of "health." For her, weight loss is an affirmation of life: It does not stem from mourning and grief but from a healthy diet. Eating vegetarian brushes off bereavement, tentatively perhaps. But placed in the context of rituals and the search for meaning amidst mourning and memories of her deceased mother, it begins to reaffirm the principle of life.

* * * *

In summer 2009, Lam wants to eat vegetarian food daily because the seventh month of the lunar calendar is the period of the Vu Lan Buddhist festival, when souls of the deceased return to earth momentarily to "visit" their relatives. This is an intensely devotional period for those who have recently lost a family member, especially for those who have lost their mother, the one who nourishes. It is important at this time for Lam to follow a vegetarian diet. This is another expression of her devotion. The point of devotion here is not religious obedience, but karmic transmission of meritorious deeds: If she follows the precepts of Buddhism carefully, she will have an opportunity to help her mother in the afterlife. I accompany her to Buddhist temples, and she prays fervently. She purchases incense and spirit money, which she burns in the receptacles installed for this purpose in temple yards. When she finishes praying, she slips money in each of the large red donation boxes placed in front of the altars. She has explained to the divinities that her mother died. She names her mother, her date and place of birth, the time and place of her death, and who she, the daughter, is. The point is for this biographical information, based on precise naming and explanation of circumstances of birth and death (and hence, rebirth), to be passed on and communicated to the large protective circle of Buddhist divinities and benevolent spirits.

For Lam, who now lives in Saigon, this time spent eating vegetarian in Hanoi during the seventh lunar month is also a form of homecoming. As she crosses the city to visit Buddhist temples and eat in vegetarian restaurants, memories of her mother resurface—memories of her childhood and the life of the family in Hanoi during the difficult post-war years. Moving through the city creates memories, or brings memories back to the surface. At meals, she doesn't talk about her mother, or Buddhism per se, but the atmosphere is suffused with the loss and with thoughts of mourning, echoed by the soft Buddhist devotional music streaming from the speakers.

She adds that until her mother's death she had never eaten vegetarian, even on the two ritual days of the lunar month when many Buddhists abstain from eating meat. Nor had she attended Buddhist ceremonies at temples. "Life then was a shade of pink," she says, suggesting that everything was rosy until her mother died. Clearly a bit of an overstatement, but within the context of mourning after the recent death of her mother, this also places vegetarianism in a new light. She describes the critical first forty-nine days of mourning, during which, according to both Buddhist doctrine and popular belief, past deeds of the deceased are evaluated and when the future of the soul of the deceased is being negotiated in the other world according to the laws of karma. Eating vegetarian at that moment begins a new cycle, and life itself—no longer rosy and now marked irremediably by the presence of death—begins to shift. Small actions begin to be thought in terms of their potential consequences, and meritorious deeds have a new urgency. New connections between events and their aftermath arise in the alien spaces that emerge in the wake of the silence and disappearance of the dead. Conversations begin to take place between the living and the deceased. In silence, by choosing to eat foods untainted by killing and blood, one communicates a wish for atonement to the dead in order to facilitate their passage to the next world.

After death, and with the help of Buddhist clergy and ritual specialists, the deceased find new abodes in several locations: in the tomb containing the corpse or in the urn holding the ashes of the cremated (which is kept in a ritual room in a Buddhist pagoda), and on an altar that now constitutes the focal point of the house. A photograph of the face of the deceased is now placed on the altar, to which Lam, like any dutiful daughter, prays daily. She lights an incense stick, joins her hands, and prays to the spirit of her mother. In the days leading to the lunar New Year, a time of intense ritual activity for each of the various worship practices in Vietnam—Buddhist, tutelary spirit, and ancestor worship—Lam places an additional bowl on the table. She fills it with rice and vegetables, and places chopsticks across it, ready to be picked up. This is the bowl that will feed the spirit of her mother. Then, toward the end of the meal, and after the offering has been "eaten" by the deceased, she shares the food in the bowl with those sitting at the table, who eat it. Food is shared, including with the dead. The same process takes place with the offerings of fruits, cookies, tea, alcohol, etcetera, placed on the altar of the deceased. Eventually, these offerings are removed from the altar and consumed by family members. Sharing food and drink between the living and the now deceased parent continues. It is a form of mourning in which separation from the dead is deferred. The dead occupy a place, both symbolic and real, in the house, and this place is given substance in terms of food. The symbolization of the connection between parents and children—and now between ancestor and descendants—is made real through the presence of food, including food that is offered to the dead and later consumed by the living. The pleasant fragrance of incense is another way to symbolize this connection: the rising incense smoke "feeds" the soul of the deceased, and is accompanied by prayer and evocation of the name, birthplace, death-place, and age at death of the deceased, as well as requests for their well-being.

* * * *

Eating vegetarian in Vietnam focuses the mind. The Buddhist practice of full vegetarianism is not widely followed, except by Buddhist clergy. Yet many women who have lost a parent or other dear relative or friend eat vegetarian on the first and the fifteenth of the lunar month, days of ritual practice and visits to Buddhist temples. The appearance of the full moon and the alternating lunar cycles hint at different realities, both cosmic and intimate in scope. Eating vegetarian can give rise to jokes, as when, incongruously, a Western man, single and apparently celibate, is given a Vietnamese Buddhist name and lives for a time in a household of fervent Buddhist vegetarian practitioners. What is disturbing here is that this contradicts the Vietnamese stereotypical understandings of Westerners and of masculinity. Eating vegetarian enabled me to position myself seamlessly in the world of Vietnamese Buddhist ritual, pilgrimages, and funerary and mourning practices—an eminently female domain. Female lay Buddhist practitioners organize most of the logistics and day-to-day activities in temples, and during family rituals and pilgrimages, including the large vegetarian banquets associated with religious and mourning festivals. The so-called "female world" to which I was granted access, because I was curious about Buddhism, easily translated into stories and memory work. Women eagerly shared their experiences of the war and post-war years, and the current "open door" period and reemergence of a consumer society in Saigon. Eating vegetarian was an entry point into these realities: I simply asked questions and ever so gently crossed gender and cultural boundaries. Women were usually happy to answer, especially since so few men asked these questions or cared about how food arrived in their bowl.

In mourning practices, however, as in the case of Lam, eating vegetarian allows for the continued presence of the deceased, the deferred recognition of their absence and of the moment of full separation. Such full separation, "letting go," is completely alien to Vietnamese (and Buddhist) ritual practices and conceptualizations of death. Since the living must, somehow, live on in the wake of the departure of the deceased, they can have recourse to a form of eating that includes the deceased; here the relationship to the dead person is re-inscribed into wider trajectories and a broader cosmic order. Eating vegetarian can also become a work of memory, and many women, including Lam, become momentarily vegetarian—for the first forty-nine days of the mourning period, during the seventh lunar month or on two days of the monthly ritual calendar.

Some, as a form of remembrance, become vegetarian for good, as a way of continuing to "feed" the soul of the departed by refraining from eating meat, thus continuing to transfer karmic merit from the world of the living to that of the dead. And, as Lam concludes, one feels "healthier and lighter"—a pragmatic way of translating into bodily terms the peaceful feeling that she seeks, to make sense of a mourning that has darkened her world and, through intense grief, temporarily rendered it uninhabitable.

Acknowledgements

I want to thank Parvis Ghassem-Fachandi for long conversations on the politics and symbolism of vegetarianism and nonviolence, and for sharing key references with me on these topics. I thank Nguyen T.T.V. for her thoughtful discussions of vegetarianism and Buddhist rituals in Vietnam.

–11–

The Food of Sorrow: Humanitarian Aid to Displaced People

Elizabeth Cullen Dunn

On a frosty day in January 2009, I first walked into Tsmindatsqali settlement. Composed of hundreds of identical small white cottages lined up along un-paved gravel roads, Tsmindatsqali was one of thirty-six new settlements meant to house more than twenty-eight thousand people, mostly ethnic Georgians, who were driven out of their homes in the breakaway province of South Ossetia during the 2008 war between Georgia and Russia. Once South Ossetia had de-clared independence and closed the unofficial border between South Ossetia and Georgia proper, Russian and Ossetian forces bombed, looted, burned, and, in some cases, bulldozed the Georgians' houses to ensure they could never return. The Government of Georgia officially classified these victims of ethnic cleansing as internally displaced people (IDPs), and, with the help of international donors, built the new settlements as a base from which the IDPs could reintegrate into Georgian society and rebuild their lives.

Guram, the first person I met in Tsmindatsqali, had been violently ejected from his village during the war. His youngest son and his son's wife had both been killed during the bombing of Gori, and a photograph of his two sons, the eldest cradling the dead body of the youngest in front of a building in flames, had be-come the defining image of the war. Guram's losses were enormous; the grief and emptiness in his life was only temporarily filled by becoming blind drunk, which he did often. Yet, on that first day, it was not the destruction of his family or the loss of his home that seemed to bother him most. It was the food-aid package that had been delivered to him in his new home. "It's New Year's! The most important day of the year; the day when we hold our biggest *supra* [ritual banquet]. But they just gave us some macaroni. That's it! Macaroni, and beyond that, nothing!"

Indeed, the World Food Program gave each IDP—man, woman, or child—one-and-a-half kilograms of macaroni in a food package, along with other staples, throughout the first year of displacement. It was enough for every person to have macaroni every day. Yet in over a year of fieldwork, although I saw macaroni piled up under beds, stacked in boxes, and sold in black markets, I almost never saw anybody *eating* it. Given that IDPs had lost nearly everything, why wouldn't they eat free macaroni? How is it that instead of being *something,* a gift from benevolent donors, macaroni came to symbolize *nothing,* the wrenching absence of all that had been lost in the war? What can the nothingness symbolized by donated macaroni show about the experience of displacement and the effects of humanitarian aid? These are important questions, despite how trivial mere pasta might seem. There are over thirty-five million displaced people in the world today, many of whom live in limbo in camps and settlements and are dependent on humanitarian aid for their survival. Understanding how humanitarian projects make *nothing* instead of *something*—foster passivity, highlight absence, and exacerbate loss—is an important means of understanding the barriers that keep displaced people from reintegrating socially, politically, and economically.

Macaroni: The Anti-Food

In the wake of the war, over $3.7 billion in foreign aid poured into Georgia. Under the auspices of the United Nations' Office for the Coordination of Humanitarian Affairs (OCHA), more than ninety-six nongovernmental organizations (NGOs) began providing relief to the displaced. Within months, most of the IDPs were resettled in one of the hastily constructed new settlements, where each family was given a small cottage or an apartment, furniture, clothing, hygiene kits, food deliveries from the World Food Program, and more. Yet despite this outpouring of aid, nearly every interview I had in the IDP settlements began with the same plaintive litany: "The government is not helping us; they do nothing for us. We are getting nothing from the NGOs, just little things that don't help much. We are alone, we are abandoned, nobody will help us, and we have nothing."

For IDPs, having nothing obviously stems from the violence of displacement. "Having nothing" was more than "never having had" something. Instead, it was the nostalgia for things they once had, and had lost. Many IDPs described their former homes to me in loving detail, from when each of the furnishings was acquired to the layout of the garden and the orchard. This way of having nothing was encapsulated in a gesture made by Tamuna, a teenager living in one of the cottages near Gori. Making coffee, she reached into a cabinet and her hand closed on nothing. "Oh!" she said, "I was reaching for the green coffee pot. But of course, it's gone now." Nothing, here, was really a "having had something."

If the problem of nothing was the fact that people used to have things, and now they didn't, it would follow that getting new things—including food—would mean they no longer had nothing. But surprisingly, as humanitarian agencies rushed to fill the property void with distributions of material goods, the problem of nothingness became paradoxically more acute. People got houses, but the grids of white, identical cottages seemed stark and bare. Inside, they were minimally furnished with twin beds, a table and backless stools, a television, and little else. All the aid that was given seemed only to point out how much had been lost: plastic wash-buckets constantly reminded women of their washing machines now looted by the Ossetians; donated secondhand clothes made people think of their own clothes left behind in closets; backless stools called up images of ornately carved dining chairs gone up in smoke as houses burned. Material humanitarian relief was an *anti-artifact,* something that didn't symbolize itself, but instead the lost things it replaced. Donated objects were thus *nothing,* markers that constantly pointed out what wasn't there and therefore made it impossible for IDPs to feel they had anything regardless of how much was given.

Macaroni soon became the quintessential anti-artifact. As part of humanitarian food packages offered by the World Food Program, the macaroni was not intended to provide essential nutrients, but to ensure that each IDP received 2,240 calories per day, thought to be the minimum for sustaining life. But in the context of Georgian cuisine, which is highly elaborate and full of spices, walnuts, pomegranates, fresh vegetables, and meats, macaroni is hardly food at all. It is not a staple starch, as bread or corn is, and it isn't served in the beautiful and complex dishes that typify Georgian cuisine. It's usually just boiled or fried, served in soup or sprinkled with sugar. Macaroni is just *calories,* something that only the poorest of the poor eat. "Look, it's UN help; it's to keep you alive," said one woman. "But there's no comfort in it." Macaroni would have been humiliating to serve to guests, much less at a ritual *supra* banquet, so the fact that people only had macaroni made it difficult for them to invite friends and relatives to meals. This made it much more difficult to reestablish the all-important relationships of extended kinship and neighborliness that define people's places in Georgian society; without the ability to be hospitable, it was difficult to rebuild the social ties that had been blown apart when people from a single village had been scattered among the settlements. This was one critical way that humanitarian macaroni was thus anti-food: food that existed, materially, that supported the essential functions of physical life, but that actively destroyed social meaning and kept people from reassuming their roles in their own extended families and village society.

Food from Nowhere and Nobody

Everything about the donated macaroni made it symbolize the nothingness of displacement. In the first place, it was food that came from nowhere. For the people from South Ossetia, like Georgians in general, food usually came with a tie to a distinct landscape. Like the French, Georgians have a concept of *terroir,* although one that is less well articulated. They believe that the specific environment where a food is grown—the slope of the land, the amount of rainfall, the way the sunshine falls on a particular segment of mountain or gorge, and particularly the unique taste of the water—all endow foods with unique tastes. People from each place in South Ossetia extolled the virtues of their home village: water that was particularly sweet or soil that gave grapes a pleasant mineral taste. Individual families told me even about the food from particular fields. The apples from Merab's orchard tasted different than those from Nona's; the bees that feasted on nectar from Dito's *tkemali* (sour plum) trees gave honey with an aroma distinct from that of the honey made by Tamuna's bees, who lived in a peach orchard. Each meal became a kind of ritualized geography, in which food linked the people who were eating it to the places where it was grown.

Macaroni was the absolute antithesis of this place-linked food. It came with only the barest of labels: "Made in Turkey," "World Food Program," or sometimes "A Gift from the American People." The labels were written in Latin letters, which most people could not read, and in English, which nobody spoke. Arriving in big plastic bags in unmarked trucks, the macaroni seemed as if it came from nowhere at all. It was the very epitome of displacement, taken in the literal sense of something removed from its place: food from no place for people who had lost their places.

Macaroni was also deeply anonymous. In the first place, it was food that came from nobody: It wasn't made by anybody that the IDPs knew personally, and they did not even know who had donated the food. While much of the feeding program had been financially supported by the United States Agency for International Development, the IDPs had no idea who that was, nor what the World Food Program was. Although the World Food Program had contracted with the NGO World Vision to distribute the food, and World Vision had hired Georgians to manage the distributions, none of the IDPs knew the young Georgians who handed out the food, and the name "World Vision" meant nothing to them. When I asked my friends in the settlement who was giving out the food, they would shrug and say either *mtavroba* (the government) or *gaero* (the United Nations). The food arrived as if from another planet, given out by people who ignored the fundamental ways food in Georgian society creates enduring bonds of reciprocity and exchange. This was food made by nobody and given out by nobody, food that arrived without the context of hospitality and which could never be repaid in kind.

This was again a strong contrast with the food the IDPs had eaten before the war. Since the demise of the USSR in 1991, most Georgians had come to depend heavily on home-preserved foods. As the Soviet economy collapsed, Georgia's fruit and vegetable canneries, which had once produced food for the entire Eastern Bloc, shut down. For most Georgians, this meant that few people could acquire industrially canned foods, since all of them had to be imported. Instead, women grew and canned their own food for their families, hundreds of jars per year. Poached pears, *adjapsandali* (a Georgian version of ratatouille), stuffed peppers, tomatoes preserved in water, *tkemali* (plum sauce), and every imaginable flavor of jam were all preserved as each fruit or vegetable was harvested.

Given the enormous shortage of cash that most rural farming families faced, all this canning was economically essential. With little hope of affording the fresh produce grown in greenhouses or imported from Turkey in the winter, most families depended on the jars in their basements to feed them throughout the winter. This dependence had become even more pronounced in the years leading up to the war. In 2006, Georgian President Mikheil Saakashvili shut down the Eredvi bazaar, the main market in South Ossetia. In retaliation, the Russian government banned the import of almost all agricultural goods from Georgia. This stranded farmers in South Ossetia, who depended on selling apples and other fruit in Russia in order to gain the cash to buy Russian imported goods in the Eredvi bazaar. With trade almost shut down, homemade foods became even more economically important.

Most of the food that the people in South Ossetian villages ate, then, was food grown and prepared on land they knew, by people they knew. It wasn't just that people ate food prepared in their own families: Food also circulated along lines of kinship, friendship, and neighborliness. After enjoying meals at somebody's house, guests almost always left with big bags of fruit, plastic soda bottles full of milk, or jars of *tkemali* and jam. Mothers, daughters, and sisters varied their families' food stores by trading products with one another. Because both ethnic Georgians and ethnic Ossetians practiced village exogamy, in which daughters from one village would marry into other villages, food flowed along these bonds of kinship from village to village. In a fundamental way, being a person in the villages of South Ossetia meant being from a place, growing food in that place, exchanging food with people affectionately regarded, and eating food made by specific others in specific places. Food embedded people in a topography not only of gardens and orchards and barns, but in a carefully noted topography of social relations.

Lost Labor

When the war came in August, it destroyed not only people's homes, but the harvest. The apple orchards that had provided most of the ethnically Georgian farmers with their only source of cash income were full of unexploded ordnance and stood behind borders zealously guarded by Ossetian militia. Fields full of ripe vegetables were mined, and even those people who dared sneak in past the border guards were too afraid to go into the fields to harvest. Crops died in the

August heat, and fruit rotted off the trees for lack of anyone to pick it. Worst of all, many women had already begun preserving fruits and vegetables that had come into season throughout the summer. When the houses were bombed and burned, most of that food was destroyed, or left in basements underneath the charred hulls of brick houses.

For the IDPs I knew in the settlements, the loss of the jars was one of the bitterest losses. It symbolized the loss of their homes, and hours of hot, sweaty labor in the fields and in the kitchens gone to waste. The loss of the glass jars themselves was economically significant. With new jars costing 1 to 3 lari each, families living on the government's subsidy to IDPs, only about 125 lari (roughly eighty dollars) for a family of five, couldn't afford to buy the hundreds of jars they would need to can for the next year. The jars were so important in both economic and symbolic terms that some people went to great lengths to try and recover them. My friend Manana Kordadze, for example, once got me to borrow a small Russian jeep and drive her to the village of Mereti, which sat right on the South Ossetian border. The trip took hours, since we had to explain to armed guards at all three checkpoints on the Georgian side of the border what we were doing. With an automatic rifle at the ready, each guard in his camouflage uniform would carefully scrutinize my passport, and the car, which had diplomatic license plates. "*Why* are you going to Mereti? To get jars? No, really, *why are you here*?" they would demand, looking skeptical as I described our plan to make jam. When we finally made it to the Ossetian border, Manana and I had lunch with her cousins, and then she disappeared, reappearing later with a huge bag of empty glass jars on her back. "Where on earth did you get those?" I asked her. "From my house!" she crowed, proud that she'd been able to scavenge them from the wreckage. As the long story unfolded, the lengths to which Manana and her husband had gone to get the jars became clear: Her husband had risked his life to cross the border on a fake Russian passport, dug through the rubble of the house, and then, in partnership with an Ossetian friend, slipped across the border under the noses of the Russian FSB (formerly the KGB), who were guarding the Ossetian side of the border, to leave them in Mereti.

Doing Nothing

Manana's overwhelming desire to get her jars back highlighted another problem caused by macaroni and the other donated food. It wasn't just that macaroni showed that the IDPs had nothing, but that it exacerbated the problem of *doing* nothing. In the Georgian villages in South Ossetia, most people had been very busy. Farming is hard, physical work, and even those people who had jobs outside farming (such as teachers, doctors, and skilled tradesmen) also worked on their family's farm evenings and weekends. There were fields to tend, and most of the work beyond plowing, such as weeding, spraying, and harvesting, had to be done by hand. Orchards required pruning, bees had to have their hives tended, cows had to be taken to pasture and milked twice a day, eggs had to be gathered, and chickens had to be fed. Once the food was grown, it had to be processed. Apples were sliced and dried, strawberries were cooked into jam, cherries were made into compote and stored in jars, and chickens were slaughtered, plucked, and roasted. Once meals were made—from scratch, three times a day—food scraps had to be carried out to the pigs. Except in the dead of winter, most people worked long days.

In the IDP settlements, though, inactivity and boredom was a constant problem. Living as they were on donated food and never-ending macaroni, the work of growing and cooking food had been dramatically reduced. In the first winter of displacement, men had no need to tend the small garden plots the IDPs had been allocated, and women had no food to preserve or store. Even the work of making meals was truncated: There was no meat to butcher or cook, since most people couldn't afford it; no cakes to bake since nobody donated ovens and everything had to be cooked on a gas burner; and in settlements where factory bread was delivered, no need to bake bread. In the absence of chores, hour after hour was spent doing nothing at all. People watched endless hours of television on the sets donated to them by the Georgian government. Men played cards listlessly in tents set up by the United Nations High Commissioner for Refugees (UNHCR) for food distribution, or they stood on the corner in *birzhas* (exchanges) and talked aimlessly. Some men drank heavily. Many people slept most of the day away, not because they were tired but as a means of alleviating boredom. There were few *supras* or communal meals, which once had taken days to make.

The donated macaroni, which was easy to cook, fast to eat if somebody felt like eating it for the hundredth time, and every bit as bland as the days in the settlement, thus came to represent doing nothing as well as having nothing and being nobody. When people from surrounding villages began coming into the settlements a few months after the IDPs arrived, offering to trade their homegrown produce for the other staples in the World Food Program packages, people leapt at the chance. Just after dawn, the still air of the settlements would be broken by the crunch of tires on the gravel roads and a voice calling, *"Rze! Rze! Rze vqidi!"* ("Milk! Milk! I'm selling milk!") or, *"Kartopili! Kartopili!"* ("Potatoes! Potatoes!"), and women would spill out of the cottages holding bags of macaroni to trade for whatever was in the trunk of the car passing through. The ratio was decidedly not in the IDPs' favor, since a kilo of macaroni never bought a kilo of carrots or apples, but the people in the settlements seemed not to care. Anything was better than more macaroni.

That spring, a few people discovered how to transform the loathed macaroni, that symbol of nothingness, into something to do. In February, each IDP had received a "winterization payment" of one hundred lari for each member of the family. It was meant to buy winter coats and boots, which the IDPs had obviously left without when they'd been displaced the previous August. But some families did not buy coats, choosing to make do by layering donated sweaters or just to remain cold. With the money, they instead bought chickens or piglets, and began raising them in pens in the small yards around the cottages. Of course, there was no way that any of the IDPs could afford commercial animal feed. Instead, they fed the livestock food scraps and boiled macaroni. While raising livestock was difficult and smelly, given that the animals had to live almost touching the houses, the activity gave people a vestige of their old livelihoods back, and, for a few brief moments, something to do.

Boomerang Food

If macaroni symbolized nothingness and the bitterness of loss, and if it could not replace the jars of food and all the ties to place and to people that they represented, there was one kind of food that could fill in the empty spaces. It was a food that was socially nourishing as well as physically nourishing, that rebuilt the links between family members and friends and reattached displaced people to their places of origin. This was what I call "boomerang food," food that came back. I learned about boomerang food in Aleko Mentashvili's cottage in Skra, an IDP settlement not far from Tsmindatsqali. In lieu of sitting on a sofa, I was perched on a twin bed shoved against the wall, eating off the wobbly table that he'd been given as humanitarian aid. As we drank *ch'a ch'a* (homemade moonshine), we ate terrible bread made by Aleko's wife from flour given out by the World Food Program. There was something wrong with the flour, and the bread would not rise, so everyone in the settlement was stuck eating bread that sat in the stomach like a lump of concrete. "It's not fit for animals," Aleko complained as we got progressively more drunk. But then, with a flash of an idea, Aleko rose unsteadily and wobbled into the kitchen. Returning with a small jar and a spoon, he said, "Taste this!" It was honey, sweet May honey fragrant with plum blossoms and fresh-cut grass. "Where'd you get that?" I asked, knowing that honey was twenty-five lari a kilo, far out of Aleko's budget. "It's *mine!* It's from my bees!"

I was utterly confused, since Aleko's house was in the village of Tamarasheni, which had been utterly destroyed. Aleko, a veterinarian, had been famous all over the Didi Liakhvi gorge as the "Bee Guy," the man who had more hives and made more honey than anybody else in the region. His honey was, in large measure, the crystallized form of his identity, the product that defined him in local society more than even his profession. He once took great pleasure in giving jars of his honey to friends and relatives. So, when Aleko was displaced, and the bees were lost, his relatives from villages inside Georgia proper, where they were able to return after the war, made the kindest gesture they could think of: They brought his honey back to him. As we drank on that cold day, we ate the honey by the spoonful. At the bottom of the jar, Aleko scraped up one last spoonful and held it out to me. "This is the last honey from Tamarasheni," he said, his eyes overflowing with sadness and drink. I declined it, and Aleko ate it slowly, savoring the last taste of his land. It was as if his displacement had not been complete, as long as the honey remained, but with the last of it gone, he became truly unmoored in space, a person who was now from nowhere.

Eating these boomerang foods—honey, jam, bottled fruit, and even homemade "white lightning"—became a ritual in many of the IDPs' cottages I visited. Almost always, the foods were accompanied by beautiful, idealized, and elegiac descriptions of the house and the land they had come from. Judging from similar villages on the Georgian side of the border, the villages in South Ossetia were probably not much to look at from the outside: ramshackle brick houses, scraggly gardens, unpaved rutted dirt roads, and un-mowed clumps of tall grass everywhere. But to those who had lost them, the houses and the land were paradise lost. As we ate the food that had been returned to those who made it, I listened to people recount the numbers of peach and cherry trees they had, describe the places where they'd hung rope hammocks out to rest and swing in, talk about the seemingly huge numbers of cows and chickens they'd raised, and tell me about the cheeses stacked up in their cellars. Boomerang foods were the opposite of anti-artifacts. Where macaroni, a hollow tube around a center of nothingness, could only trace the outlines of what had been lost and point to the space it once occupied, boomerang foods truly filled the holes left by what had been lost, if only for a moment. As they circulated back to their makers, the returning jars and bottles called up memories of place and reconnected people to them emotionally, while closing the loop of reciprocity that connected givers and receivers.

Conclusion

It might be easy to argue that in planning for emergency humanitarian aid, the cultural meanings that people endow food with are not important. After all, in the midst of a war or in the aftermath of massive displacement, it is difficult for aid agencies to factor in the complexity of local cuisines and symbolic systems. The food that is given out as aid needs to be cheap to buy, easy to store and move, and easy to distribute. If the mission is to keep people from starving, the argument goes, it doesn't have to taste good or make people feel good or help bring people together again. It only has to provide the brute calories needed to keep them alive. From this utilitarian perspective, macaroni is an ideal food. It doesn't require refrigeration or a lot of complex equipment to prepare, and as a simple starch, it provides a lot of calories in a small package.

This perspective, one focused purely on the biological survival of the displaced, comes from a focus on what philosopher Giorgio Agamben has called "bare life," human beings taken only as physiological organisms that humanitarians must struggle to keep alive. In this minimalist view, the cultures, languages, cuisines, politics, and social ties of displaced people do not matter. All that matters is sustaining their physical lives.

In the last few years, though, humanitarian agencies have moved away from this focus on sustaining bare life. Realizing that displaced people can be trapped in the limbo of refugee camps without much attention given to the complex ways that they interact with the communities where they resettle, humanitarian agencies such as UNHCR, and the International Organization for Migration, CARE International, and World Vision have all begun to push for "social reintegration" programs for the displaced. Under the framework of social integration, these agencies have begun making concerted efforts to help displaced people find jobs, start businesses, send their children to local schools, and participate in community organizations. The goal is to remake the displaced into full, functioning social beings, something far beyond bare life.

If social reintegration is the goal for the displaced, though, their cultural practices and beliefs, their emotional states and their social worlds matter. If they are supposed to start businesses and get jobs, for example, having strong social networks is the key to raising capital, finding customers, and advertising via word of mouth. If they are supposed to parent well and provide communities that will discourage militarism and ethnic hatred (two things that often fester in refugee camps), staving off depression and hopelessness is important. And if the displaced are supposed to create community organizations to articulate their needs to the authorities, strong communal bonds are essential. In Georgia, where food, eating, and the *supra* banquet are the building blocks of social life, having food that reminded people of loss and discouraged sociality only posed barriers to social reintegration.

Yet, outside the framework of humanitarian aid, the food that enabled those bonds circulated, in small quantities of precious foods from home that made their way through the webs of kinship and friendship to return to their owners. The sweet taste of home, for many IDPs, was the beginning of making their own food again, and attaching to their new homes. As spring came to Tsmindatsqali, as people planted and tended gardens, and then harvested fruit and vegetables in the late summer, they began eating more of their familiar foods. People from different villages, now neighbors in the settlements, began to get to know one another, at first over sunflower seeds and other snacks shared outside, and then later over meals in each others' cottages. There were even *supras* again—less lavish than before the war, to be sure, but important occasions nonetheless.

Late in the summer of 2009, I was invited to the first wedding thrown by the people from the village of Ksuisi since the war. The banquet hall was full with over three hundred people. The bride floated in on a haze of white tulle and silver tinsel, gliding on the arm of her new husband, who had met her while randomly dialing telephone numbers and waiting for girls to answer. As the band played and the wine flowed, we got up to dance the *lezginka,* a traditional dance of the Caucasus performed with arms high in the air. And when we returned to the long banquet tables, exhausted and giddy from the dance, we saw the tables laden with literally hundreds of dishes full of fish and fruit, spinach and eggplant *pkhali,* chunks of boiled meat and cones of fresh cheese, and dozens of tiny cakes glittering in frosting. There was not a plate of macaroni to be seen.

Guide to Further Reading

Leo Coleman

Scholars from many disciplines research and write about food, in all its various transformations—from agricultural product to nutritional value, packaged commodity, delicacy or luxury good. The boundaries between these categories are, naturally, constantly crossed in practice (as when you pick an apple from a tree and savor it, transforming it from agricultural product to delicacy in the process; meanwhile, what is a luxury in one context can be a banality in another). Researchers who pursue insights into food and its social uses likewise cross boundaries. Nutritionists who are concerned about the limits of a purely biophysical approach to health and the medicinal benefits of food can be found writing about the social contexts of food consumption and agricultural policy, and the symbolic values different foodstuffs gain through advertising and placement in the supermarket (e.g., Nestle 2007). Meanwhile, anthropologists most concerned with local systems of morals and meaning, concepts of personhood, and economic and social relations, also engage with nutritional standards, food-safety systems, and the political economy of food production (see, e.g., Dunn 2004; cf. Jones 2007). Contemporary studies of food often return to or reproduce, deliberately or by fortuitous convergence, classic approaches to food and eating in anthropology. Some of those genealogical connections are introduced below, tracing abiding concerns and connections between classic and contemporary works.

Each of the essays in this volume, further, draws on a deep ethnographic archive of descriptions of cultural patterns, folkways, and foodways. The essays, that is, refer implicitly and explicitly both to the ethnography of an area or region of the world, which describes its particular complex of religions, histories, and cultures, and to the long history of anthropological research into food that focuses on "meal patterns," repertoires of behavior, and the ideas about health, medicine, and well-being characteristic of particular food cultures across time and in different places (see Douglas 1984 for a classic methodological statement; cf. Farquhar 2002). Each cultural area or set of practices addressed in the essays—from Austrian epicureanism, to Amazonian ideas of contagion, to Georgian banqueting, to Middle-Eastern hospitality—is worth further study in its own right. This guide, thus, is deliberately selective, but aims to provide readers with furrows to follow as they orient themselves in the fields of food studies and anthropology.

More comprehensive reviews of recent work in the anthropology of food can be found in the following: Mintz and Dubois (2002), which focuses on work since the 1980s; Sutton (2010) reviews sensory approaches in ethnography, while his other work focuses on food and memory (2001); Counihan (1999) includes key review essays and guides to heterogeneous literatures on food, gender, and the body; Lien and Nerlich (2004) offer a rich set of readings exemplifying current approaches to the political economy of food production and food safety, many based on ethnographic studies; while Watson and Caldwell's (2005) reader collects articles with a focus on the politics of consumption and globalization.

Meanwhile, there is a vast array of sources on ethnography as a research method; *Food Studies: A Guide to Research Methods* (Miller and Deutsch 2009) offers a basic introduction to that and other methods current in the field for beginning researchers. For more advanced engagement with ethnography as a research method in anthropology, see Borneman and Hammoudi (2009); the collection edited by Faubion and Marcus (2009), which collects narratives from dissertation fieldwork reflecting on the process of organizing experiences and composing a written ethnography; and Goulet and Miller (2007), which highlights extraordinary experiences and the challenge to ordinary reason presented by ethnographic encounters.

Food to Think

The first anthropological studies of food are found in nineteenth-century studies of comparative religion and ritual, which surveyed food taboos, dietary laws, the use of animals and plants as totems, ritual sacrifices, and celebratory meals as they were found in ancient sources and in the then-contemporary observations of missionaries and colonial travelers. In the middle of the twentieth century, Claude Lévi-Strauss examined the anthropological literature on the use of food, plants, and animals as symbols of both individual and corporate identity—a heterogeneous group of social practices from many cultures analyzed under the name of "totemism"—and concluded that animals and other natural products were used as symbols of social differences not just because they were "good to eat," but more fundamentally because they were "good to think"—useful, and indeed, necessary objects in speculative systems (Lévi-Strauss 1963: 89). In his view, animals, plants, and their parts provided metaphors though which social, or even cosmological, contradictions were either consciously or unconsciously expressed and worked out, a point he pursued across his four-volume study of mythological systems in the Americas, the *Mythologiques*.

In *The Origin of Table Manners* (1978), Lévi-Strauss includes a "short treatise on culinary anthropology," which extends his insights from earlier in his career about the way in which transformations of food products from "raw" to "cooked" help people think about social relations. He attempts a systematic synthesis of the conceptual operations involved in cooking, and the ways in which particular ways of cooking and preparing food assign particular dishes, people, and indeed whole societies to one side or another of a fundamental set of evaluative contrasts (nature/culture; raw/cooked). While many of Lévi-Strauss's theses appear, in retrospect, ad hoc and often worked up to resolve an immediate problem of interpretation, his broader insight that food and cooking are means by which cultural and political problems are made tangible (or "concrete") in everyday thought, and made amenable to reformulation and reconsideration, have proved very durable.

Other anthropologists have focused on specific foods in given cultural contexts in more detail, concerned not so much with basic contrasts, but with why one food is counted as "raw" in one place, and as "cooked" in another, why a particular food is taboo and another desired. As Mary Douglas, in another context, vigorously argued, the *content* of these contrasts is culture-specific (see "The Meaning of Myth," collected in Douglas 1999). Yet her long-term analyses of food prohibitions and taboos from many cultures, with a special focus on the Old Testament dietary laws, likewise emphasizes that the structured opposition between pure and impure foods we find across all such systems is a means of ensuring social order and social reproduction (see "Interpreting a Meal," in Douglas 1999).

Lévi-Strauss's and Douglas's work jointly established the intellectual stature and social importance of all the daily practices involved in food preparation and commensality, removing them from the realm of the simply material or the superfluously ritual and religious, and placing them among the great imaginative achievements of humans in society. Meanwhile, their work and the long-term interests of anthropologists in the ritual and religious work that people do with food—through sacrifices or acts of communion—encourage an abiding anthropological focus on the social uses of food, which does not contradict but rather complements other approaches to food safety, nutritional values, and the substantial qualities of foods. Indeed, a focus on the cultural patterning, uses, and meanings of foods in the present is relevant even in seemingly technical domains such as food policy.

Food Policy as Social Philosophy

The challenge of discerning large-scale social and cultural meanings in American and European debates over food policy is taken up systematically in Sheila Jasanoff's comparative sociology of biotechnology and food regulations in Europe and the United States, *Designs on Nature: Science and Democracy in Europe and the United States* (2005). Jasanoff highlights different policy outcomes in the regulation of biotech and manufactured foods in Europe (comparing Britain and Germany) and the United States, showing how these policy disputes are cultural arenas in which both nature and society are simultaneously debated and constructed (see especially Chapter 5). Her period of research spanned the 1990s, and her book reanimates many significant food-related controversies, now faded from public memory, as the site of key decisions about our food supply that continue to affect both the regulation of food as well as our ability to recognize and conceive of new boundaries between the natural and the technological.

Congruent arguments about the intertwining of law, policy, and science in the contemporary American culture of producing and eating food are exemplified by Pollan's account of "four meals," of the varieties of food available in contemporary America, and how and why they vary (2006). Despite different aims and procedures, both of these accounts reveal very forcefully how thought about food is also, at large, thought about social, political, and cultural relations.

Consumption and Politics

The cultural study of food practices and habits in North America has grown immensely in the past two decades, with a crop of new journals providing homes for professional writing on food, ranging from the literary (such as *Alimentum: The Literature of Food*), to the multidisciplinary, but still disciplined (*Food, Culture, and Society*; *Food and Foodways*), to the glossy, comprehensive, and essential *Gastronomica*. These journals are one indication among many of how food has become a political and cultural subject of intense importance, in part due to the recent scholarly focus on consumption, identity, and status. Much of this work, directly or indirectly, is indebted to the poststructuralist theories of practice and habitus developed by the sociologist Pierre Bourdieu, which linked bodily habits and desires to political life and identity.

Bourdieu (1984) examined taste—meaning the whole evaluative panoply of discriminations that constitutes "good taste" and "bad taste"—as a means of social judgment, making and marking distinctions between people. His primary target was to reveal the ways in which class statuses are lived and made real in contemporary capitalist society, becoming habitus—or engrained, durable dispositions, not mere optional "identities." Moving away from an idea of class and social identity as rooted in one's relationship to work—either a worker or a leisured aristocrat—Bourdieu provided new tools for thinking about differentiation in consumer society, while also introducing more flexibility, strategy, and negotiation into the kinds of "codes" studied by Lévi-Strauss and Douglas.

Food-studies scholars have taken up various elements of this two-pronged theory of habitus and distinction in order to broach a wide range of other boundaries marked by food practices, including gender, sexuality, race, ethnic identity, and even citizenship (Counihan and Van Esterik's 2008 reader on food and culture includes many essays that follow this approach). Krishnendu Ray (2004) writes about Bengali kitchens and cooking as the site of the making of both assimilation and memory for immigrants to the United States, while Manpreet Janeja (2009) follows the local complexities of food transactions in shaping relations across the political boundary between India and Bangladesh.

Judith Farquhar's (2002) study of life in post-reform China focuses precisely on the modifications and manipulations of appetite, taste, and desire as a way to understanding the experience of both communist rule and market-oriented reforms in the recent history of that country (themes also broached, for other post-socialist societies which are being slowly, and with disruption, "reformed" toward integration into global capitalist circuits, in Caldwell 2004, 2009). As Farquhar demonstrates for China, even relatively short histories can produce habits and longings, though such novelties usually draw, albeit selectively, on long-standing cultural archives of classifications, meanings, and practices.

Hunger, Desire, and Disgust

One of the great sociological observations encouraged by the study of food, thus, is how malleable human hungers, tastes, and desires can be, and yet how deeply felt and natural-seeming food habits, customs, and even sensory reactions to certain foods can also be. Both sides of the observation are equally important: Food is an eminently cosmopolitan thing, shared and shareable, and yet tastes are highly localized and deeply rooted. The learning and love with which we come to appreciate certain foods (individually and collectively), and the places and times past we associate with them, is as much (if not more so) a part of their appeal as their given pleasurable qualities. Hunger and disgust, meanwhile, can be potent motivating factors in political life, and the material of subtle manipulations to highlight certain boundaries or to challenge existing organizations of power.

Among the great political leaders of the twentieth century, M. K. Gandhi's fasts and extensive writings on diet were central to his challenge to British power in India, and to the communication of his political message to Indian audiences (Roy 2010). Political hunger and its uses as protest in the prisons of 1980s

Northern Ireland is harrowingly presented in the British artist Steve McQueen's recent film *Hunger* (2008). But the use of foods to motivate and demonstrate commitment is not limited to fasting or protest, or anger at established powers. Ghassem-Fachandi (2009a: 42) reports encountering "idioms of diet and sexuality" whenever he discussed intercommunal violence with interlocutors in India. He grounds his interpretation of this violence in distinctions between vegetarian and non-vegetarian that have become highly politicized, and argues that the violence gathers some of its force and emotional justification from processes that identify groups of other people with "disgusting" practices like meat-eating (2009b).

These latter studies return to the connections long explored by anthropologists (and others, including Freud) among food, socialization, and ritual, and to a tradition that examines food, eating, and taste as fundamental tools for navigating the social world. As Zabusky shows in her study of ritual contexts of European identity-production (2006), it is the materiality of food and the range of ritual contexts in which it is emplaced—which can include restaurants or other venues of consumption, but are not limited to them—that puts food and identity into such close connection, and makes food useful for making, challenging, and reforming political identities.

Globalization and Consumption

As has been widely observed, novel consumer opportunities are ever more apparent and accessible in China, India, and elsewhere, and this is a significant aspect of globalization, which is understood to involve new tastes, as well as new distinctions and discriminations. Globalization has come to be associated with a few prominent food-and-lifestyle corporations: McDonald's, Starbucks, and KFC now have a global presence, and even more high-end packaged or "theme" restaurants are making their way into the global market.

Watson's volume *Golden Arches East* (2006; first published in 1997) documents the cultural adoption of, and adaptation to, American fast food in East Asia, emphasizing how Chinese and other Asian consumers put their own set of values and understandings on what, in the local context, are often rather expensive dining options. In her now widely anthologized essay on fast food in Beijing, Yan (2000) points out that the first phase of fast-food acculturation in China saw the use of the fast-food restaurant as, paradoxically, a place to *linger* and enjoy the new space and symbolic practice of consumption. Only more recently, she notes, has the urban middle-class, who seek out such venues for status-building display and consumption, found new outlets, while the growing ubiquity of fast-food chains in Chinese cities made them a more banal place for everyday consumption. The global proliferation of fast food has fostered opposition, of course, in localist claims and discourses and the now-global Slow Food movement. Slow Food has attracted a growing array of commentators focused on how it, too, represents a politics of identity and consumption, marking new distinctions and forms of protest, but also fostering an equally global set of economic and social networks (see the contributors to Wilk 2005).

Stability and Change

A very influential voice in the contemporary North American debate about how we should raise, process, and choose our foods, Pollan (2008) tries to argue that "food" is something we can recognize and deal with in the raw (as it were), as opposed to technologically produced, processed, or manufactured "food-like substances," and he thus creatively reproduces current American distinctions between whole and processed foods. As Jordan points out here, Pollan's (and others') arguments often rely on a contrast with an imagined European (or "preindustrial") food culture, which is stable, local, and sustainable. These assumptions and contrasts demand further inquiry, especially since Jasanoff and others have shown that the European food system is just as much a result of legal, political, and technological interventions as the American one. (For a view into the industrialized core of food production in Europe, there is no better source than Nikolaus Geyrhalter's 2005 documentary, *Our Daily Bread*; see also Harding 2010).

Moreover, the ideal of some pristine, stable food culture in preindustrial places or times, in harmony with its environment and with human needs, can serve—even when applied with intent to praise—to hide the real sources of that stability in historical inequalities and power relations. Anne Meneley (2007), thus, asks how much of the "stable food culture" of Europe relies on cheaply available fruits and vegetables from across the Mediterranean. She examines the place the Mediterranean has taken in recent accounts of systems of food production, and how the reality of olive-oil production is both transnational and industrial, encompassing many countries not conventionally counted as "Mediterranean," including Palestine, and many forms of labor not usually thought of as "artisanal." Paxson (2010) offers a related critique of the category of the so called artisanal in the context of cheese production in the United States, exploring the ambiguities of the term and the forms of production that it devalues despite their long, local lineages in the United States.

Similar lessons are reinforced in Deborah Gewertz and Frederick Errington's study of the sugar industry in Papua New Guinea (PNG), as well as their more recent study of the regional trade in cheap meats in the Pacific (Errington and Gewertz 2004; Gewertz and Errington 2010). They aim to provide a nondeterministic, fully historical and human, account of the development of different food cultures, taking into account actors in positions of power within the global economy, the desires and habits of a developmentalist national elite in PNG, as well as "local" preferences and customs, including how the latter change and incorporate global commodities into long-standing patterns.

What these writers share is an interest in tracing the relations hidden behind apparently transparent labels and attributes of foods; what do we mean when we say something is "organic," "artisanal," or "cheap"? How can we understand the mutability of these definitions over time, and the kinds of opportunities and crises different interpretations of these labels bring? How do some foods, and not others, get singled out for local valuation and global circulation? The problem is much the same when we are looking at national cuisines, which are seldom as stable and immemorial as they are thought to be. How does pork fat become Italian (Leitch 2003), or how did Chicken Tikka Masala become the national dish of England? Richard Wilk's long-term study of cross-cultural influence and change in the food culture of Belize, *Home Cooking in the Global Village* (2006), follows this approach to a "national cuisine," examining how it was cooked up, out of what ingredients, and what the consequences of packaging it and marketing it globally are.

Substances and Senses

All recent scholarship on the political economy of food production *and* consumption (showing how the two are so intimately intertwined; see Heath and Meneley 2007), on food and politics, and food and identity, is indebted to the pioneering work of Sidney Mintz. His *Sweetness and Power* (1985) tells the story of the rise of sugar as a commodity in the world economy, focusing on a pan-Atlantic (and later much more extensive) political and economic system in which sugar was intensively extracted and refined to be traded for slaves, guns, and rum. Mintz showed how a whole cultural history of capitalism, spanning the extractive labor regimes of the Caribbean and the cheap, nonnutritive diets of the English working classes, could be constructed by following the exchange relations out of which a single commodity was produced. However, Mintz not only tracked otherwise concealed connections between national economies and cultures over the long term; he also argued that sweetness itself became newly demanded and desirable after the advent of large-scale production of highly refined sugars, leading to the cultivation of new tastes and experiences, new ways of eating.

This latter insight into the production—some would say fabrication—of qualities and desires in global capitalist circuits informs Don Kulick and Anne Meneley's (2005) edited volume *Fat: The Anthropology of an Obsession*. Kulick and Meneley focus on the multiple appearances and qualities of fat in foods, in bodies, and in circulation as an ideal and as a feared and denied substance. Lofgren and Wilk (2006), meanwhile, offer tools for a new anthropology of cultural processes which would focus on such inner qualities—exemplified by sensations and qualities such as "creaminess"—as they are abstracted and experienced in various kinds of products and encounters.

These latter approaches might take the study of food into new terrain. Adjacent fields remain productive, in which scholars examine the local meanings of particular foods; significant relations between foodstuffs, or the use they are put to, symbolizing and constituting social relationships and identities; change and stability over time; and the political uses of food and its incorporation into individual and social bodies. But the inner manipulation and alteration of foods, the spread of genetically modified crops, and the fabrication of new tastes and sensations both in the laboratory and in high-end restaurants devoted to molecular gastronomy, point to a new social reality of transformations acting at more fundamental levels than previously imaginable. Studies that focus on these inner transformations in particular substances and qualities intrinsic to food— no longer whole commodities, such as sugar or salt, nor even "foodways"— will create an archive of cultural knowledge about food suited to the current technological, economic, and political era. Even the most synthetic, creative, and critical of this work, however, will start where good ethnography always does: with encounters between people in which the food they share is their first object of social interest and exchange.

Select Bibliography

Bestor, T. C. (2004), *Tsukiji: The Fish Market at the Center of the World,* Berkeley: University of California Press.

Borneman, J., and Hammoudi, A. (eds.) (2009), *Being There: The Fieldwork Encounter and the Making of Truth*, Berkeley: University of California Press.

Bourdieu, P. (1984), *Distinction: A Social Critique of the Judgement of Taste*, R. Nice (trans.), Cambridge: Harvard University Press.

Caldwell, M. L. (2004), *Not by Bread Alone: Social Support in the New Russia*, Berkeley: University of California Press.

Caldwell, M. L. (ed.) (2009), *Food and Everyday Life in the Postsocialist World*, Bloomington: Indiana University Press.

Caton, S. (2005), *Yemen Chronicle: An Anthropology of War and Mediation,* New York: Hill and Wang.

Child, J., and Prud'homme, A. (2007), *My Life in France*, New York: Anchor Books.

Collier, S., Lakoff, A., and Rabinow, P. (2004), "Biosecurity. Towards an Anthropology of the Contemporary," *Anthropology Today*, 20: 5–7.

Counihan, C. (1999), *The Anthropology of Food and Body: Gender, Meaning, and Power*, New York: Routledge.

Counihan, C., and Van Esterik, P. (eds.) (2008 [1997]), *Food and Culture: A Reader*, 2nd ed., New York: Routledge.

Crawford, D. (2008), *Moroccan Households in the World Economy: Labor and Inequality in a Berber Village*, Baton Rouge: Louisiana State University Press.

Cronon, W. (1991), *Nature's Metropolis: Chicago and the Great West*, New York: W. W. Norton.

Da Matta, R. (1973), "Panema: Uma Tentativa de Analise Estrutural," in *Ensiaos de Antropologia Estrutural.* Rio de Janeiro: Vozes.

de la Pradelle, M. (1996), *Les vendredis de Carpentras: Faire son marché en Provence ou ailleurs*, Paris: Fayard.

Dening, G. (1980), *Islands and Beaches*, Chicago: The Dorsey Press.

Descola, P. (2005), *Par delà nature et culture*, Paris: Gallimard.

Douglas, M. (1984), "Standard Social Uses of Food: Introduction," in M. Douglas (ed.), *Food in the Social Order: Studies of Food and Festivities in Three American Communities*, New York: Russell Sage Foundation.

Douglas, M. (1999 [1975]), *Implicit Meanings: Selected Essays in Anthropology*, 2nd ed., New York: Routledge.

D'Souza, B. (2008), *Harnessing the Trade Winds: The Story of the Centuries-old Indian Trade with East Africa, using the Monsoon Winds*, Nairobi: Zand Graphics.

Dunn, E. (2004), *Privatizing Poland: Baby Food, Big Business, and the Remaking of Labor*, Ithaca: Cornell University Press.

Du Pont De Bie, N. (2004), *Ant Egg Soup: The Adventures of a Food Tourist in Laos*, London: Hodder and Stoughton.

Errington, F. K., and Gewertz, D. (2004), *Yali's Question: Sugar, Power, History*, Chicago: University of Chicago Press.

Farquhar, J. (2002), *Appetites: Food and Sex in Post-Socialist China*, Durham: Duke University Press.

Faubion, J. D., and Marcus, G. E. (eds.) (2009), *Fieldwork is Not What It Used To Be: Learning Anthropology's Method in a Time of Transition*, Ithaca: Cornell University Press.

Fielding, R. (2005), "Avian Influenza Risk Perception, Hong Kong," *Emerging Infectious Diseases,* 11/5: 677–82.

Fisher, M.F.K. (1943), *The Gastronomical Me*, New York: Duell, Sloan & Pearce.

Garrett, P., and Baquedano-López, P. (2002), "Language Socialization: Reproduction and Continuity, Transformation, and Change," *Annual Review of Anthropology*, 31: 339–61.

Gewertz, D., and Errington, F. K. (2010), *Cheap Meat: Flap Food Nations in the Pacific Islands,* Berkeley: University of California Press.

Geyrhalter, N. (dir.) (2005), *Unser Täglich Brot* (Our Daily Bread). Icarus Films.

Ghassem-Fachandi, P. (2009a), "*Bandh* in Ahmedabad," in P. Ghassem-Fachandi (ed.), *Violence: Ethnographic Encounters*, Oxford: Berg Publishers.

Ghassem-Fachandi, P. (2009b), "The Hyperbolic Vegetarian: Notes on a Fragile Subject in Gujarat," in J. Borneman and A. Hammoudi (eds.), *Being There: The Fieldwork Encounter and the Making of Truth*, Berkeley: University of California Press.

Goossaert, V. (2005), *L'interdit du bœuf en Chine: Agriculture, éthique et sacrifice,* Paris: De Boccard.

Goulet, J.-G. A., and Miller, B. G. (eds.) (2007), *Extraordinary Anthropology: Transformations in the Field*, Lincoln: University of Nebraska Press.

Greger, M. (2006), *Bird Flu. A Virus of Our Own Hatching,* New York: Lantern Books.

Hammoudi, A. (2009), "Textualism and Anthropology: On the Ethnographic Encounter, or an Experience in the Hajj," in J. Borneman and A. Hammoudi (eds.). *Being There: The Fieldwork Encounter and the Making of Truth*, Berkeley: University of California Press.

Handlin Smith, J. F. (1999), "Liberating Animals in Ming-Qing China: Buddhist Inspiration and Elite Imagination," *Journal of Asian Studies*, 58/1: 51–84.

Handy, E.S.C. (1923), *The Native Culture in the Marquesas*, Honolulu: Bishop Museum.

Harding, J. (2010), "What We Are About to Receive," *The London Review of Books*, 32/9: 3–8.

Heath, D., and Meneley, A. (2007), "Techne, Technoscience, and the Circulation of Comestible Commodities: An Introduction," *American Anthropologist*, 109/4: 593–602.

Heldke, L. (2003), *Exotic Appetites: Ruminations of a Food Adventurer*, New York and London: Routledge.

Janeja, M. K. (2009), *Transactions in Taste: The Collaborative Lives of Everyday Bengali Food*, New Delhi: Routledge.

Janowski, M., and Kerlogue, F. (eds.) (2007), *Kinship and Food in Southeast Asia*, Copenhagen: NIAS Press.

Jasanoff, S. (2005), *Designs on Nature: Science and Democracy in Europe and the United States*, Princeton: Princeton University Press.

Jones, J. (2008), *The Tenth Muse: My Life in Food*, New York: Anchor Books.

Jones, M. O. (2007), "Food Choice, Symbolism, and Identity: Bread-and-Butter Issues for Folkloristics and Nutrition Studies," *Journal of American Folklore*, 120/476: 129–77.

Jordon, J. A. (2007), "The Heirloom Tomato as Cultural Object: Investigating Taste and Space," *Sociologia Ruralis*, 47/1: 20–41.

Keck, F. (2008). "From Mad Cow Disease to Bird Flu: Transformations of Food Safety in France," in S. Collier and A. Lakoff (eds.), *Biosecurity Interventions: Global Health and Security in Question*, New York: Columbia University Press.

Keck, F. (2009), "The Contaminated Milk Affair," *China Perspectives* 2009/1: 88–93.

Kirkpatrick, J. (1983), *The Marquesan Notion of the Person*, Ann Arbor: UMI Research Press.

Kolata, G. (2006), *Flu. The Story of the Great Influenza Pandemic and the Search for the Virus that Caused It*, New York: Simon and Schuster.

Krahn, J. (2005), "The Dynamics of Dietary Change of Transitional Food Systems in Tropical Forest Areas of Southeast Asia: The Contemporary and Traditional Food System of the Katu in the Sekong Province, Lao PDR," Unpublished dissertation, Bonn, Rheinische Friedrich-Wilhelms Univeritaet.

Kulick, D., and Meneley, A. (eds.) (2005), *Fat: The Anthropology of an Obsession*, New York: Tarcher/Penguin.

Leitch, A. (2003), "Slow Food and the Politics of Pork Fat: Italian Food and European Identity," *Ethnos* 68/4: 437–62.

Lévi-Strauss, C. (1963), *Totemism*, R. Needham (trans.), Chicago: University of Chicago Press.

Lévi-Strauss, C. (1973), *Tristes Tropiques*, J. and D. Weightman (trans.), New York: Penguin.

Lévi-Strauss, C. (1978), *The Origin of Table Manners* (*Mythologiques,* vol. 3), J. and D. Weightman (trans.), Chicago: University of Chicago Press.

Lien, E. R., and Nerlich, B. (eds.) (2004), *The Politics of Food*. Oxford: Berg.

Limbert, M. (2010), *In the Time of Oil*, Stanford: Stanford University Press.

Liu, T.-S. (2008), "Custom, Taste and Science: Raising Chickens in the Pearl River Delta Region, South China," *Anthropology & Medicine*, 15/1: 7–18

Lofgren, O., and Wilk, R. (2006), *Off the Edge: Experiments in Cultural Analysis*, Copenhagen: Museum Tusculanum Press.

Maclagan, I. (2000), "Food and Gender in a Yemeni Community," in S. Zubaida and R. Tapper (eds.), *A Taste of Thyme: Culinary Cultures of the Middle East*, London: Tauris.

Mayfair, M. Y. (1994), *Gifts, Favors and Banquets: The Art of Social Relationships in China*, Ithica: Cornell University Press.

McQueen, S. (dir.) (2008), *Hunger*. Film4/Pathé.

Meneley, A. (1996), *Tournaments of Value: Hierarchy and Sociability in a Yemeni Town*, Toronto: University of Toronto Press.

Meneley, A. (1998), "Analogies and Resonances in the Process of Ethnographic Understanding," *Ethnos*, 63: 202–26.

Meneley, A. (2007), "Like an Extravirgin," *American Anthropologist*, 109/4: 678–87.

Miller, J., and Deutsch, J. (2009), *Food Studies: An Introduction to Research Methods,* Oxford: Berg.

Mintz, S. W. (1985), *Sweetness and Power: The Place of Sugar in Modern History*, New York: Viking.

Mintz, S. W., and DuBois, C. M. (2002), "The Anthropology of Food and Eating," *Annual Review of Anthropology,* 31: 99–119.

Nestle, M. (2007), *Food Politics: How the Food Industry Influences Nutrition and Health*, revised ed., Berkeley: University of California Press.

Ochs, E., Pontecorvo, C., and Fasulo, A., (1996), "Socializing Taste," *Ethnos*, 61/1–2: 7–46.

Ochs, E., and Schieffelin, B. B. (2010), "Language Socialization: An Historical Overview," in P. Duff and N. Hornberger (eds.), *Encyclopedia of Language and Education*, vol. 8, Dordrecht: Kluwer Academic Publishers.

Paugh, A., and Izquerdo, C. (2009), "Why is This a Battle Every Night?: Negotiating Food and Eating in American Dinnertime Interaction," *Journal of Linguistic Anthropology*, 19/2: 185–204.

Paxson, H. (2010), "Cheese Cultures: Transforming American Tastes and Traditions," *Gastronomica* 10/4: 35–47.

Pollack, N. (1992), *These Roots Remain: Food Habits in Islands of the Central and Eastern Pacific since Western Contact*, Honolulu: University of Hawaii Press.

Pollan, M. (2006), *The Omnivore's Dilemma: A Natural History of Four Meals*, New York: Penguin Press.

Pollan, M. (2008), *In Defense of Food: An Eater's Manifesto*, New York: Penguin.

Ray, K. (2004), *The Migrant's Table: Meals and Memories in Bengali-American Households*, Philadelphia: Temple University Press.

Riley, K. C. (2001), *The Emergence of Dialogic Identities: Transforming Heteroglossia in the Marquesas*, PhD dissertation, New York, CUNY Graduate Faculty.

Riley, K. C. (2007), "To Tangle or Not to Tangle: Shifting Language Ideologies and the Socialization of Charabia in the Marquesas, French Polynesia," in M. Makihara and B. B. Schieffelin (eds.), *Consequences of Contact: Language Ideologies and Sociocultural Transformations in Pacific Societies*, New York: Oxford University Press.

Riley, K. C. (2008), "Language Socialization," in B. Spolsky and F. M. Hult (eds.), *Handbook of Educational Linguistics*, Malden: Blackwell.

Riley, K. C. (2009), "Who Made the Soup? Socializing the Researcher and Shaping her Data," *Language and Communication*, 29/3: 254–70.

Roy, P. (2010), *Alimentary Tracts: Appetites, Aversions, and the Postcolonial*, Durham: Duke University Press.

Sahlins, M. (1972), *Stone Age Economics*, New York: Aldine de Gruyter.

Schieffelin, B. B., and Ochs, E. (eds.) (1986), *Language Socialization Across Cultures*, Cambridge: Cambridge University Press.

Schieffelin, B. B. (1990), *The Give and Take of Everyday Language*, Cambridge: Cambridge University Press.

Senders, S., and Truitt, A. (2007), "Introduction," in S. Senders and A. Truitt (eds.), *Money: Ethnographic Encounters,* Oxford: Berg Publishers.

Shortridge, K. F., and Stuart-Harris, C. H. (1982), "An Influenza Epicentre?" *Lancet*, 320/8302: 812–13.

Simmons, F. J. (1991), *Food in China: A Cultural and Historical Inquiry,* Boston: CRC Press.

Sing, P. (1981), *Traditional Recipes of Laos*, A. and J. Davidson (eds.), London: Prospect Books.

Striffler, S. (2005), *Chicken: The Dangerous Transformation of America's Favorite Food*, New Haven: Yale University Press.

Suggs, R. (1966), *Marquesan Sexual Behavior*, New York: Harcourt, Brace and World.

Sutton, D. E. (2001), *Remembrance of Repasts: An Anthropology of Food and Memory*, Oxford: Berg.

Sutton, D. E. (2010), "Food and the Senses," *Annual Review of Anthropology*, 39: 209–23.

Thomas, N. (1990), *Marquesan Societies: Inequality and Political Transformation in Eastern Polynesia*, Oxford: Clarendon Press.

Thu, H. (2010), *100 Món Ăn Á-Âu Ngon Miệng*, Hà Nôi: Nôi: Nhà Xuất Bản Thời Đại.

Trân, N. T. (2000), "Trong lối ăn của người Việt" ("The Vietnamese way of eating"), in Huy Xuân (ed.), *Văn Hóa Ẩm Thực & Món Ăn Việt Nam*, Ho Chi Minh City: Nhà Xuất Bản Trẻ.

Van Esterik, P. (2008), *Food Culture in Southeast Asia*, Westport: Greenwood Press.

Watson, J. L., and Caldwell, M. L. (eds.) (2005), *The Cultural Politics of Food and Eating: A Reader*, Oxford: Blackwell.

Watson, J. L. (ed.) (2006), *Golden Arches East: McDonald's in East Asia*, 2nd ed., Stanford: Stanford University Press.

Wedeen, L. (2008), *Peripheral Visions: Publics, Power, and Performance in Yemen*, Chicago: University of Chicago Press.

Wilk, R. (ed.) (2005), *Fast Food/Slow Food: The Cultural Economy of the Global Food System*, Lanham: Altamira Press.

Wilk, R. (2006), *Home Cooking in the Global Village: Caribbean Food from Buccaneers to Ecotourists*, Oxford: Berg.

Xuân, H. (2000), *Văn Hóa Ẩm Thực & Món Ăn Việt Nam*, Ho Chi Minh City: Nhà Xuất Bản Trẻ.

Yan, Y. (2000), "Of Hamburger and Social Space: Consuming McDonalds in Beijing," in D. S. Davis (ed.), *The Consumer Revolution in Urban China*, Berkeley: University of California Press.

Yeung, E. (1956), "Poultry Farming in Hong Kong," Unpublished undergraduate essay, Department of Geography and Geology, University of Hong Kong.

Zabusky, S. E. (2006), "Food: National Identity, and Emergent Europeanness at the European Space Agency," in T. M. Wilson (ed.), *European Studies 22: Food, Drink and Identity in Europe*, Amsterdam: Rodopi.

Index

Agamben, Giorgio, 148
alcohol, 26
    drinking of, 31, 73–4, 129
    varieties of, 40, 114
animals, 11, 55–8, 62, 130, 146, 152–3
    humans and, 12–13, 49–50, 58
    spirits and, 42–4, 47, 57

biosecurity, 11–12, 49, 54, 58
    see also food safety
biotechnology, 154
    see also industrial food production
body, *see* embodiment
Bourdieu, Pierre, 154–5
    see also habitus
Brazil, 9, 39–47 passim
Buddhism, 12, 15–16, 55–7, 128–37
Bush, George H. W., 28

Caldwell, Melissa, 2, 152, 155
Canada, 9, 19, 24, 26
Caton, Steven, 21
Child, Julia, 69
China, 13, 49–58 passim, 155–6
    see also Hong Kong
commensality, 1, 64–6, 92–6 passim, 114,
    132, 153
comparison, 6, 9, 50, 70
    cross-cultural knowledge and, 23–4,
    28, 67, 99, 129, 131
consumers and consumption, 8, 14, 46, 57,
    77–81, 107–8, 114, 152
    theories of, 154–8
    see also markets; shopping
cooking, 2–3, 10–11, 14–15, 46, 97–8,
    118–22, 143–5, 153

ethnographer's skill at, 23, 90, 106–7
household division of labor and, 20–1,
    33–5, 85–7, 94, 105, 121
    see also gender
Counihan, Carole, 2, 152, 155

disease, *see* illness
Douglas, Mary, 6, 152–3, 155

embodiment, 1–2, 5, 13–14, 16, 43–5, 47,
    60–1, 65–6
Errington, Frederick, 157–8
ethnography, 8–10, 50, 151
    encounter-based, 2, 4–6, 8, 12–15, 159
    fieldwork and, 4–5, 10, 13–14, 60–1,
    94–6, 111–12, 152
    history and, 39, 45
    method of, 3–4, 70, 75, 77–81, 123, 152
    see also embodiment; exchange; gifts
    and reciprocity
etiquette, *see* table manners
Europe, 69–71, 74, 79–80, 112–14, 154,
    156–7
    see also Paris (France); Vienna (Austria)
exchange, 5–7, 13–15, 19, 25, 56–7,
    112–13, 115–17, 142
    see also gifts and reciprocity
exoticism, 5, 25, 59, 67, 100, 105

Farquhar, Judith, 6, 155
fieldwork, *see* ethnography
Fisher, M.F.K., 16
food safety, 9, 12–13, 64–7, 152
    see also biosecurity
food security, 12–13, 59–60, 64–7, 120
    defined, 60

167